Cultural and Religious Boundary-Crossing
in Early Modern Spain

D1796291

Miriam Bodian
Editor

Cultural and Religious Boundary-Crossing in Early Modern Spain

Previously published in *Jewish History*
"Special Issue: Cultural and Religious
Boundary-Crossing in Early Modern Spain"
Volume 35, issue 3-4, December 2021

Springer

Editor
Miriam Bodian
History Department
University of Texas
Austin, TX, USA

Spinoff from journal: "Jewish History" Volume 35, issue 3-4, December 2021

ISBN 978-3-031-18426-0

This Springer imprint is published by the registered company Springer Nature Switzerland AG
The registered company address is: Gewerbestrasse 11, 6330 Cham, Switzerland

Contents

Jewish History (2021) 35: 229–239
https://doi.org/10.1007/s10835-021-09421-3

Introduction: Cultural and Religious Boundary-Crossing in Early Modern Spain

MIRIAM BODIAN

University of Texas at Austin, Austin, TX, USA
E-mail: bodian@austin.utexas.edu

Accepted: 14 July 2021 / Published online: 17 December 2021

This issue of *Jewish History* brings together the work of scholars who are exploring the entanglement of traditions and identities among the three major religio-ethnic groups in early modern Spain. These scholars are participating in a broad shift in early modern Spanish historiography in recent decades. It challenges a traditional conception according to which the historical trajectories of "Old Christians," judeo-conversos (henceforth "conversos"), and moriscos (baptized Muslims and their descendants) were essentially separate. According to this conception, each population developed within its own rather fixed psychic and cultural boundaries.

The scholarly segregation of these populations has been the norm in both of the major traditional conceptualizations of early modern Spanish history. One, which goes back to medieval times and held sway in the conservative academic culture of modern Spain, perpetuates a view of Spain as inherently Catholic and European. The other, with deep roots in the Protestant world, presents early modern Spain as a stagnant backwater where cultural creativity and dissent were crushed by a repressive church, state, and inquisition. Different as they are, both conceptualizations have had the effect of submerging early modern Spain's religio-ethnic minorities beneath the surface of "mainstream" Spanish history.

It is true that the influential, if idiosyncratic, work of Américo Castro in the 1940s and 50s challenged both paradigms. Castro envisioned Spanish society and culture as having been shaped from the Reconquista onward not, as others would have it, by the dominance of the majority population of Spanish Catholics, but by the dynamic interactions of Catholic, Jewish, and Muslim "castes." Today, the speculative, tendentious approach of Castro, with its thinly-veiled racism, has been largely discredited; however, in its time, Castro offered a precocious vision of a Spain whose major, enduring contours emanated from a mixing of cultures.

Chapter 1 was originally published as Bodian, M. Jewish History (2021) 35: 229–239. https://doi.org/10.1007/s10835-021-09421-3.

1  Springer

Jewish Historiography

Traditional Jewish scholarship produced an alternate perspective on early modern Spain. It has focused on a single population (the conversos), a single institution (the Inquisition), and a single form of religious dissent (crypto-Judaism). It has represented the history of the forcibly baptized Jews and their descendants in the Iberian Peninsula as an intrinsic part of centuries-long Jewish diaspora history. It served to corroborate the familiar contours of Jewish history, resonating with the themes of persecution and resistance in Jewish collective consciousness. Whether we read the work of major Jewish historians who have studied Spanish converso experience (Cecil Roth, Yitzhak Baer, Yosef Hayim Yerushalmi, Benzion Netanyahu, and David Nirenberg, among others) or textbooks and popular narratives of Jewish history, we are presented with a relationship between the dominant Spanish-Catholic population and descendants of baptized Jews that was relentlessly antagonistic.

This is hardly surprising. The broad contours of Jewish/converso existence in early modern Iberia *were* defined by the traumatic experiences of coerced mass conversion, systematic inquisitorial persecution, expulsion, and racial discrimination. The sources include a large corpus of virulent anti-converso propaganda as well as an ample stockpile of bitterly anti-Catholic converso utterances; these too have reinforced the image of Old Christians as persecutors and of conversos as victims. Among Jewish scholars active in the post-Holocaust period, a focus on the traumatic aspects of converso existence (including exclusion based on "purity of blood" laws) was understandable. Yet there was a more fundamental reason for the highlighting of Old Christian persecution and converso resistance, namely the persistence of a long historiographical tradition that holds Jewish society to be existentially at odds with Christendom.

It was only in the 1980s and 1990s—at a time when historians across fields were becoming aware of the degree to which scholars had tended to "essentialize" ethnoreligious groups, overlooking the frequent everyday intimacy among them—that scholars of Jewish history began acknowledging the fluidity and variability of Jewish-Christian relations, even in periods when intergroup tensions ran high.[1] The growing prevalence in these years of a theoretical notion of "identity" that was inherently unstable and multilayered, along with the increasing perception of group boundaries as being malleable and constantly negotiated, further eroded the clear-cut distinctions that once prevailed.

---

[1] Perhaps the most influential revision of thinking about the contours of Jewish-Christian relations in Spain has been David Nirenberg, *Communities of Violence: Persecution of Minorities in the Middle Ages* (Princeton, 1996; rev. ed. 2015).

Despite the overall shift toward a less monochromatic representation of conversos, a new current of scholarship emerged in the 1990s that once again depicted conversos in essentialist terms—not, as had earlier been the case, as a defamed and persecuted population, but as a population with unique and identifiable cognitive and psychic characteristics. Scholars pursuing this line of inquiry used the term "marranism" to refer to the psychic phenomenon they described. Some regarded "marranism" as nothing less than a precursor to "modernity" itself (in the sense of a modern sensibility).[2] To be sure, this body of scholarship acknowledged—indeed, required—a conceptualization of individual identity as potentially conflict-ridden and unstable. Yet, by singling out conversos as the exclusive bearers of a "marrano" sensibility, it had the effect of giving new life to a view of the conversos as a distinct and unique population.

Hispanists who have devoted essays and monographs to converso history have also, like scholars of Jewish history, tended to study conversos in isolation from other populations. But they have done much to mitigate the once conventional image among Jewish scholars of the conversos essentially as a population of crypto-Jews. While there is no single thrust to their work—their assumptions, methodologies, and interests vary widely—they have played an important role in throwing light on the otherwise neglected lives of *assimilated* conversos, relying on local and regional archival documents as well as Inquisition files.[3] They have shown that some converso families, faced with stigma and discrimination, succeeded in gaining official certification that their blood was "pure," and that others married into the nobility, entered the Church, gained privileged positions on municipal councils, or otherwise blended into Old Christian society.

While such studies have served to balance the picture, some have overemphasized converso assimilation, representing converso identity in strictly socioeconomic terms. *"La clase social de los conversos"*—the title of an important work published in 1955 by Antonio Domínguez Ortiz—is an early

---

[2] The most influential work in this vein is Yirmiyahu Yovel, *The Other Within: The Marranos; Split Identity and Emerging Modernity* (Princeton, 2009). For critical reviews of the work see David Nirenberg, "Unrenounceable Core," *London Review of Books* 31, no. 14 (2009): 16-17; Miriam Bodian, *American Historical Review* 115 (2010): 616–18; and Yitzhak Melamed, *Journal of Modern History* 83 (2011): 198–200.

[3] An early contribution is that of Francisco Márquez Villanueva, "Conversos y cargos concejiles en el siglo XV," *Revista de Archivos, Bibliotecas y Museos* 63 (1957): 503–40. For a more recent study in English, see Linda Martz, *A Network of Converso Families in Early Modern Toledo: Assimilating a Minority* (Ann Arbor, MI, 2003). For a discussion of the use of non-inquisitorial documents for the study of conversos, see Enrique Soria Mesa, "Los judeoconversos granadinos en el siglo XVI: Nuevas fuentes, nuevas miradas," in *Estudios sobre Iglesia y Sociedad en Andalucía en la Edad Moderna* (Granada, 1999): 101–9.

example of this approach. The author describes the New Christian population as an "educated, wealthy and active minority" that was concentrated in urban areas and in certain occupations (administrative functions, commerce, crafts) and that was separated from the majority society by "an invisible frontier" of discrimination.[4] Let me add that Domínguez Ortiz was by no means doctrinaire, and what he meant by "social class" was rather vague. In a far more dogmatic vein, the Portuguese scholar António José Saraiva published a work in 1956 that made the radical and controversial argument that the Portuguese Inquisition was in effect an instrument of class struggle. His work dismissed as disingenuous the religious or racial justifications that contemporaries gave when anti-converso measures were adopted. In his view the Portuguese New Christian mercantile bourgeoisie threatened the ruling aristocratic class, which fought back by establishing an institution that, while claiming to be a guardian of Catholic orthodoxy, in fact aimed to crush the power of the class of New Christians of Jewish descent.[5] Whether "social class" has been conceived loosely or dogmatically, however, the use of this term has served to support the impression that Iberians with Jewish ancestry, scattered throughout the Peninsula, comprised a cohesive and rather homogeneous urban stratum.

In fact, the trajectories of assimilation were myriad. As early as the fifteenth century many conversos in Spain were conforming—and sometimes deeply committed—Catholics. But they were not necessarily *conventional* Catholics. It is well known that conversos played an entirely disproportionate role in fifteenth- and sixteenth-century circles where new, interior forms of Catholic spirituality were developed, forms that harked back to Pauline teaching but also drew from Reformation currents.[6] Recent work has helped elucidate how the social degradation experienced by conversos provided a motivation for adopting this new, egalitarian spiritual orientation.[7] Crypto-Jews could also be attracted to it. It was by reading Catholic spiritual literature in this vein (about which see the essay of Mercedes García-Arenal in this issue) that the dogmatizing judaizer Luis Carvajal integrated aspects of this

---

[4] Antonio Domínguez Ortiz, *La clase social de los conversos en Castilla en la edad moderna* (Madrid, 1955), 139–54, quotes at 139–40.

[5] The first edition of this quite polemical work was published in Portuguese as *Inquisição e cristãos novos* (Lisbon, 1956), and was followed by five subsequent editions. It has been published in English as *The Marrano Factory: The Portuguese Inquisition and Its New Christians 1536–1765*, trans. Herman Prins Salomon and Isaac S. D. Sassoon (Leiden, 2001).

[6] Marcel Bataillon brought this to light in his magisterial work, *Erasme et l'Espagne* (Paris, 1937).

[7] See Stefania Pastore, *Una herejía Española: Conversos, alumbrados e Inquisición (1449–1559)* (Madrid, 2010).

spirituality into his followers' practice and understanding of Judaism.[8] Research on this protean trend, which drew richly from wider European trends, and for convenience is referred to as *alumbradismo*, has served to underscore the vitality of religious innovation in early modern Spain, as well as the need to look across religoethnic divides in order to grasp its contours.

Morisco Historiography

Scholarship on moriscos has long been similarly partitioned off from the study of other Iberian populations. (Not coincidentally, my own assessment here relies heavily on the work of others.[9]) As with conversos, scholars have tended to treat the history of the moriscos as a distinct subfield with its own contours. To be sure, a few scholars have skillfully examined both converso and morisco minorities.[10] Yet until recently they have usually done so in separate studies dedicated to one group *or* the other. It is true that scholars have noted the evident, if partial, parallels between morisco and converso history.[11] But, in general, as James Amelang has observed, conversos and moriscos have been treated in "two largely separate historiographies that often seem to … live largely with their backs to each other."[12]

The historical trajectory of the moriscos differs most strikingly from that of the conversos in that the former were forcibly expelled en masse from Spain. Despite the fact that they had been baptized for generations, they were uprooted in the years 1609–1614 and scattered mainly to Muslim lands. In contrast to the conversos, much of whose history has been written by Jewish scholars, morisco history has overwhelmingly been written by Spanish historians (or other western Hispanists). This has not been due to Arab historians' lack of interest in Spain's Muslim population. However, most works written in Arabic on Muslim Spain have dealt with the centuries when that

---

[8] See Miriam Bodian, *Dying in the Law of Moses: Crypto-Jewish Martyrdom in the Iberian World* (Bloomington, IN, 2007), 47–78.

[9] I am particularly indebted to the review essay by Mercedes García-Arenal, "Religious Dissent and Minorities: The Morisco Age," *Journal of Modern History* 81 (2009): 888–920.

[10] Mercedes García-Arenal points to the "distinguished exceptions" of Julio Caro Baroja, Antonio Domínguez Ortiz, and Francisco Márquez Villanueva in her "Religious Dissent and Minorities," 902–3. For further works that have dealt with both populations, see James S. Amelang's pioneering work, *Historias paralelas: Judeoconversos y moriscos en la España moderna* (Madrid 2011), 183–84.

[11] For a deft and concise analysis of parallels and differences, see James S. Amelang, *Parallel Histories: Muslims and Jews in Inquisitorial Spain* (Baton Rouge, LA, 2013), the abridged English translation of *Historias paralelas*.

[12] Amelang, *Parallel Histories*, x.

society flourished; few have been dedicated to the century of decline after the mass conversions of the sixteenth century. This has produced different fault lines in converso and morisco history, respectively. While in the case of converso scholarship there has sometimes been a struggle between two competing national narratives (Jewish and Spanish), in the case of the moriscos the struggle has mainly been over the shape of one national narrative—the Spanish. Traditional early modern Spanish historiography, which viewed Spain as fundamentally European and Christian, rendered moriscos, in one scholar's words, as "exotic and strange, almost out of place in their own homeland, and marginal to the great events of the Hispanic imperial drama."[13] However, a cluster of scholars in recent decades (including several featured in this issue) have challenged this view, envisioning Spain as the moriscos' homeland, a region where their ancestors had put down extensive roots many centuries earlier.

The need to reconceive Spanish history in a way that demarginalized moriscos was articulated in an influential work by Francisco Márquez Villanueva, who since 1960 sought to demonstrate how little early modern Spain conformed to its fixed historiographical image.[14] Márquez argued that the necessity felt by Spaniards to justify the expulsion of hundreds of thousands of baptized persons whose only crime was their Muslim ancestry had shaped the historical narrative about the morisco presence from the start. According to the prevailing narrative, he noted, there was never really any other option but to expel the moriscos, because they had proved unassimilable. This convenient assumption about the moriscos persisted even well after the emergence of modern Spanish scholarship in the nineteenth century.

Márquez also argued (as have others) that disproportionate reliance on Inquisition documents has reinforced the stereotype of the unassimilable morisco. Much as in converso scholarship, reliance on the plentiful files of the Inquisition to study moriscos, who were typically charged with adhering to Muslim practices, has tended to magnify the conflictive aspects of morisco/Old Christian relations. It is no accident that historical overviews of Spanish history often deal with moriscos mainly as a "problem" for Spanish society. To be sure, more progressively minded historians, critical of the religious and cultural coercion exercised by Spanish authorities in early modern Spain, have viewed morisco resistance sympathetically. Either way, however—that is, whether moriscos are viewed as troublemakers or victims seeking justice—they appear in a posture of conflict with Old Christian society.

---

[13]L. P. Harvey, *Muslims in Spain (1500–1614)* (Chicago, 2005), viii.
[14]Francisco Márquez Villanueva, *El problema morisco* (*Desde otras laderas*) (Madrid, 1998), 98–195.

That many people imagine the morisco population to be an undifferentiated mass—poor, rural, Arabic-speaking, resistant to Spanish-Catholic culture, and inclined to ally themselves with Muslim powers—also has to do with the fact that scholars have tended to focus on the dense, rural, and unintegrated moriscos of Valencia and Granada (where moriscos launched a serious rebellion in 1568–70, after the use of Arabic was banned), to the neglect of the more assimilated moriscos of Castile and Aragon, who are often difficult to identify. Summarizing an agenda that she has singularly advanced, Mercedes García-Arenal a decade ago wrote of the need to "endow Morisco history with a complexity it currently lacks."[15] Recent research has brought into view the activity of moriscos who were no longer the manual workers and farm laborers they had been at the time of the mass conversions, but whose ranks included priests, university graduates, nobles, and civic functionaries. A trove of local documents has revealed the considerable social mobility over the course of the sixteenth century of the moriscos in the Castilian village of Villarrubia, as well as these moriscos' readiness to take action to preserve their rights.[16] An outstanding example elsewhere of morisco activism is that of the Granadine morisco Francisco Núñez Muley, who wrote a trenchant memorandum to Crown officials protesting the restrictions placed on traditional morisco customs and habits that did not violate Christian norms.[17]

The work of revision has entailed turning to new sources and expanding the field of study. A particularly rich source for recent research is the *aljamiado* literature, a morisco literature in vernacular Spanish with Arabic elements, written in Arabic script. Although *aljamiado* texts were systematically confiscated by the Inquisition, some two hundred of them, hidden away, have survived. These texts reveal a creative vitality in the morisco orbit that has often been assumed not to exist. In the wake of a massive assault on their sense of collective identity, authors of this literature engaged in a process of recovery and reconstruction, one that entailed the linguistic and cultural hispanization of Islam (a phenomenon with parallels in crypto-Jewish circles) in

---

[15]García-Arenal, "Religious Dissent and Minorities," 892.

[16]For a work that aims to demonstrate the diversity of morisco voices, see Bernard Vincent, *El río morisco* (Saragossa, 2006). See also the revealing research of Trevor J. Dadson, *Tolerance and Coexistence in Early Modern Spain: Old Christians and Moriscos in the Campo de Calatrava* (Woodbridge, UK, 2014).

[17]See Vincent, *El río morisco*, 89–104, chapter titled "Algunos voces más: De Francisco Núñez Muley a Fátima Ratal." And see, in English, the introduction by Vincent Barletta to his translation of this work, *A Memorandum for the President of the Royal Audiencia and Chancery Court of the City and Kingdom of Granada* (Chicago, 2007), 1–54.

an effort to preserve the traditions of Muslim Spain.[18] Of particular interest, also, is a set of forged lead tablets found in Granada shortly before the start of the expulsion in 1609, which have now been closely studied.[19] These texts, written in Arabic, were supposedly authored in the first century by disciples of Saint James, who according to tradition had brought Christianity to Iberia. They offer a narrative of the Spanish past in which Arabic culture—including the Arabic language and elements of Islam—are integrated into a Christian framework. The morisco forgers of these tablets perhaps hoped to mitigate Crown and Church measures that were intended to eliminate Arabic and cultural habits associated with Islam (about which see David Scotto's article in this issue).

Interest also has turned to the experience of moriscos *after* their expulsion from Spain. Here, again, there is a parallel with converso history. However, while sources abound and much has been written on the ex-converso diaspora, morisco exile sources—and research based on them—is more limited, partly because the great majority of the morisco exiles were absorbed relatively quickly into the Muslim cultures of their places of settlement. Yet recent work by scholars, building on the work of Mikel de Epalza, has contributed to a multifaceted picture of morisco life after the expulsion, not only in North African and Ottoman lands but in Spain, where some returned or managed to remain. The fact that morisco exiles had lost so many of their traditions that they had to undergo a process of "islamization" (akin to the "rabbinization" of ex-conversos), along with the fact that they continued to write in Spanish and sometimes identified as Andalusian nobles, attests to the degree to which they had been hispanized.[20]

This Issue

In sum, recent studies have produced a wealth of evidence that, despite the Crown's enormously powerful apparatus of religious control, early modern Spain was a site of considerable religious ferment. The sometimes-radical

---

[18] See Luce López-Baralt, *La literature secreta de los últimos musulmanes de España* (Madrid, 2009), and the introduction to María Teresa Narváez Córdoba, ed., *Tratado (Tafsira) del Mancebo de Arévalo* (Madrid, 2003).

[19] See Mercedes García-Arenal and Fernando Rodríguez Mediano, *Un oriente español: Los moriscos y el Sacromonte en tiempos de Contrarreforma* (Madrid, 2010); English translation, *The Orient in Spain: Converted Muslims, the Forged Lead Books of Granada, and the Rise of Orientalism*, trans. Consuelo López-Morillas (Leiden, 2013).

[20] See, inter alia, Luis Bernabé Pons, *Los moriscos: Conflicto, expulsion y diaspora* (Madrid 2009); Mercedes García-Arenal and Gerard Wiegers, eds. *Los moriscos: Expulsión y diáspora: Una perspectiva internacional*, 2nd ed. (Valencia, 2016).

reevaluation of religious assumptions in early modern Spain, to some degree fed by humanist and Italian-Catholic innovations from abroad, had much to do with the exposure of Spaniards to three religious traditions. The discovery of manifold permutations of belief (or unbelief) in all sectors of society has contributed to what Seth Kimmel has called "a dramatically revised sense of the place of Spain ... within the broader European history of religious reform."[21] The Inquisition, however long its reach, could not prevent human minds from productively violating the orthodoxies it tried to enforce. The very existence of competing faiths in a Spain that systematically persecuted infidels and heretics—that was still, in effect, a multireligious society—had an impact, however immeasurable, on the way Spaniards of all backgrounds interpreted their experience.[22]

This issue of *Jewish History* grew out of two panels at the annual meeting of the Renaissance Society of America Annual Meeting in New Orleans in March 2018. The essays it includes explore the impact of cross-religious interchange in the life and imagination of early modern Spanish subjects. The authors, while attentive to research that has already been done, ask new questions and work with new sources. For readers who are unfamiliar with this relatively new vein of scholarship, the essays in this issue can serve as an introduction. For specialists, they further elaborate an emerging cultural landscape that has proved to be anything but stagnant.

The opening article is by Mercedes García-Arenal, a leading scholar of morisco history and an important proponent of an integrated approach to the spiritual and intellectual history of early modern Spain. The mass conversions of Jews and Muslims were followed by the confiscation of their religious texts, depriving the converts and their descendants of access to the foundational texts of their traditions. In her essay, García-Arenal gleans from the riches of the inquisitorial archives to examine a specific phenomenon found among judaizing conversos. Lacking access to Jewish texts, the latter made use of Catholic sources (among them, polemical and inspirational works) to learn about Judaism, reading them "against the grain." So important was this stratagem that inquisitors began to discern, on the basis of their interrogations, a specific repertoire of such texts. To prevent their use by judaizers, the Inquisition added many of these essentially orthodox works to indexes of forbidden books. The removal of access to these works had the unintended

---

[21] Seth Kimmel, "The Morisco Question: Methodology and Historiography," *History Compass* 17, no. 4 (2019): 6.

[22] See Felipe Pereda, *Images of Discord: Poetics and Politics of the Sacred Image in 15th Century Spain* (London, 2018), for a discussion of how the choice of religious statuary used in evangelizing the forced converts and their descendants had an impact on Old Christian piety. And see the contribution to this issue of Mercedes García-Arenal for a parallel phenomenon related to book censorship.

consequence of altering the religious experience even of pious, conforming Catholics. García-Arenal examines this phenomenon, which she richly illustrates, in the broader context of an intensely polemical and evangelizing early modern Spanish environment.

Yonatan Glazer-Eytan, in his essay, explores how Spanish-Catholic narratives and images sometimes depicted Muslims or moriscos committing imagined acts of sacrilege of a kind typically associated exclusively with Jews or conversos—in particular the supposed act of desecrating the host. He assembles evidence showing that on some occasions the Inquisition, too, accused moriscos of host sacrilege. Although Muslims lacked the motive that best "explained" Jewish behavior in host desecration narratives—that of deicidal impulses—they nevertheless appeared analogous to Jews in their stubborn infidelity, their hostility to Christianity, and their supposed skill at practicing magic. The author suggests that in tales whose fundamental aim was to prove the truth of the doctrine of transubstantiation (through a miracle that followed the desecration), the religio-ethnic identity of the infidel who perpetrated the crime might be of secondary importance. Widening his lens, Glazer-Eytan demonstrates how Jews and Muslims were lumped together in other contexts as well, including that of medieval restrictive legislation. Analyzing images and texts dating from the thirteenth to the seventeenth centuries, he suggests an association of Muslims and Jews in the Christian imagination, despite the crucial differences in Christian attitudes toward each of these religious minorities.

The following essay by Davide Scotto deals with a quite different case of Christian thinking that also, however, analogized Jews and Muslims. Scotto examines the evangelization strategies of the prominent Hieronymite friar Hernando de Talavera, archbishop of Granada, and challenges the accepted scholarly view that Talavera adopted a uniquely tolerant attitude toward coercively baptized infidels. In fact, he argues, Talavera's approach to conversion was in some respects quite compatible with that of his contemporaries. Scotto analyzes in detail the taxonomy of ritual practice and worship as it emerges from Talavera's program of evangelization for both conversos and moriscos. What he perceives underlying Talavera's works is a universal template of religious behavior, one that Talavera applied to both Judaism and Islam (and perhaps to infidel religions in general). The plan was not geared to effecting a spiritual conversion in the hearts and minds of forced converts. Rather, it aimed to eliminate the everyday rites and customs that had been integral to the converts' previous lives, replacing them with Christian practices. Scotto makes the argument that Talavera's supersessionist understanding of his plan, though rhetorically Pauline, in fact represented a basic deviation from the teachings of Paul.

In the final essay, Miriam Bodian opens with a historiographical survey showing how, from the 1980s onward, scholars have come to recognize the pervasiveness, richness, and fluidity of heterodox ideas in early modern Iberia. The same ideas that, when conversos spoke them, were categorized by inquisitors as "judaizing" could also be found among heterodox Old Christians—though in the latter case they would likely be categorized as "blasphemy" or heretical "*proposiciones*." Skeptical ideas—once largely absent from the history of early modern Spain—have been found scattered in Inquisition documents, uttered by Old and New Christians alike. The profusion of such evidence has led scholars to think more deeply about the paths by which heterodoxy originated and circulated. Bodian's essay continues with an examination of a set of unresolved issues raised by this evidence. Do the popular criticisms of Catholic doctrine uncovered by the Inquisition precociously anticipate the European Enlightenment, or did such criticisms perhaps exist, though undocumented, everywhere in Reformation Europe? Put differently, was the Inquisition uncovering religiously skeptical and relativistic currents that were latent and ubiquitous in European cultures, or did these currents first appear in Iberia, where they signaled an early shift in the direction of "modernity"? Can we reliably explain what lay behind the heterodox expressions recorded by the Inquisition? And are we able accurately to assess their scope?

Publisher's Note   Springer Nature remains neutral with regard to jurisdictional claims in published maps and institutional affiliations.

Jewish History (2021) 35: 241–263
https://doi.org/10.1007/s10835-021-09423-1

Reading Against the Grain, Readings of Substitution: Catholic Books as Inspiration for Judaism in Early Modern Iberia

MERCEDES GARCÍA-ARENAL

Consejo Superior de Investigaciones Científicas, Madrid, Spain
E-mail: mercedes.garciaarenal@cchs.csic.es

Accepted: 15 July 2021 / Published online: 17 December 2021

Abstract Forced conversion produced a large number of converts, many or at least some of whom sought to continue to practice their former religion. For many crypto-Jews and crypto-Muslims, polemical literature was actually a source of knowledge about their old religion—sometimes the *only* source. It was not unusual for Iberian New Christians, lacking access to Jewish or Islamic books, to make use of Catholic works either to gather information about Judaism and Islam or to borrow from their expressions of spirituality and piety. In this essay I explore the unintended readings and reception of polemical works among converts, in particular the Christian books of piety and devotion that persons of converso origin read and used in their own writings. In the end most of these books were included by the Inquisition and Church censors in the *Index of Forbidden Books*, affecting in this way the perception of these orthodox books by Catholic Church authorities. On the one hand, I am interested in how a heterodox (or Jewish or Muslim) spirituality could be constructed using Catholic books; on the other hand, in how this phenomenon had an impact on orthodox Catholics. I argue that Catholic books were sometimes condemned to the *Index* simply because they were read by New Christians who the Inquisition considered to be judaizers or crypto-Muslims.

Keywords Early modern Iberia · Forced conversion · Religious polemics · Crypto-Islam ·
Crypto-Judaism · Conversos · Religious dissent

This essay addresses questions pertaining to the social, religious, and cultural consequences of the forced conversions that took place in Iberia in the fifteenth and early sixteenth centuries.[1] In that period, through a series of royal decrees, Iberia was transformed from the religiously plural society that it had been during the Middle Ages into a mono-confessional one. Judaism and Islam were forbidden, as were their sacred texts. The change from a religiously plural society to a mono-confessional one was of tremendous consequence and took place in conjunction with the establishment of the Inquisition and the crisis produced by the Protestant Reformation, which questioned

---

Chapter 2 was originally published as García-Arenal, M. Jewish History (2021) 35: 241–263.
https://doi.org/10.1007/s10835-021-09423-1.

[1]For a contextualization, see Mercedes García-Arenal, ed., *After Conversion: Iberia and the Emergence of Modernity* (Leiden, 2016), and Mercedes García-Arenal and Yonatan Glazer-Eytan, eds., *Forced Conversion in Christianity, Judaism and Islam: Coercion and Faith in Premodern Iberia and Beyond* (Leiden, 2020).

the sources of religious authority. Public indoctrination, evangelization, religious polemics—including attacks on Judaism and Islam and refutation of the arguments of Judaism and Islam against Catholicism—all became part of everyday life for the inhabitants of Iberia. The forced conversions made necessary a degree of disputation and evangelization that led to some of the conflicts analyzed in this paper.

In recent work I have argued that widespread conversion created knowledge of, and even familiarity with, the religions of the former minorities. Paradoxically, as a result of the contact between religious faiths that had each previously been confined to a community of believers, forced conversion gave rise to a multiplicity of religious options. The three religions each affected the development of the others over time. Iberia became a polemical arena, and polemical social, cultural, and political fields became factors in the way the three religious communities interacted in the many diverse regions of the Peninsula.[2] Polemics was part of a theological discourse, but it was also a form of social practice that carried with it real consequences in the field of interreligious encounters. Polemics largely reflect changing relations among the three communities, but also internal apologetic needs.

Forced conversion produced a large number of converts, many of whom tried to continue to practice their former religion or the religion of their forefathers, becoming crypto-Jews or crypto-Muslims whose access to the sources and Scriptures of Judaism and Islam was very limited. Despite the fact that chairs of Arabic and Hebrew existed in the universities, the former was forbidden to moriscos (converted Muslims) and the latter was the object of deep suspicion. In the last ten years of the fifteenth century, Ferdinand of Aragon and Isabella of Castile forbade all vernacular translations not only of the Hebrew Bible and the Talmud, but also of the Christian Bible that includes the New Testament. St. Jerome's Latin translation, known as the Vulgate, was to be the only translation permitted to the inhabitants of Iberia, whether converts or Catholics. The Inquisition was particularly vigilant and persecuted the possession of all sacred scriptures in Romance languages. From the middle years of the sixteenth century it also promoted the censorship of religious texts and the inclusion of forbidden works in the various consecutive *Indexes*.[3] The difficulties in reading the Bible affected even the educated elites, beginning with the categorical interdiction of vernacular

---

[2]Mercedes García-Arenal and Gerard Wiegers, eds., "Introduction" to *Polemical Encounters: Polemics between Christians, Jews and Muslims in Iberia and Beyond* (Leiden, 2019), 1–21.

[3]Virgilio Pinto Crespo, *Inquisición y control ideológico en la España del siglo XVI* (Madrid, 1983); Rafael M. Pérez García, *La imprenta y la literatura espiritual castellana en la España del Renacimiento, 1470–1560: Historia de una emisión cultural* (Gijón, 2006), 119–74; Jesús Martínez de Bujanda, ed., *Index des livres interdits: Index librorum prohibitorum 1600-1966*, 11 vols. (Montreal, 1985–2002).

Bibles in the *Index* of 1551, and then with the *Censura Generalis* of 1554 onwards.[4] In 1552–53 the Inquisition set about feverishly confiscating all the Bibles in vernacular languages that it could find. Special officers were situated at frontier custom points to prevent any translated Bibles from being brought in from abroad.[5] The zeal shown by the Inquisition in confiscating and destroying most medieval and vernacular Bibles, considered as tokens of crypto-Jewish traditions and later as dissemination of Reformed ideas, is demonstrated by the scarce number of surviving copies.[6]

With the nearly insurmountable difficulty of accessing the sacred texts in the vernacular, for many converts polemical literature became an important source of knowledge about their old religion. I argue here that the Inquisition—and the Church in general—was conscious of the dangers posed by the information included in written works, sermons, and sentences that condemned Judaism, Islam, Protestantism, or other forms of deviance or dissent from Catholic orthodoxy. On the basis of Inquisition trials, I examine the problem of how converts could learn about the religion of their forefathers once Judaism had been forbidden, mainly through polemical works against Judaism and through Christian works of piety and spirituality. The converted Jews, as I show, were keen on a fixed repertoire of Catholic books that they used as inspiration for their own covert Judaism. I examine how this fact, this reading against the grain, may have affected not only Iberian crypto-Judaism but also Catholicism. I question the extent to which post-Expulsion Iberian Judaism was constructed on Christian texts and religious notions. Further, I argue that Catholicism, in its attempt to draw clear boundaries separating it from Judaism, reacted by forbidding and including in the *Index* some Catholic books that had become particularly popular among converts. Clerics and inquisitors also introduced changes in the way these texts were used in polemicizing and evangelizing. In other words, I suggest that the removal of Catholic books that Judeo-converts sought out and read from the Catholic mainstream allowed crypto-Judaism to affect and condition the definition of Spanish Catholicism itself.

Knowledge and Belief

Certain changes in early modern Catholicism provide important context, particularly the emergence of conceptions about faith and belief that impinge

---

[4]Martínez de Bujanda, *Index des livres interdits*, 5:276–302, 604.

[5]Angel Alcalá Galve, *Literatura y Ciencia ante la Inquisición Española* (Madrid, 2003), 67.

[6]Gemma Avenoza, "Las traducciones de la Biblia en castellano en la Edad Media y sus comentarios," in vol. 1, pt. 2 of *La Biblia en la literatura española*, ed. Gregorio del Olmo Lete (Madrid, 2008), 13–75.

upon the fields of religious polemics, censorship, and the indexes of forbidden books. These changes in Catholicism also were reflected in the way Jews thought about Judaism.

The measure of allegiance that Catholicism demanded from the believer increased after the late Middle Ages. Coinciding with the period of forced conversions, the expectation was that a Christian be knowledgeable in order to believe; the comfortable faith in the ancestral traditions of one's family or group (*habitus*) was no longer enough.[7] The new religious situation in Iberia demanded that all people (not only converts) be familiar with religious dogma in order to be considered good Catholics. Simple adherence to the faith no longer sufficed, since the mass conversions were accompanied by the imposition of a particular version of Catholicism, the one elaborated and defined at the Council of Trent in the middle decades of the sixteenth century.[8] While this deeper knowledge was required, it was also deemed to be dangerous, because it called into question not only authority but also loyalty, adhesion, and obedience. As Cavaillé, Wirth, Schmitt, Vega Ramos, and Mothu have have shown, Catholicism places value on the so-called *foi du charbonnier*, "the coalman's faith," or the faith of the ignorant and simple. [9] At the same time it requires this *charbonnier*—when he is suspected of heresy or irreligion—to demonstrate perfect theological orthodoxy and a complete absence of doubt.[10] Knowledge was thus both a problem and the remedy for the task that Schmitt has termed "faire croire."[11] The Inquisition considered

---

[7]Thomas Kselman, ed., *Belief in History: Innovative Approaches to European and American Religion* (Notre Dame, IN, 1991), especially John van Engen, "Faith as a Concept in Medieval Christendom," 19–67; John H. Arnold, *Belief and Unbelief in Medieval Europe* (London, 2005).

[8]See Fernando Bouza, Pedro Cardim, and Antonio Feros, eds., *The Iberian World: 1450–1820* (London, 2019), esp. 79ff.

[9]Jean-Pierre Cavaillé, "La Question de l'irréligion populaire, à la rencontre de l'histoire et de l'anthropologie," *Institut d'Histoire de la Réformation, Bulletin annuel* 36 (2015): 55–69, at 68; Jean Wirth, "La naissance du concept de croyance (XII–XVII siècles)," repr. in idem, *Sainte Anne est une sorcière et autres essais* (Geneva, 2003), 113–76; Alain Mothu, "De la foi du charbonier à celle du héros (et retour)," *Les dossiers du Grihl*, "Libertinage, athéisme, irreligion: Essais et bibliographie" (Dec. 6, 2010), https://journals.openedition.org/dossiersgrihl /3393.

[10]María José Vega Ramos, "The Coalman and the Devil: *Carbonaria Fides* and the Limits of Religious Knowledge," in *Religious Connectivity in Urban Communities* (1400–1600)*: Reading, Worshipping, and Connecting in the Continuum of Sacred and Secular*, ed. Suzan Folkerts (Turnout, 2021), 239–62, and eadem, "Coram simplicibus: Disputatio y diálogo doctrinal en el pensamiento censorio del siglo XVI," in *Diálogo y censura en el siglo XVI (España y Portugal)*, ed. Ana Vian Herrero, María José Vega Ramos, and Roger Friedlein (Madrid, 2016), 73–104.

[11]Jean-Claude Schmitt, "Du bon usage du 'Credo'," in *Faire croire: Modalités de la diffusion et de la réception des messages religieux du XIIe au XVe siècle* (Rome, 1981), 337–61.

interior conversion and full adherence to the entire corpus of Catholic belief to be imperative. To believe was to obey. This fact, as well as the story of the coalman, was an example that the morisco Ibrahim Taybili, exiled in Tunis at the beginning of the seventeenth century, cited as proof of the ignorance that Catholics had of their own faith. Taybili shows that the story of the coalman was a well known motif among the different religious groups of Iberia.[12]

Just how much the uneducated needed to know about religion had long presented a dilemma. The *Summa Theologica* expressly condemns laypeople disputing with heretics because it had the potential to lead to confusion and heresy. Thomas Aquinas believed that it was also illicit to hold any disputation about the faith "in the presence of simple people" (*pericolosum est disputare de fide coram simplicibus*) since their faith would be sturdier if they never heard anything other than what they were supposed to believe.[13] This idea is commonplace in Catholic theology throughout the fifteenth and sixteenth centuries. Many Catholic writers were of the opinion that one reason the Reformation had spread was precisely because the common people had gained access to spiritual debates and biblical interpretation.[14] Because of their emphasis on direct access to Scripture, Iberian Judaism and Lutheranism were often lumped together or connected in the mind of the Inquisition: two heresies that had merged from the time of the Pre-Reformation.[15] Indeed, from the end of the fifteenth century Spanish theologians had established a link between Jewish enthusiasm for printing and distributing the Bible and the work carried out by contemporary Christian Bible scholars and, in general, with the movements sparked off by the European Pre-Reformation.

In a key article on the subject, Eleazar Gutwirth also has shown that late medieval Spanish Jews shared with Christians an anticlericalism that was on the rise throughout Christian Europe in the years leading up to the Reformation. Clerical authority (that of the rabbis, in this case) was challenged

---

[12] Ibrahim Taybili, *Contradicción de los catorce artículos de la fe Cristiana* (1628), fols. 68v–69r. "Esta quimera y vano fundamento / en la fe que el cristiano idiota se ase/es la fe que celebran de aquel cuento / del carbonero que muriendo estaba / y la fe que sabía confesaba. / Preguntó el confesor en qué creía / respondió: 'padre mío solo creo / en lo que manda y al cristiano guía la santa madre iglesia'." I am grateful to Teresa Soto for giving me this passage of Taybili. See also Teresa Soto, "Poetics and Polemics: Ibrahim Taybili's Anti-Christian Polemical Treatise in Verse," in García-Arenal and Wiegers, *Polemical Encounters*, 331–56.

[13] John Tolan, "*Ne de fide presumant disputare*: Legal Regulations of Interreligious Debate and Disputation in the Middle Ages," in *Interreligious Encounters in Polemics between Christian, Jews, and Muslims in Iberia and Beyond*, ed. Mercedes García-Arenal, Gerard Wiegers, and Ryan Szpiech (Leiden, 2018), 14–28, esp. 23–24.

[14] Vega Ramos, "The Coalman and the Devil," 17.

[15] García-Arenal, "Introduction" to *After Conversion*, 1–19.

and confronted by direct readings of the Scriptures. The Christian religious crisis was reflected, according to Gutwirth, among the Jewish population, an argument that has helped Gutwirth shed new light on a number of texts.[16] This crisis was also an underlying factor in some voluntary and individual conversions of Jews to Christianity, as part of a current that rejected rabbinic authority and the preeminence of the Talmud over the Hebrew Bible.[17] Such is the case of Joshua ha-Lorki, a Jewish physician from Alcañiz in Aragon, who after conversion took the name Jerónimo de Santa Fe and wrote a treatise against the Talmud.[18]

At the same time, the way in which Catholics conceptualized religion had an impact on Judaism. Scholars like David Graizbord have argued that starting in the late Middle Ages in Iberia, Judaism and Jewish culture—the *ley de Moisés* that had previously been considered a law, a habitus, a way of life—was transformed into a "faith" and, therefore, in competition with Christianity. The public *Disputatios* in which late medieval Iberian Jews were forced to participate impelled Jewish religious authorities and intellectuals to echo the terms of Christian debate. Thus, whether for the purposes of disputation or out of true conviction, some Jewish scholars tacitly adopted the Christian definition of Jews' way of life as a "faith" founded on theological propositions and hence analogous to Christianity, in a sense a sort of inverted mirror-image of Christianity.[19]

As an illustration of the high degree to which Jewish scholars became accustomed to debating their ancestral law in conceptual terms that scholastic anti-Judaism had provided, both Graizbord and Benjamin Gampel have pointed to the aforementioned Joshua ha-Lorki who would later convert and become Jerónimo de Santa Fe.[20] His is one among the many cases that show how the rhetoric and images of Catholic religiosity permeated Iberian Ju-

---

[16]Eleazar Gutwirth, "Conversions to Christianity amongst Fifteenth-Century Spanish Jews: An Alternative Explanation," in *Shlomo Simonsohn Jubilee Volume: Studies in the History of the Jews in the Middle Ages and Renaissance Period*, ed. Daniel Carpi et al. (Tel Aviv, 1993), 97–121.

[17]Piero Capelli, "Jewish Converts in Jewish-Christian Intellectual Polemics in the Middle Ages," in *Intricate Interfaith Networks in the Middle Ages: Quotidian Jewish-Christian Contacts*, ed. Ephraim Shoham-Steiner (Turnhout, 2016), 33–83.

[18]Moisés Orfali, "Jerónimo de Santa fe y la polémica contra el Talmud," *Annuario di Studi Ebraici* X (1984): 157–78.

[19]David Graizbord, "The Fracturing of Jewish Identity in the Early Modern Jewish Diaspora: The Case of the *Conversos*," in *Paths to Modernity: A Tribute to Yosef Kaplan*, ed. Avriel Bar-Levav, Claude B. Stuczynski, and Michael Heyd (Jerusalem, 2018), 85–119.

[20]Benjamin R. Gampel, "A Letter to a Wayward Teacher: The Transformations of Sephardic Culture in Christian Iberia," in *Cultures of the Jews: A New History*, ed. David Biale (New York, 2002), 389–447.

daism.[21] The acceptance of Christian theological notions and propositions would be reinforced by the fact that the Latin Vulgate would soon become the only version of the Bible that Spanish Jews would be able to access. In short, the particular Catholic culture of the sixteenth and seventeenth centuries produced significant innovations in Spanish conversos' literary culture, rhetorical expression, and ideological content.[22]

Polemical Literature as an Agent of Conversion

The authorities' dissemination of knowledge about "heretical religions" had consequences—unintended and without a doubt indirect—on the Spanish public. The focus here is on information to be found in three sources: polemical works; the public "edicts of faith"; and the sentences read out publicly by the Inquisition. How did the Inquisition, and in general the Church, address the need to inform and evangelize and, in so doing, clearly demarcate what constituted the Catholic faith, while at the same time seeking to prevent this information from spreading dangerous ideas, raising doubts, or fostering irreligious personal opinions? It was a difficult balance to strike. The Inquisition had a powerful pedagogical role: it produced "edicts" in which different heresies, including Judaism and Islam, were described, as well as their practices and identifying signs. These edicts were read in public in cities and villages throughout Spain so that the common people could recognize heretics and denounce them. The Edicts of Faith included lists of Jewish and Muslim customs and rituals, and were published widely as an aid to identify judaizers or crypto-Muslims. This pedagogical role was indeed effective, if one is to judge from the Inquisition trials, which reveal the pervasiveness of the vigilance and denunciations. But it also spread knowledge about the repudiated religions and aroused doubt and even sympathy in dissenters or among people who were opposed to the inescapable power of the Church.

In fact, documents show that judaizers actually talked about their reliance on the Edicts of Faith. An example is offered by a case in Castile, in the community in Quintanar, in which the Inquisitor asked Antonio, the son of Juan de Mora, how he knew that the ritual decapitation of birds was an act of heresy. He replied that he had "heard it read aloud from an edict of the Holy Office and that he had done it so many times before that he did not even know

---

[21] David M. Gitlitz, *Secrecy and Deceit: The Religion of the Crypto-Jews* (Albuquerque, NM, 1996), 468–72; Miriam Bodian, *Dying in the Law of Moses: Crypto-Jewish Martyrdom in the Iberian World* (Bloomington, IN, 2007), 58.
[22] Carsten L. Wilke, *The Marrakesh Dialogues: A Gospel Critique and Jewish Apology from the Spanish Renaissance* (Leiden, 2014); Soto, "Poetics and Polemics," 331–56.

whether it was good or bad."[23] When, in 1643, Juan de León was accused in Mexico of teaching Judaism to the sisters Blanca de Rivera, he replied that "they knew more than he did about when certain celebrations took place, because in the Edicts of Faith that were publicly read you could hear all the rites and ceremonies of the Law of Moses."[24]

The autos-da-fé, in which detailed lists of accusation and offenses of heretics were read aloud to the public, were similar sources of knowledge. Belchior Fernandes was accused in Coimbra in 1574 of having said that if he knew about the Laws of Moses "it was from having heard them read in the copies of the sentences that the students from the village of Sea wrote down from the autos-da-fé in this city" and then read to him and others. In 1646 a witness in Mexico described how he had learned to Judaize when the Inquisition began to hold the autos-da-fé in the city.[25] The Suprema (supreme council) of the Inquisition concluded by recommending that the public readings of the sentences of those accused by the Inquisition appearing in a public auto-da-fé include as little about the prisoners' ideological justifications as possible. And so the Council of the Inquisition insisted:

> It is important to make sure that the rulings [of the Inquisition trials] do not state the motives and reasons provided by the prisoner, and which they use to defend their errors, nor those testified to by heretics, nor other things that might offend Catholic ears, nor which pose or might pose an opportunity to teach or learn something of these ideas or come to doubt anything; and this must be borne closely in mind, because it is said that some have learned from hearing these rulings.[26]

---

[23] Archivo Diocesano de Cuenca [ADC], Leg. 324, exp. 4652; Vincent Parello, "Inquisition and Crypto-Judaism: The "Complicity" of the Mora Family of Quintanar de la Orden (1588–1592)," in *The Conversos and Moriscos in Late Medieval Spain and Beyond*, ed. Kevin Ingram (Leiden, 2009), 187–210, esp. 198; Charles Amiel "Crypto-judaisme et Inquisition: La matière juive dans les édits de la foi des Inquisitions ibériques," *Revue de l'histoire des religions* 210 (1993): 145–68.

[24] Gitlitz, *Secrecy and Deceit*, 233 and 241; "lo sabían mejor que este confesante y cuando caía la dicha pascua y que en los edictos de la Fe que se publicaban oían todos los ritos y ceremonias de la dicha Ley de Moisés."

[25] Gitlitz, *Secrecy and Deceit*, 241; "Disse que elle nunqua for a judeu nem fizera cousas da ley de Moyses e que se algumas sabía, era por has ouvir lerem treslados de sentenças que os estudantes da villa de Sea tomavao nos autos de Fe e has hiao ler"; "Cuando se empezaron a hacer autos de la fe por los años cuarenta y seis poco más o menos, en esta ciudad, la dicha persona oía leer los ritos y ceremonias que hacían los judíos, lo cual todo procuraba hacer."

[26] Pablo García, *Modo di processare nel Tribunale del Santo Officio della Inquisizione di questo regno di Sicilia* (Palermo, 1714), 66; cited in Salvatore Caponetto, "Origini e caratteri della Riforma in Sicilia," *Rinascimento* 7 (1956): 219–341, quote at 252. "Hase de aduertir,

Polemical works were also a source of information. They could inform persons of Muslim or Jewish descent, but they could also arouse the curiosity or doubts of Old Christians, as illustrated with a few case studies. I begin by revisiting a very famous case, the trial of Lope de Vera.[27]

Lope de Vera was an Old Christian who converted to Judaism and died at the stake for maintaining and defending his beliefs. He was arrested in 1639 while he was at the University of Salamanca, where he had studied Hebrew. His intimate acquaintance with the Hebrew Bible and his recognition of the inadequacy of the Vulgate as a faithful translation, a conclusion he had arrived at by reading the forbidden works of Erasmus, along with his contacts with Portuguese conversos studying in Salamanca, had triggered his doubts about the tenets of the Catholic Church. He was struggling with doubt and trying out other religions in the hope of arriving at certainty. Of particular interest here is the fact that one main source for Lope's arguments against Catholicism was Alonso de Espina's *Fortalitium fidei*, a fifteenth-century book that was widely disseminated in Spain.[28] This book is a polemic against Christian heresy, Judaism, and Islam. In accordance with the standard scholastic methodology, Espina starts by citing their respective arguments against Catholicism in order to refute them afterwards. The Jewish arguments turned out to be more convincing for Lope de Vera than their Catholic refutations, which made the work counterproductive from the Church's perspective. This same book by Espina was also pivotal, a generation later, for the converso Isaac Orobio de Castro, who settled in Amsterdam and became a New Jew.[29]

Lope de Vera's case is far from unique. Juan de Prado turned from crypto-Judaism to a form of skeptical Deism while still in the Iberian Peninsula. According to the testimony given to the Inquisition by Baltasar (later Isaac) Orobio de Castro in Seville in 1643, Prado had adopted a skeptical view of all religions including Judaism as a result of reading polemical works. As for Francisco Maldonado, a Catholic of Jewish descent and a physician, he

---

que en las sentencias no se saquen las causas y razones que da el Reo, en que se funda para tener aquellos errores, ni las que dan los hereges, ni otra cosa que ofenda los oydos de los Católicos, ni que sea, ni pueda ser ocasión, que por ello sean enseñados, o que aprendan algunas cosas de aquellas, o vengan a dudar en algo; y esto se deue mirar y considerar mucho, porque se afirma que algunos se han enseñado, oyendo estas sentencias."

[27] Analyzed by Miriam Bodian, *Dying in the Law of Moses*, 156–77, and published in part by Kenneth Brown, *De la cárcel inquisitorial a la sinagoga de Amsterdam* (*Edición y estudio del "Romance a Lope de Vera" de Antonio Enríquez Gómez*) (Toledo, 2007).

[28] Alonso de Espina, *Fortalitium fidei* (Nuremberg, 1494); Ryan Szpiech, *Conversion and Narrative: Reading and Religious Authority in Medieval Polemic* (Philadelphia, 2012), 144.

[29] Yosef Kaplan, *From Christianity to Judaism: The Study of Isaac Orobio de Castro*, trans. Raphael Loewe (Oxford, 1989) 77, 102–104.

encountered a book in his father's library that was to have a profound effect on him—the *Scrutinium scripturarum*, by the converted Jew Pablo de Santa María.[30] The former rabbi addressed the work, written in 1432–34, to his former coreligionists in order to convince them that Christianity was the true religion. He sought to remove the basic theological obstacles to the Jewish reception of Christianity. On the other hand, he made use of Talmudic literature as a source of polemical truths. As much as Christians intensified their campaigns for conversion on the base of rabbinic testimonies, they did propagate anti-Christian features of rabbinic Judaism.[31] The structure of the first part of the book, a dialogue between Paul, the Christian, and Saul, the Jew, allows Saul to ask some pointed questions on key issues in the long history of medieval Jewish anti-Christian polemics. In his inquisitorial trial, Maldonado confessed that, after having read "some questions that Saul had asked in defense of the Law of Moses, which Paul had responded to in defense of the Law of Jesus Christ," he found that he was dissatisfied with Paul's replies. Santa María recognized that the Jews' strongest polemical edge was their insistence on a straightforward, if not strictly literal, interpretation of the biblical text. When Maldonado read this work, according to what he told the inquisitors, it seemed to him that the Jewish position was stronger than the Christian one.

Another work that had an influence on Francisco Maldonado was Fray Luis de León's *De los nombres de Cristo*. David Gitlitz has suggested that this work may have been attractive to judaizers because of the abundant citations of Old Testament material. Fernando Rodríguez Mediano has argued in a recent essay that Fray Luis de León's trial by the Inquisition revolved not so much around the fact of his having translated biblical texts into the vernacular (though, of course, this was one of the charges), as around his criticism of the Vulgate and his defense of a literal rather than an allegorical interpretation.[32] Francisco Maldonado had also read Fray Luis de Granada's *Introducción al Símbolo de la Fe* and written a refutation of it. Maldonado's arguments for the truth of the Law of Moses rested entirely on medieval Jewish anti-Christian polemics, as was the case with Isaac Cardoso and his *Excelencias de los Hebreos*, according to Yerushalmi.[33]

[30] Yosi Yisraeli, "From Christian Polemic to a Jewish-Converso Dialogue: Jewish Skepticism and Rabbinic-Christian Traditions in the *Scrutinium Scripturarum*," *Medieval Encounters* 24 (2018): 160–96.

[31] Ibid., 195.

[32] Fernando Rodríguez Mediano, "Biblical Translations and Literalness in Early Modern Spain," in García-Arenal, *After Conversion*, 66–94.

[33] Yosef Hayim Yerushalmi, *From Spanish Court to Italian Ghetto. Isaac Cardoso: A Study in Seventeenth-Century Marranism and Jewish Apologetics* (New York, 1971).

This reversal in the role of Christian polemical literature is also observed in the case of the converted Muslims known as moriscos. There are many Inquisition trials in which a morisco is accused of having in his possession the famous anti-Islamic polemical treatise *Antialcorano* by Bernardo Pérez de Chinchón (1535). This book contained extensive information on Islamic beliefs and practices and included many literal translations of Qur'anic *suras* as well as the interpretation given to them by the canonical authors of *tafsir*. One such example is the trial of Luis de Córdoba, which took place in the village of San Clemente. Luis de Córdoba had borrowed a Qur'an in Arabic and paid to have it copied because he knew no Arabic. He also was in possession of Pérez de Chinchón's *Antialcorano*, which formed one of the charges against him. One possible explanation for his possession of this work is that he was trying to follow his Arabic Qur'an with the help of the translations and glosses provided by Pérez de Chinchón. The morisco Jesuit Ignacio de las Casas mentions this reading of *Antialcoranes* by moriscos in his *Memorial* to Cristóbal de los Cobos. Las Casas remarks on how many moriscos used the *Antialcorano* to gain doctrinal information about Islam and bought the book not to be convinced of the superiority of Catholicism but to learn more about Islam.[34]

The Church considered as dangerous polemical literature that could be used as a source for converts to learn about the religion of their forefathers. In addition, these works included the arguments of other religions against Catholicism. Were the Inquisition and the Church sensitive to the dangers and unintended effects of polemical works? The answer is undoubtedly "Yes." In his *Cathólica impugnación* (Salamanca, 1487)[35] Hernando de Talavera, the well-known bishop of Granada, authored a book of polemics against the "judaizing heresy" as it was formulated in anonymous pamphlet that appeared in Seville. This pamphlet, now lost, that Talavera called the *libelo* was written

---

[34]"Aunque an salido varios cathecismos o contra alcoranes, son en lenguas que ni éstos saben ni ven y los que para los de España an salido en la nuestra, an sido tales que, méritamente, an sido prohibidos, así porque guiándose los autores dellos por solas relaciones y por lo que hallan en otros libros atribuyen a la secta lo que no admite o niegan lo que admite, como por lo principal que se a esperimentado que, no siendo los argumentos tales que valgan a convencerlos bastamente, lo que dellos los v[e]ían, se mofavan de todo y, citando costumbres y lugares del Alcorán, los compravan (más para enterarse en sus ceremonias y costumbres, que las hallaban allí juntas, ya que no les permitían tenerlas de otra manera) que para convencerse." Youssef El Alaoui, "El jesuita Ignacio de las Casas y la defensa de la lengua árabe: Memorial al padre Cristóbal de los Cobos, provincial de Castilla (1607)," *Áreas: Revista Internacional de Ciencias Sociales* 30 (2011): 11–28, esp. 16–17.

[35]Hernando de Talavera, *Cathólica impugnación del herético libelo maldito y descomulgado que fue divulgado en la ciudad de Sevilla*, ed. Francisco Márquez Villanueva and Stefania Pastore (Córdoba, 2012).

by Jewish converts who thought that they could become Christians but retain parts of Judaism.

In *Cathólica impugnación* Talavera explicitly follows the principle of not spreading heretical doctrine but, rather, summarizing it only to the extent that it can ultimately be refuted and, hence, eradicated. Hernando de Talavera says:

> Now let us come to refuting [the libel] by examining some of its words and briefly showing through commentary that it is all madness, foolishness, heresy, and vain speech. The entire wicked libel is not given here *de verbum ad verbum* in order not to engage those who would want to read this and the vain and inconsequential speech that it contains without any purpose or connection, and also because heresies ought not be seen or heard beyond what is necessary to refute and destroy them.[36]

But despite the explicit precautions taken by Talavera, the *Cathólica impugnación* was included in the *Index* of forbidden books of 1559 together with the *Antialcorano* of Pérez de Chinchón and other polemical works that contained too much information about the religion under attack and its arguments against Catholicism. These included Lope de Obregón's *Confutación del Alcorán* (Granada, 1555) and Juan Andrés's *Confusión o Confutación de la secta mahomética y del Alcorán* (Valencia, 1515), works that had been written for the evangelization of the Muslims of Granada and Valencia. Later they also would include a work by Jerónimo Gracián de la Madre de Dios, a Carmelite friar and confessor of Teresa de Ávila. His *Diez lamentaciones del miserable estado de los ateístas de nuestros tiempos* (Brussels, 1611), which deals with different Protestant sects, as well as with libertines and skeptics, was included in the *Index* of 1632. The prologue of the 1559 *Index* expressly stated that all books containing attacks on Catholicism written by Protestants, Jews, and Muslims, as well as "disputes and controversies of a religious nature between Catholics and heretics as well as refutations of Muhammad in the vulgar tongue" were forbidden.[37] It had become necessary to put an end to the spread of any and all heretical doctrines.

---

[36] *Cathólica impugnación*, 15: "Ahora vengámonos a lo impugnar (el libelo) examinando algunas de sus palabras y mostrando brevemente como por vía de comento que todas son locuras, necedades, herejías y hablas vanas. No se pone aquí todo su mandito libelo *de verbum ad verbum* por no ocupar a los que esto quisieren leer con muchas vanas y livianas hablas que contiene sin propósito y sin concierto; y aún porque las herejías, ni deben ser vistas ni oídas, más de cuanto es menester para que sean impugnadas y destruídas."

[37] "Las disputas y las controversias de carácter religioso entre católicos y herejes así como las refutaciones de Mahoma en lengua vulgar." *Index Librorum Prohibitorum* (1559).

Catholic Books Favored by Jewish Converts

To this point the focus has been on the reading of books "against the grain"—selective reading of fragments from a specific type of book. This sort of reading disregards the work's main argument and magnifies the aspect of the work that the dissident reader sets out to refute. While some of the books now to be discussed can be included among works that were read "against the grain," the focus here will be readings of these books that involved substitution and appropriation.

Literacy among Judeo-Conversos was high, reaching 72% in the case of men. This is an extremely high figure as compared to the mere 34% among Old Christians.[38] While many were moderately affluent artisans and shopkeepers, as well as contractors and businessmen, their relationship with written culture is also worth considering. Books with title and author were recorded in the inventory of sequestered items of some defendants of the Inquisition.[39]

Many trials of judaizers record the titles of the books in the defendant's possession, as well as the books that the defendant had heard others read out loud in his or her community. Reading aloud was often a shared, lived activity performed by specific individuals who played an important role in their community. Catholic works read from a Jewish perspective constituted the largest category of books mentioned in the Inquisition trial documents. It is important to bear their titles in mind (usually just the title is given) because they constitute a repertoire that, while relatively small, reappears throughout Spanish lands, from Majorca to Lima, over the course of approximately two centuries.[40] Among them are books containing stories of the prophets or stories from the Old Testament more generally.[41] Such is the case of *La torre de David* by the Jeronymite friar Juan de Lemos and *David perseguido* by Cristóbal Lozano. In seventeenth-century Cuenca, Antonio Enríquez de León reported that at his father's house he had read a book

> called *Cronicón* ..., the first part of which deals with the entire Old Testament, and the second part with the New. Because of the

---

[38] Sara T. Nalle, "Literacy and Culture in Early Modern Castile," *Past and Present* 125 (1998): 65–96.

[39] Miriam Bodian, "An Inventory of an Inquisitorial Prisoner's Possessions: An Introduction," *Early Modern Workshop: Jewish History Resources, vol. 4, Jewish Consumption and Material Culture in the Early Modern Period*, 2007, University of Maryland, https://fordham.bepress.com/cgi/viewcontent.cgi?article=1057&context=emw.

[40] Charles Amiel, "Les cent voix de Quintanar: Le modèle castillan du marranisme," *Revue de l'histoire des religions* 218 (2001): 195–280, at 218, and 487–577, esp. 516–34.

[41] Bernardo López Belinchón, *Honra, libertad y hacienda (Hombres de negocios y judíos sefardíes)* (Alcalá de Henares, 2001), 361.

information that Moses gives about his Law and [information it offers] about other prophets, he bought it on the advice of his father, *licenciado* Méndez de León, and of his stepmother, and after getting married he read it to his people many times.[42]

Another book belonging to this genre is the *Sumario de la vida y excelencia de trece patriarcas del Testamento Nuevo*, by the Dominican Domingo de Valtanás. Valtanás was a close friend of both Fray Luis de Granada and Juan de Ávila, who were in favor of reading the Bible in Spanish. His book was banned in the *Index* of 1582.[43] Most of these books included references to or quotations from the Old Testament, or bits of information about the history of the people of Israel.[44] History was a very important bone of contention among groups of different religious origins in Iberia. Pedro Onofre, a Chueta (converso) from Majorca, was knowledgeable about the history of the Jews and held gatherings in his house in which he expounded on it, "since he appears to have read about it in the *Flos Sanctorum* or in the book called *Monarchía Ecclesiástica*."[45]

There are multiple books bearing the title *Flos Sanctorum*. The *Index* of 1559 banned a *Flos Sanctorum* printed in Zaragoza in 1558, but without indicating the author's name. According to Gitlitz, in trials against judaizers, the one of these works most commonly mentioned by the Inquisition was the *Flos Sanctorum* of Alonso de Villegas. It was a compilation of lives of saints that included various figures from the Old Testament. In Veracruz in 1646 the Portuguese converso Duarte Rodríguez declared that he had often read Villegas's book and the lives of "the patriarchs and prophets, Judith and Esther."[46] Gonzalo Váez, who was burned at the stake in a 1649 auto-da-fé in Mexico, described it as a missal in the vernacular tongue. In Majorca in 1678, Pedro Onofre stated that the book's popularity among judaizers was due to the fact that it contained "different chapters dealing with some of the blessings that

---

[42]"ansi llamado *Cronicón* ... el cual trata en la primera parte de todo el testamento viejo y en la segunda del nuevo y por la noticia que da Moisés de su Ley y de otros profetas le compró este a instancia de su padre, el licenciado Méndez de León, y de su madrastra y este después de casado se lo leía a su gente muchas veces." ADC, Leg. 404, exp. 5714, and Leg. 492, exp. 6569.

[43]"por haverlo leydo, a lo que pareze, en el *Flos Sanctorum*, o en el libro llamado *Monarchía Ecclesiástica*." Alcalá Galve, *Literatura y Ciencia*, 53.

[44]Manuel Peña Díaz, "Libros permitidos, lecturas prohibidas (siglos XVI–XVII)," *Cuadernos de Historia Moderna. Anejos* 1 (2002): 85–101, at 92.

[45]Manuel Peña Díaz, *Escribir y prohibir: Inquisición y censura en los Siglos de Oro* (Madrid, 2015).

[46]Gitlitz, *Secrecy and Deceit*, 430.

God gave to the people of Israel and to the patriarchs of the Old Law."[47] These were books that were widely read among judaizers in Majorca. Pedro Onofre himself admits to having gone back to Judaism because of his reading:

> As I was inclined to read books, reading the lives of the holy patriarchs in the *Flos Sanctorum*, in the *Monarchia ecclesiástica*, and in the *Gobernación Christiana* and other curious books, seeing that they were good and that they had been saved by keeping the law of Moses and performing his ceremonies, this confessor was deceived by the devil and believed that he too could be saved by performing the same ceremonies that they performed in observance of the law of Moses.[48]

Monarchia ecclesiastica is the most frequently mentioned book in Inquisition trials from Majorca between 1670 and 1689. This is probably a reference to the *Monarquía eclesiástica o Historia universal del mundo desde su creación*, by the Franciscan Juan de Pineda, published in 1576. It is a work of Renaissance erudition that cites important authors from antiquity and contains a wealth of material on the Old Testament.

In the home of another judaizer, a witness claimed in 1691 that "they used to read, in a book ... called Josepho, *De Bello Judaico*, different things about the Jews."[49] *De bello judaico*, by Flavius Josephus, was translated by Alfonso de Palencia and published in Seville (1492), Antwerp (1555) and Madrid (1557).[50] It shows up in numerous Inquisition trials, from Lima to Majorca. In the trial held in 1691 of Diego Forteza, from Majorca, many witnesses stated that judaizers frequently read this book.[51] The Spanish translation of

---

[47] "diferentes capítulos que tratan de algunos beneficios que Dios hizo al pueblo de Israel y a los Padres de la ley antigua." See Blanca Vizán, "Lecturas criptojudías y la *Introducción al Símbolo de la Fe* de fray Luis de Granada," in *Las razones del censor: Control ideológico y censura de libros en la primera edad moderna*, ed. Cesc Esteve and Cristina Luna (Bellaterra, 2013), 195–216, at 202.

[48] "Como era inclinado a leer libros, leyendo el *Flos Sanctorum*, en la *Monarchía ecclesiástica* y en la *Gobernación Christiana* y otros libros curiosos las Vidas de los Santos Padres, viendo que eran buenos y que se habían salvado guardando la ley de Moysés y haciendo sus ceremonias, a este confesante le engañó el demonio y creyó que también podría salvarse haciendo las mesmas ceremonias que ellos hazían en observancia de la ley de Moyses." Angela Selke, *Los chuetas y la Inquisición: Vida y muerte en el ghetto de Mallorca* (Madrid, 1972), 40–41 and 113.

[49] "Solían leer en un libro ... llamado Josepho, *De Bello Judaico*, diferentes cosas de judíos." Manuel Peña, "Libros permitidos, lecturas prohibidas," 91.

[50] Julian Weiss, "Flavius Josephus, 1492," *International Journal of the Classical Tradition* 23 (2016): 180–95.

[51] Selke, *Los chuetas y la Inquisición*, 42.

Josephus's work was included in the *Index* starting in 1559. Indeed all of the above-mentioned titles were included in the indexes of prohibited books of Spain and Portugal. Such was the case of the *Flos Sanctorum*, included in the *Index* from 1559, and of *Monarchía Ecclesiástica* (1583) or the *Cronología de los hebreos* by Gilbert Génébrard.[52] In 1592, censor Hernando del Castillo wrote that:

> Gilber Genebrardo, whose account this is, is a very Catholic man and he has demonstrated this in his writings. He is curious about history. The *Chronologia de los hebreos* is nothing but a translation by him, from Hebrew into Latin. [It] is an interesting thing but since it is full of Judaic lies, I know not if any good can come of it in the Church. Rather, I believe that the book's purpose is for converts, whose blood still boils, to learn new prayers, rites, ceremonies, doctrines, offices of the dead, symbols and supplications taken from the books of the Talmud and from other rabbinical [books], which many will read and understand in the Latin tongue, but few or none [would understand] the original in the Hebrew, even if they were learned in Hebrew, but these books are not allowed in Spain, and being in Latin everyone can surely have them and read them.[53]

Converts were eager to learn and to hear about the history of Israel, with which they identified and which gave them a sense of pride. Even Catholic iconography in paintings and tapestries could be used to learn of "the wonders that God had worked with his people" (Israel). A niece of Ana Sánchez de Guevara said that her Jewish faith had been strengthened

---

[52] Jesús Martínez de Bujanda, *El Índice de los libros prohibidos y expurgados de la Inquisición española (1551–1819)* (Madrid, 2016), 504, 562, 588. On the use by crypto-Jews of another work by Génébrard, see Bodian, *Dying in the Law of Moses*, 132.

[53] Archivo Histórico Nacional [AHN], Inquisición, 4436/8: Calificaciones de Gilber Gene-brardo, *Cronología de los hebreos*. "Gilber Genebrardo cuya es esta historia es hombre muy cathólico y lo ha mostrado en sus escritos. Es curioso en la historia quanto el que más en nuestros tiempos. La *Chronología de los hebreos* no es sino traducción que él hizo de hebreo en latín, cosa curiosa pero como está llena de mentiras judaicas no sé qué provecho pueda hazer en la Iglesia. Antes creo que es libro ocasionado para que los conversos, a quienes todavía hierve la sangre, sepan nuevas oraciones, ritos, ceremonias, doctrinas, officios de defunctos, símbolos y plegarias sacadas de los libros del Talmud y de otros rabinos que en la lengua latina los podrán leer y entender muchos, y en la hebraica su original pocos o ninguno, y aunque fuesen doctos en hebreo, pero estos libros no se consienten en España, y estando en latín pueden los tener y leer todos seguramente, y assí aunque a la opinión de Genebrardo no toque nada, sino averlo traduzido, sería muy acertado prohibir esto todo de los hebreos, si otros mejores votos no tuvieren lo contrario. Esto me parece en Valladolid, 15 de octubre de 1592. Fray Hernando de Castillo."

upon seeing paintings in certain countries where there are street painters, how they had painted the story of King Pharaoh and the dinner of King Balthazar, and also since she had a tapestry with a depiction of the main story of Solomon when he ordered the boy to be cut in two, based on this and on sermons they heard about the patriarchs, they gathered enough information to start talking about the said law of Moses.[54]

Other texts that show up repeatedly in Inquisition documents are *Espejo de consolación* and *Gobernador Cristiano*. There was also a so-called "book of Mary Magdalene," which contained the Psalms of David in Romance. It was probably *La conversión de la Magdalena* (1588) by Pedro Malón de Chaide.[55] Also appearing frequently in converso bookselves is *El gobernador cristiano, deducido de las vidas de Moisés y Jesucristo*, published in 1612 and authored by the ascetic writer Juan Márquez. The author's aim in this book, written against Maquiavelo, was to draw the paradigmatic Christian governor based on the Bible and particularly on the figures of Moses and Joshua. As for *Espejo de consolación de tristes*, by the Franciscan Juan de Dueñas, it was printed multiple times between 1540 and 1591. It is a typical work of the *speculum* genre of literature intended for personal edification, and certain passages of the Bible are offered as a mirror in which to see oneself reflected.

These examples demonstrate that, according to Scripture, life's ills are preferable to worldly riches. This point is illustrated with clear examples from the Hebrew Bible: better the blindness of Tobias than the sight of David, Susana's imprisonment than Dinah's freedom, and so on, in a long list that nearly amounts to an encyclopedia of the Old Testament. The *Espejo* is mentioned in countless Inquisition cases in Spain and the New World.[56] In March 1595 the inquisitors of the tribunal of Mexico informed the Suprema that it was common among the judaizers of New Spain to read the *Espejo*, and that as such it should be included in the *Index*. In Portugal it was included in the *Index* in 1564, and in Spain would finally be included in 1632.[57] These repeated warnings coming from Mexico support the principal argument presented here: that certain books were the preferred readings of judaizers was

---

[54]"de ver pintado en algunos países que ponen los pintores en las calles en que estaba pintada la historia del Rey Faraón y en otros la cena del rey Baltasar y también tener esta en su tapicería pintada la historia de Salomón principal cuando mandó hacer partir al niño y de esto y de oír los sermones de los padres antiguos tomaron noticia para empezar a hablar de la dicha ley de Moisés." ADC, Leg. 484, exp. 6521.

[55]ADC, Leg. 481, exp. 6504; Leg. 492, exp. 6570; Leg. 477, exp. 6491; Leg. 484, exp. 6521.

[56]Amiel cites various Inquisition trials from Lima and Mexico that mention judaizers reading the *Espejo de Consolación*. See Amiel, "Les cent voix de Quintanar," 530–31.

[57]Martínez de Bujanda, *El Índice de los libros prohibidos*, 1079.

sufficient cause to land them on the *Index*, regardless of the book's Catholic orthodoxy.

An important category of works that judaizers accessed and read from works produced for Catholics were the Psalms. Of course, the Psalms had been popular among Catholics in the Middle Ages; since the Reformation they were routinely read by Catholics and Protestants alike. For this reason they were readily available in the Iberian Peninsula, and it is not surprising that they are frequently mentioned as texts judaizers turned to, particularly those psalms that Scripture ascribed to David. Pilar Huerga, in her monograph on the judaizers of Extremadura and Salamanca, shows that the Catholic version of the Psalms was the main source of prayers for the crypto-Jewish communities, with the exception of certain phrases, such as the closing *Gloria Patri*, which were omitted.[58] Indeed, this omission became a sign of "judaizing."

Unfortunately, Inquisition trials do not specify which particular Psalms an accused judaizer was said to have recited. However, they contain abundant references to the "syete salmos penitenciales," the seven penitential psalms, that is, Psalms 6, 31, 37, 50, 129, and 142 according to the enumeration of the Vulgate. Ironically, the Inquisition had prisoners who had confessed and repented, and recited these very psalms during the ceremony of penitence.[59]

Spanish translations of Psalms were particularly valuable to judaizers who did not know Latin. Although Spanish translations of the Bible were forbidden in the Iberian Peninsula, they could be smuggled across borders. Amiel argues that the most widely used version was the *Psalterio de David* published in Antwerp in 1555, and included in the *Indexes* from 1559 on.[60] Other psalms were available from a work entitled *Epístolas y Evangelios*, by Ambrosio de Montesinos, originally published in 1512 and subsequently reprinted several times. It contains texts from the gospels and epistles addressing different needs throughout the liturgical year.

We may recall that the *Index* of 1559 included the stipulation that translations of the New Testament in Spanish should be submitted to the Inquisition for inspection, and the *Index* of 1583 renewed that prohibition, extending it to include Bibles in any vernacular language. Judaizers tried to import Spanish translations of the entire Bible, even of the Gospels—in particular those made by Francisco Enzinas, a Protestant from Burgos, published in Antwerp

---

[58]Pilar Huerga Criado, *En la raya de Portugal: Solidaridad y tensiones en la comunidad judeoconversa* (Salamanca, 1994).

[59]Jacqueline Genot-Bismuth, "Recherche sur les fonctions de la prière individuelle en milieu marrane aux alentours de 1492: Prière et salut," in *Prière, Mystique et Judaïsme: Colloque de Strasbourg, 10–12 septembre 1984*, ed. Roland Goetschel (Paris, 1987), 174.

[60]Amiel, "Les cent voix de Quintanar," 519.

in 1543, along with Psalters published in Flanders.[61] The Judeo-Converso communities in the Peninsula went to great pains to smuggle in the *siddurim* that had been so abundantly published in Castile prior to the expulsion.[62] However, the focus here is not the Jewish books that judaizers tried to bring into the Iberian Peninsula—a real and important phenomenon—but rather the orthodox Catholic books that they kept and read.

Interest in the Psalms was probably the reason behind the success of the so-called *Ramillete de flores*. Gitlitz had previously identified this book with Isaac Matatia Aboab's *Peraḥ Shoshan* (Amsterdam, 1687).[63] However, a recent article by Vega Ramos has attributed it to Pedro Ruiz de la Visitación, whose *Ramillete de Flores* was published in Majorca in 1589.[64] This book does not include a Romance translation of the Psalms, but rather a vernacular description of them, along with their sequence, uses, and relationship to other passages from the Old Testament. A letter from the Hebrew alphabet precedes each octonary in the *Ramillete*. The lengthiest part of the book consists of in-depth explanation of the meaning of the Hebrew letters and provides a great deal of information about Jewish mysticism. It is a book that offers a reading by substitution, recounting the psalms without daring to print them, concealing the literal meaning and instead offering summaries. *Ramillete de flores*, as Vega Ramos proposes, belongs to the body of readings by substitution, such as the texts of Juan de Dueñas, Juan de Pineda, or Fray Luis de Granada, to whom I will refer below. A similar case is to be found in the Books of Hours, which were also very popular among judaizers, since they included psalms of penitence as well as other material from the Old Testament. They, too, were included in the Spanish and Portuguese indexes.

Perhaps the work one was most likely to find on the bookshelves of the Judeo-Conversos was Fray Luis de Granada's *Introducción al Símbolo de la Fe*.[65] The *Introducción* contains five parts. The first four were published in

---

[61] An interesting example is to be found in an inquisitorial exchange detailing a 1614 raid that took place at the port of Camariñas in Galicia. Aboard a boat with a Portuguese captain, manned by a group of moriscos and sailing from France, the authorities found books in Spanish deemed to be Jewish. The books included a translation of the Gospels, the Psalms of David in Castilian verse, and a *Sedur de las oraciones del mes con mucha diligencia visto y enmendado, ympreso por industria y despensa de Yom Tob Atias* (Ferrara, 5312 [1552]). There is also a "Calendar of the Hebrew holidays," which Fernando Bouza says he is unable to identify among pre-1614 editions, but that could correspond to the *Calendario de ros hodes, fiestas y aynos que los hebreos celebran cada año* (Amsterdam, 1663).

[62] Genot-Bismuth, "Recherche sur les fonctions de la prière individuelle," 164–70.

[63] Gitlitz, *Secrecy and Deceit*, 379.

[64] María José Vega Ramos, "Lecturas criptojudías en los siglos aúreos: El *Ramillete de Flores*," *Studia Aurea* 4 (2010): 37–51.

[65] Vizán, "Lecturas crypto-judías."

1583 and were not mentioned in the *Índice de libros prohibidos* published that year by the inquisitor Gaspar de Quiroga. Fray Luis had already experienced run-ins with the Inquisition, and several of his works had already found their way onto the *Index*. However, in the case of the *Introducción* he decided to take all possible precautions, starting with dedicating the work to Quiroga, the inquisitor tasked with updating the 1559 index of the inquisitor Valdés. Despite dedicating the book to Quiroga and explicitly stating that he will not mention the lies of the heretics so that they will not ensnare the common folk, Fray Luis does include a long chapter on the Talmud, entitled "De las mentiras, falsedades y desvaríos del Talmud." [66] Fray Luis employs the dialogue genre, with the teacher espousing the orthodox point of view and the catechumen voicing small hints of heterodoxy in the form of doubts, masked by the character's clear ignorance. In this chapter the teacher expounds upon the errors of the Jews who, he explains, have been deceived by the Talmudists. In other words, this chapter falls into the body of polemical works discussed in the preceding section of this article, which, in order to confute the tenets of a religion, ended up describing them one by one. Fray Luis's chapter on the Talmud goes one step further, in that each statement is accompanied by a precise reference to the relevant text and chapter of the Talmud, including summaries and quotations, thus providing the judaizers among his readership with invaluable information.

Where did Fray Luis get this information on the Talmud if, as Gitlitz argues, there is no evidence of any conversos having access to the Talmud after 1480? Fray Luis himself explains, stating that he read the anti-Talmud treatise *De Iudaicis Erroribus ex Talmud* by Jerónimo de Santa Fe, the converso we saw at the beginning of this article, originally named Joshua ha-Lorki. Santa Fe had been asked to write the book by Pope Benedict XIII, along with another one arguing that the Scriptures foretold the coming of Jesus, *Tractatus contra perfidiam Iudaeorum*. They were translated into Spanish as one book, *Azote de los Hebreos*; a Portuguese edition was printed in Goa in 1565. Fray Luis de Granada's work also included a long description of the history of the Jews according to the Old Testament and to Josephus. There was much in this extensive work that could be appealing to converts, and not only to converts. *Introducción al Símbolo de la Fe* was an extraordinary best

---

[66]"Although this text (which declares the truth) condemns the falsehoods and errors of the heretics, we will not mention them [the falsehoods and errors] because it would not be fitting to break the common people's fast from these deceptions. Because they are much less likely to fall for them if they have never heard of them." In *Introducción al Símbolo de la Fe*, Parte Primera, "Al Ilustríssimo y Reverendíssimo Señor Don Gaspar de Quiroga." Apud Vizán, "Lecturas crypto-judías," 206.

seller for the entire early modern Hispanic world. [67]About sixteen editions of it were produced in the sixteenth century alone.

A complete list of the judaizers who read Fray Luis de Granada would be exceedingly long; we cite just a few examples. In Cuenca, Jerónimo de Parra held that Jesus was not the son of God "and that to bring his law into the world he had made use of ignorant men like the apostles, who were fishermen and not men of letters."[68] He claimed to have formed this idea by reading Fray Luis de Granada's *Símbolo de la fe*, particularly those passages in which Fray Luis describes the dialogue between a catechumen and his teacher.[69] In another case, from 1658, Lorenzo Escudero, a morisco from Seville who went to Amsterdam to practice Judaism, stated that "reading the books of Fray Luis de Granada had made him become Jewish."[70] Another case is that of a man named Manuel de Lucena, accused by Luis de Carvajal "el mozo" of being a judaizer and burned at the stake by the Mexican Inquisition in 1596. One of the books he used to teach the Law of Moses was the *Introducción*. By Carvajal's account, Manuel de Lucena recommended the *Introducción* to an Old Christian friend of his, Juan de Cassal. This came after Cassal, in prior conversations, had voiced doubts about the "law under which he lived."[71] This is why Cassal eventually asked Manuel de Lucena, a New Christian, to procure the book for him. Luis de Carvajal had studied at the Fransiscan school of Santiago de Tlatelolco in Mexico City with friar Pedro de Oroz, and confessed to the Inquisition that he had studied the Bible, including the Apocrypha, Ribadeneyra's *Espejo de Consolación*, Fray Luis de Granada's *Guía de Pecadores* and *Introducción al Símbolo de la fe*, Maimonides' *Thirteen Principles of Jewish Faith*, and Nicholas of Lyra's *Postillae*.[72] These readings gave Luis de Carvajal the background he needed to write brief treatises and religious poems that he distributed among his judaizing friends.

[67]Alex Kaplan Szyld, "¿Una alternativa pedagógica en tiempos inquisitoriales?: La cuarta parte de la *Introducción al símbolo de la fe* (1583)," in *La Monarquía Hispánica y las minorías*, ed. Ana Isabel López-Salazar and Francisco Moreno Díaz del Campo (Madrid, 2019), 409–30.

[68]"y que para introducir su ley en el mundo se había valido de unos hombres ignorantes como habían sido los apóstoles los cuales habían sido pescadores y no hombres de letras." ADC, Leg. 478, exp. 6494.

[69]ADC, Leg. 478, exp. 6494.

[70]"el aber leydo en los libros de fray Luis de Granada le havía hecho judío." AHN, Inquisición, Leg. 1123.

[71]Bodian, *Dying in the Law of Moses*, 71.

[72]Cohen, 1973, 201–03; Seymur B. Liebman, *The Jews in New Spain: Faith, Flame, and the Inquisition* (Coral Gables, FL, 1970), 153.

Counterfacting Christianity into Judaism

In summary, what we have surveyed is a set of polemical works read against the grain, a series of books from which judaizers were able to glean knowledge about the history of the people of Israel, and a number of Catholic devotional works that judaizers used by way of substitution or with their own particular interpretations. Those are the ones I refer to as counterfacting Christianity into Judaism.[73] Counterfacting is a literary technique closely connected to the concept of mimesis. The term was coined by Bruce W. Wardropper in his seminal study on early modern Spanish *a lo divino* poetry, in which he defined it as the rewording a secular literary text to transform it into a religious text.[74] Here I suggest applying the term to religious texts of one religion which are counterfacted into religious texts of another religion. As a consequence all of these works, which fell within the bounds of Catholic orthodoxy, ended up on the indexes of forbidden books, thereby—among other things—having an impact on the devotional practices of Catholic believers, as well as on their knowledge of the Old Testament. The systematic censure of Catholic devotional literature—books of devotion and books of hours—was to have a profound effect on Catholic believers. As argued by Vega Ramos and Peña Díaz, whose works I have drawn on in abundance, the loss of these instruments of everyday piety forced Catholics in turn to devise their own religious readings and practices of substitution. It also had an impact in the creation on an hermeneutic of suspicion that constantly invited doubts as to the real sense of one book.[75] This suspicion activates elements of the text that in other, less harsh circumstances would have passed inadverted. It contributed, as Vega Ramos has shown, to the *malitia temporum* collaborating to create a particular way of reading.

Moreover, because the readings crop up again and again over such a vast swath of time and space, one cannot help but infer the presence of community leaders and *dogmatistas* who guided the faithful and recommended readings—figures who were, in turn, in contact with one another. These *dogmatistas* would have had a certain degree of religious education, giving them influence and relevance within their immediate group. And yet there is considerable evidence that such individuals used these very Catholic devotional texts to educate judaizers, as well as to coax members of the converso community back into Judaism. Pedro Onofre, the aforementioned Chueta from

---

[73] Taking the term from Teresa Soto. For the parallel process, counterfacting Christianity into Islam, see Soto "Poetics and Polemics," 331–56, esp. 336ff.

[74] Bruce W. Wardropper, *Historia de la poesía lírica a lo divino en la cristiandad occidental* (Madrid, 1958), 5–7.

[75] María José Vega Ramos, *Disenso y censura en el siglo XVI* (Salamanca, 2012), 31.

Majorca, was clearly one such figure, as was Diego de Mora, in Quintanar, who hosted gatherings at his house where he would read the books we have identified to his guests and comment aloud on them.[76] Similarly, people would go to *licenciado* Méndez de León's house so that he would read and explain "certain parts of the Bible and show them pictures of it, telling them many things about the patriarchs and the prophets." Méndez de León, in turn, was in contact with other people versed in the Law of Moses, such as Doctor Pereda, who had shown him a Bible in Latin, without a doubt the Vulgate.[77]

At the same time, the fact that judaizers used this repertoire of Catholic books across such a great expanse of time and space suggests that they had made them their own, adopting them as a part of their heritage, as an ingredient of their particular tradition and religiosity. The counterfacting of these books was a way of erasing, rewriting, and correcting a Christian text but also a form of imitation and incorporation. In the end, what this essay shows is the profound imbrications in early modern Iberia of two religious groups—Catholics and crypto-Jews—that have long been regarded as theologically entirely distinct. Through appropriation and rejection, "judaizers" in particular, but also pious Catholics, shaped together their respective ways of understanding and living religion.

Acknowledgments The research leading to this study was funded by the European Research Council under the European Union's Seventh Framework Program (FP7/2007–2013) / ERC Grant Agreement number 323316; project CORPI "Conversion, Overlapping Religiosities, Polemics, Interaction. Early Modern Iberia and Beyond"; and by Proyecto MINECO "Orientalismo y verdad: la influencia de la erudición oriental en el desarrollo del pensamiento crítico en la España Moderna" (FFI2017-86538-P). A earlier version of this paper was presented at the conference "Agents of Conversion," organized by the Center for the Study of Conversion and Inter-Religious Encounters, Ben Gurion University of the Negev (May 2017), and at the Renassaince Society of America annual conference in New Orleans, 2017.

Publisher's Note Springer Nature remains neutral with regard to jurisdictional claims in published maps and institutional affiliations.

---

[76] Amiel, "Les cent voix de Quintanar," 529–30; ADC, Leg. 331, exp. 4734: "While in the town of Quintanar, at the home of said Isabel de Mora, his aunt, he read from *Espejo de consolación*. . . . 'I have here a book . . . so that you read from it and see how those holy ancient prophets of the Old Testament lived,' to better attract and endear this witness to the Law of Moses."

[77] ADC, Leg. 404, exp. 5714.

Jewish History (2021) 35: 265–291
https://doi.org/10.1007/s10835-021-09424-0

Conversos, Moriscos, and the Eucharist in Early Modern Spain: Some Reflections on Jewish Exceptionalism

YONATAN GLAZER-EYTAN

Magdalene College, Cambridge University, Cambridge, UK
E-mail: yg382@cam.ac.uk

Accepted: 14 July 2021 / Published online: 3 December 2021

Abstract Sacrilegious attitudes toward the Eucharistic host are one of the most commonplace accusations leveled against Jews in premodern Europe. Usually treated in Jewish historiography as an expression of anti-Judaism or antisemitism, they are considered a hallmark of Jewish powerlessness and persecution. In medieval and early modern Spain, however, Jews and conversos (Jewish converts to Christianity and their descendants) were not the only proclaimed enemies of the Eucharist. Reports about avoidance, rejection, criticism, and even ridicule and profanation of the consecrated host were similarly leveled against Muslims and moriscos (Muslim converts to Christianity). This essay seeks to assess the parallels and connections between the two groups through a comparative examination of accusations of sacrilegious behavior towards the host. The first part of the essay analyzes religious art, legal compendia, and inquisitorial trials records from the tribunals of Toledo and Cuenca in order to show some evident homologies between the two groups. The second part of the essay focuses on the analysis of the works of Jaime Bleda and Pedro Aznar y Cardona, two apologists of the expulsion of the moriscos, and draws direct connections between Jewish and morisco sacrilege. By exploring the similarities and differences between accusations against conversos and moriscos, this essay aims to offer a broader reflection on Jewish exceptionalism.

Keywords Iberian Jews · Conversos · Iberian Muslims · Moriscos · Christian-Jewish relations · Christian-Muslim relations · Eucharistic miracles · Inquisition · Jewish historiography

In 1597, a miracle occurred in the Spanish city of Alcalá de Henares. According to several seventeenth-century chapbooks, it all began when a band of New Christians who were wandering through Castile stole from local churches monstrances (*custodias*) that contained Eucharistic hosts. Being "people with no faith," as the accounts described the band of thieves, they disparaged the consecrated wafers and threw them on the ground.[1] One of the bandits, the only one described as an "Old Christian," repented and returned a number of hosts to a local priest. The priest in turn consulted his

---

Chapter 3 was originally published as Glazer-Eytan, Y. Jewish History (2021) 35: 265–291. https://doi.org/10.1007/s10835-021-09424-0.

[1] See, for instance, *Relación breve, y verdadera del milagro de las sagradas formas, que estan, y se ven en el colegio de la Compañia de Iesus de Alcala de Henares; Y testimonio que del dio el ilustrissimo señor D. Francisco de Mendoza, obispo, y gouernador del arçobispado de Toledo* (Alcalá de Henares, 1634), fol. 1a, Biblioteca Nacional de España, VE/181/38.

37    Springer

superior, who warned him that "such wicked people" were prone to poison Old Christians and, therefore, it was better to place the returned wafers in a decent place and to allow the "accidents" of the Eucharist to decay. After that, the superior continued, they could dispose of them, as was usually done with consecrated hosts. The local priest did as he was told and placed the hosts in a secure place in the church. Yet something drew the priest to keep visiting them. To his great amazement, he found that these consecrated wafers resisted not only the bandits' attempts to physically destroy them but also the forces of nature. As the printed chapbooks announced in excitement, these wafers proved to be unharmed by the passing of years and the difficult weather conditions. The priest informed his superior about the supernatural occurrence, and the latter invited higher ecclesiastical authorities to inspect the incorruptible wafers. After examination, these hosts were proclaimed an "evident miracle." Printed "true accounts" (*relaciones verdaderas*) helped propagate this Eucharistic miracle throughout the Iberian Peninsula and declared that this was a refutation of the "heretics" and a testimony of Christ's Real Presence in the Eucharist. Eventually, the so-called Sacred Forms of Alcalá became the subject of several religious plays, devotional images, and an enduring cult. Although the original miraculous hosts were lost during the Spanish Civil War, they are still venerated today in Alcalá in the special chapel commemorating the miracle.[2]

The history of the Sacred Forms of Alcalá can be conveniently divided into three distinct phases. A sacrilege was committed upon the host in at least two senses of the term: the sacred object was taken from its designated place and was then mistreated. This rejection of the sacredness of the host was then followed by a demonstration of its miraculous power, proving that, like Christ whose body it contained under the accidents of bread, it could not be destroyed. The story ends with the emergence of a new cult centered around a Eucharistic relic. In this sense, the narrative of the Sacred Forms of Alcalá is no different from various other tales of Eucharistic miracles that served as foundation myths for the establishment of shrines across Catholic Europe. As is widely known, in a significant number of these narratives Jews figured prominently as those who profaned the host. Some scholars have explained this tendency as a sort of defense mechanism. In this view, Christians projected their theological doubts and sentiments of guilt onto Jews, who then provided a confirmation of the complex doctrine of the Eucharist, as well

---

[2]For general information on the development of the cult, see María Evangelina Muñoz Santos, "La recuperación de una devoción secular: El culto a las 24 Santas Formas de Alcalá de Henares. Génesis y vicisitudes," in *Patrimonio inmaterial de la Cultura Cristiana*, ed. Francisco Javier Campos y Fernández de Sevilla (San Lorenzo del Escorial, 2013), 193–214.

as their compulsion to reenact the deicide.[3] Israel Jacob Yuval has added an important and suggestive perspective to this issue, demonstrating that the host profanation accusation developed in a context of a polemical dialogue between Christianity and Judaism.[4] Further, Miri Rubin, in her magisterial analysis of the symbolic significance of these tales, has shown that as the Eucharist became a symbol of Christian communal identity, Jews were increasingly labeled as the archenemies of the Eucharist. Given that Jews had an ambiguous status in premodern Europe—living outside the Church but within Christian society, in the words of Gilbert Dahan—they proved to be a fruitful "object to think with" in order to mark difference.[5] In that sense, Rubin argued, Jewish host profanation was a story Christians told themselves in order to define what it meant to be a Christian.[6]

Rubin's broad survey follows the development of this anti-Jewish narrative from the early Middle Ages to the beginning of the modern era across Latin Christendom, including the Iberian Peninsula. In post-1391 Iberia, after the mass conversion of Jews to Christianity, a variant of this anti-Jewish narrative appeared when the accusation of host profanation was leveled against those Christians who were descendants of Jews. These New Christians, or conversos as they were commonly referred to, were frequently suspected of maintaining allegiance to the faith of their ancestors. As such, it was generally believed that like their forefathers, they, too, rejected Christ and the Eucharist and aimed to profane it. Against this backdrop, one may assume that the miracle of the Sacred Forms of Alcalá is yet another tale of Jewish/converso host profanation. Yet the printed accounts that spread the news about the miracle in Alcalá did not target New Christians whose ancestors were Jews. Rather, they specified that these New Christians were of Muslim origin. That is, they were what contemporaries labeled pejoratively moriscos, a term that modern scholars embrace as a convenient name for the Spanish Muslims who were forcibly converted to Christianity by royal decrees between 1502 and 1526, only to be ultimately expelled between 1609 and 1614.

---

[3] Gavin I. Langmuir, "The Tortures of the Body of Christ," in *Christendom and Its Discontents: Exclusion, Persecution, and Rebellion, 1000–1500*, ed. Scott L. Waugh and Peter D. Diehl (Cambridge, UK, 2002), 287–309. And see similar claims in Peter Browe, "Die Hostienschändungen der Juden im Mittelalter," *Römische Quartalschrift für Christliche Altertumskunde und Kirchengeschichte* 34 (1926): 167–97; Lester K. Little, *Religious Poverty and the Profit Economy in Medieval Europe* (Ithaca, NY, 1983), 52–54.

[4] Israel Jacob Yuval, *Two Nations in Your Womb: Perceptions of Jews and Christians in Late Antiquity and the Middle Ages*, trans. Barbara Harshav and Jonathan Chipman (Berkeley, 2008), ch. 5.

[5] Gilbert Dahan, *Les intellectuels chrétiens et les juifs au Moyen Âge* (Paris, 1990), 104.

[6] Miri Rubin, *Gentile Tales: The Narrative Assault on Late Medieval Jews* (Philadelphia, 2004), 5.

The reference to the moriscos in the chapbooks propagating the miracle of the Sacred Forms of Alcalá was not an exceptional case. On the contrary, the evidence mustered in the following pages testifies to the regularity with which Christians described Muslims and moriscos as enemies of the Eucharist in the late medieval and early modern Iberian Peninsula. The issue at stake, I believe, bears importance for broader consideration of Jewish exceptionalism in premodern Europe. As it stands, the history of the accusation of host profanation is by and large a history told from the point of view of increasingly conflictual relations between Christians and Jews. Rubin, for instance, has shown how the role of the Jew in these narratives changed throughout the Middle Ages from witness of Eucharistic miracle and, therefore, convertible to Christianity, to a bitter enemy of the host, who must be punished by death. More generally, scholars classify the host profanation accusation as part of the broader category of anti-Jewish libels. These hateful narratives that portrayed Jews as desecrating religious images, blaspheming against Christ and Christianity, poisoning wells and, of course, ritually murdering Christian children, were frequently used to justify violence against Jewish communities. Gavin I. Langmuir viewed these libels as an indication of the rise of "irrational" hatred towards Jews in the Middle Ages and as an important step on the road to modern antisemitism.[7] But what happens to this grand narrative if these accusations were leveled against non-Jews as well?

Historians of Christian-Jewish relations in premodern Europe tend to gloss over the existence of accusations of host desecration leveled against non-Jews. Yet other groups, such as witches, heretics and, as we shall immediately see, Muslims, were occasionally charged with profaning the Eucharist. This very fact raises further questions that only a comparative perspective can fully answer. Were these accusations against the different groups essentially one and the same thing? Can we detect mutual influences between accusations leveled against one specific group and those made against others? And, finally, were accusations of host profanation leveled against non-Christians ultimately derived from the particular conditions of Christian society, regardless of the group accused? As a first attempt at exploring these questions, this essay interrogates some of the parallels and intersections between accusations of Jewish/converso host profanation and those leveled against Muslims and moriscos.

Thus far, not all attempts to examine the reciprocal interactions between Christian anti-Muslim and Christian anti-Jewish discourses have proved fruitful. In one such case, Allan and Helen Cutler dramatically asserted that "medieval anti-Semitism (and thus, indirectly, modern anti-Semitism as well,

---

[7]Gavin I. Langmuir, *Toward a Definition of Antisemitism* (Berkeley, 1990).

which to a significant extent stems from medieval anti-Semitism) was primarily a function of medieval anti-Muslimism."[8] This sweeping statement, widely rejected in the scholarship due to its shaky methodological grounds, makes the need for a more careful historical analysis of the ways Christian-Jewish and Christian-Muslim relations inform one another all the more urgent. More rigorous scholarly efforts have pointed to the changing status of the Jew in Christian polemics and theology after the twelfth century. These changes were related to broad structural transformations in European societies, including the struggle against Christian heresy but also, significantly, the intensification of the encounter with Islam.[9] Studies devoted to what Jeremy Cohen has labelled "the Muslim Connection," however, have tended to explore influences in a single direction, namely from Christian polemics against Islam to Christian *Adversus Iudaeos* literature. This essay inverts this perspective and asks in what ways the anti-Jewish host profanation libel informed and intersected with similar accusations against Muslims and moriscos.

Some scholars of Christian-Muslim relations have pointed to Christian texts and images that represent Muslims as enemies of the Eucharist or as "infidel" witnesses to the truth it bears.[10] In early modern Iberia, those focusing on what Louis Cardaillac once labeled the "polemical confrontation" between moriscos and Christians have long noted the aversion and even ridicule moriscos were reported to express towards the Eucharist.[11] Nevertheless, to the best of my knowledge, there have been no attempts to view alleged

---

[8] Allan Harris Cutler and Helen Elmquist Cutler, *The Jew as Ally of the Muslim: Medieval Roots of Anti-Semitism* (Notre Dame, IN, 1986), 97. And see the criticism of Jeremy Cohen, "The Roots of Anti-Semitism?" *Judaism* 37 (1988): 240–42; Gilbert Dahan, "Cutlers' 'The Jew as Ally of the Muslim'," *Jewish Quarterly Review* 79 (1989): 370–77.

[9] See Jeremy Cohen, "The Muslim Connection or On the Changing Role of the Jew in High Medieval Theology," in *From Witness to Witchcraft: Jews and Judaism in Medieval Christian Thought*, ed. Jeremy Cohen (Wiesbaden, 1996), 141–62; idem, *Living Letters of the Law: Ideas of the Jew in Medieval Christianity* (Berkeley, 1999), 156–57; Ryan Szpiech, "Rhetorical Muslims: Islam as Witness in Western Christian Anti-Jewish Polemic," *Al-Qantara* 34 (2013): 153–85.

[10] See, for instance, Bernard Flusin, "Démons et Sarrasins: L'auteur et le propos des 'Diègemata stèriktika' d'Anastase le Sinaïte," *Travaux et mémoires* 11 (1991): 381–409; Arietta Papaconstantinou, "Saints and Saracens: On Some Miracle Accounts of the Early Arab Period," in *Byzantine Religious Culture: Studies in Honor of Alice-Mary Talbot*, ed. Denis Sullivan, Elizabeth A. Fisher, and Stratis Papaiaonnou (Leiden, 2012), 323–38; Nirit Ben-Aryeh Debby, "St. Clare Expelling the Saracens from Assisi: Religious Confrontation in Word and Image," *Sixteenth Century Journal* 43 (2012): 643–65; Kristen Van Ausdall, "Art and Eucharist in the Late Middle Ages," in *A Companion to the Eucharist in the Middle Ages*, ed. Ian Christopher Levy, Gary Macy, and Kristen Van Ausdall (Leiden, 2012), 541–617, esp. 591–92.

[11] For some important points of departure, see Louis Cardaillac, *Moriscos y cristianos: Un enfrentamiento polémico (1492–1640)*, trans. Mercedes García-Arenal (Madrid, 1979),

Jewish/converso hostility towards the Eucharist in Iberia in conjunction with those texts and images that depicted Muslims and moriscos as enemies of the host. The problem, it would seem, is much wider than the specific issue of shared alleged hostility toward the Eucharist. In a pioneering essay, James Amelang described the separate historiographies of Jews/conversos and Muslim/moriscos as living "with their backs to each other."[12] Thus, although both ethnoreligious groups experienced forcible conversion to Christianity, inquisitorial persecution, and expulsion in the same geographical space and in adjoining time periods, a comparative or holistic view has rarely been offered.[13] For Amelang, in the final analysis, the histories of these two minorities, while comparable, were essentially distinct. There are good reasons to concur with this conclusion. Yet as scholars have recently demonstrated, there were also intersections and mutual influences between these histories.[14] This essay presents further evidence along these lines, showing that in premodern Iberia, Christians grouped together these two minorities, compared and connected them, and even conflated them.

The Eucharist and the Christian Imagination: Associations and Variations

The emergence of the accusation of host profanation in medieval Europe is intertwined with the development of Eucharistic devotion. While the Eucharist was the focus of various rituals as well as a subject of intense theological discussion in the early and High Middle Ages, it was only in the thirteenth century that Eucharistic devotion gave birth to the accusation of Jewish host profanation. Two significant events mark the thirteenth century as the historical watershed of what came to be known as the Most Blessed Sacrament. In 1215, the Fourth Lateran Council declared that the consecrated wafer and wine were transubstantiated in the Eucharist into Christ's actual

---

290–301; Mercedes García-Arenal, *Inquisición y moriscos: Los procesos del Tribunal de Cuenca* (Madrid, 1978), 103–5.

[12] James S. Amelang, *Parallel Histories: Muslims and Jews in Inquisitorial Spain* (Baton Rouge, LA, 2013), x.

[13] The important exception is David Nirenberg's *Communities of Violence: Persecution of Minorities in the Middle Ages* (Princeton, 1996), which remains a fundamental point of departure to the study of the intersections between Christian, Jewish, and Muslim histories in premodern Iberia.

[14] See, for example, Isabelle Poutrin, "The Jewish Precedent in the Spanish Politics of Conversion of Muslims and Moriscos," *Journal of Levantine Studies* 6 (2016): 71–87; François Soyer, "The Recycling of an Anti-Semitic Conspiracy Theory into an Anti-Morisco One in Early Modern Spain: The Myth of El Vengador, the Serial-Killer Doctor," *eHumanista* 4 (2016): 233–55.

body and blood; they were "truly contained in the sacrament of the altar under the forms of bread and wine."[15] In 1264, Pope Urban IV instituted Corpus Christi, a highly solemn celebration including a Eucharistic procession, as a feast for the entire Catholic Church. With its incorporation into the collection of canon law known as the *Clementines*, which was issued in 1314 by Pope Clement IV and published by Pope John XXII in 1317, the feast of Corpus Christi became a truly universal celebration across Roman Catholicism.[16] These doctrinal and liturgical developments were accompanied, indeed propagated, by a proliferation of Eucharistic miracles. In these miracles, which were included in compilations of exempla used by preachers as well as recorded in chronicles and displayed in visual representations, the consecrated host demonstrated supernatural powers: it cured the sick, was venerated by animals, and "behaved" like an animate being—bleeding, sweating, transforming into a child, and so forth—thus proving that the Eucharist indeed performed a miracle and transformed the bread and wine into something wholly different.

Within this genre, a specifically anti-Jewish accusation emerged, according to which Jews procured the Eucharistic host in order to abuse it, in clear repetition of the Passion. In these narratives, the abused host reacted miraculously to its profanation, thus leading to the conversion or the punishment of the Jew. The most famous of these tales, known as the "*Billettes* affair" of Paris, 1290, can serve as a general model for the entire subgenre.[17] In most versions of the tale, it was a Christian woman who procured the consecrated host for the Jew. This woman was described as either the Jew's servant or, in the most influential version of the tale, the wife of a Christian debtor who was pushed to give the Jewish moneylender a consecrated host as pawn. Once the Jew acquired the host, he began to exercise his malicious plan against the body of Christ and, more broadly, against Christianity. In the Paris accusation, the Jew is described as abusing the host, stabbing it with a knife, throwing it into a fire and then into a cauldron of boiling water. The host bled in reaction to the knife attacks and, in some of the versions, was transformed through the encounter with fire and boiling water into flesh and blood. Christian authors offered different endings to this narrative. In some, the miracle of the host caused the Jew and his family to convert to Christianity. In yet other versions, after the sacrilege was discovered, the Jew was punished and

---

[15] Norman Tanner, ed., *Decrees of the Ecumenical Councils*, vol. 1, *Nicaea I to Lateran V* (London, 1990), 230.

[16] For a broad overview of the development of Eucharistic devotion and legislation, see Miri Rubin, *Corpus Christi: The Eucharist in Late Medieval Culture* (Cambridge, UK, 1991); Thomas M. Izbicki, *The Eucharist in Medieval Canon Law* (Cambridge, UK, 2015).

[17] For an overview of the "*Billettes* affair," see Rubin, *Gentile Tales*, 40–48.

his house was transformed into a church. This last version reflects a certain historical reality: in 1295 Pope Boniface VIII authorized the Bishop of Paris to establish a church on the site of the alleged profanation. For centuries, this Parisian church kept a relic of the host believed to have been profaned by Jews. As in parallel cases, the accusation of Jewish host profanation served as a foundation myth for the erection of a Christian shrine which attracted devotees and pilgrims for its miraculous host-relic.[18]

This well-known narrative was widely disseminated throughout premodern Europe, where it appeared with adaptations in most of western and central Europe before the sixteenth century and later on mostly in eastern Europe. It became as well the subject of religious imagery, most famously Paolo Uccello's *predella* for the Corpus Domini Altarpiece in Urbino (1467–1468).[19] A century before the Urbino Altarpiece was created, however, this anti-Jewish Eucharistic tale was already present in the Iberian Peninsula, where it appeared in judicial accusations against Jews and informed works of religious art.[20] A visually striking example of this can be found in the Altarpiece of the Virgin attributed to the Serra brothers and made for the cloistered female convent of Santa María in Sigena (Huesca). The centerpiece of the painting presents the Virgin with the Christ Child holding a flower, surrounded by Saint Catherine of Alexandria, Mary Magdalene, and the portrait of the altarpiece's donor, Fray Fontaner de Glera, who was the convent's commander between 1365 and 1373 (fig. 1). While the Virgin occupies the center of the painting, the broader pictorial program of the altarpiece transmits strong Eucharistic resonances. At the center of the *banco*, that is, the lower panel of the altarpiece known in Italy as the *predella*, there is a Last Supper scene. Christ blesses a chalice above which appears a host, clearly in reference to the institution of the Eucharist (Mark 14:22–24; Matt 26:26–28; Luke 22: 19–20). Flanking the Last Supper are depictions of four Eucharistic miracles that were known to late fourteenth-century viewers. To the left of the Last Supper panel, the Serra brothers depicted two Eucharistic tales, the Miracle of the

---

[18] See Mitchell B. Merback, *Pilgrimage and Pogrom: Violence, Memory, and Visual Culture at the Host-Miracle Shrines of Germany and Austria* (Chicago, 2012); Caroline W. Bynum, *Wonderful Blood: Theology and Practice in Late Medieval Northern Germany and Beyond* (Philadelphia, 2007).

[19] Marilyn Aronberg Lavin, "The Altar of Corpus Domini in Urbino: Paolo Uccello, Joos Van Ghent, Piero della Francesca," *Art Bulletin* 49 (1967): 1–24. See also Dana E. Katz, *The Jew in the Art of the Italian Renaissance* (Philadelphia, 2008), ch. 1.

[20] For a discussion of the complex history of the circulation of the host profanation accusation in late medieval Iberia, see Yonatan Glazer-Eytan, "Jews Imagined and Real: Representing and Prosecuting Host Profanation in Late Medieval Aragon," in *Jews and Muslims Made Visible in Christian Iberia and Beyond, 14th to 18th Centuries: Another Image*, ed. Borja Franco Llopis and Antonio Urquízar-Herrera (Leiden, 2019), 40–69.

Figure 1. Jaume Serra, Altarpiece of the Virgin, ca. 1367–1381, Museu Nacional d'Art de Catalunya (Barcelona). https://www.museunacional.cat/en/colleccio/altarpiece-virgin/jaume-serra/015916-cjt

Bees and the Miracle of the Fisherman. In both of these widely circulated tales, the consecrated host is prompting natural miracles: bees become hyperproductive after the host is placed in a hive; a fish is returning the host to a once sinful, now repentant fisherman who had thrown the consecrated wafer into the sea years before.[21] To the right of the Last Supper panel there are two panels representing Eucharistic miracles happening after a profanation

---

[21] See discussion, with further references to textual sources and visual parallels, in Paulino Rodríguez Barral, *La imagen del judío en la España medieval: El conflicto entre cristianismo y judaísmo en las artes visuales góticas* (Barcelona, 2008), 197–200.

Figure 2. Jaume Serra, Altarpiece of the Virgin, detail, Museu Nacional d'Art de Catalunya (Barcelona)

of the host. In the panel closer to the Last Supper, the Serra brothers depicted the Paris host profanation tale (fig. 2). The panel presented the narrative in two steps. On the left, the sacrilegious transaction takes place between the Christian woman and the Jewish moneylender. On the right, the Jew stabs the host, which bleeds in response. The host was also thrown into a cauldron of boiling water, where it was transformed into a child, a recurring trope in Eucharistic miracles. The Jew's wife and child are depicted somewhat passively as witnesses to the desecration and miracle, leaving them potentially open to conversion to Christianity.

This representation of host profanation is quite similar to many others throughout the Christian world. Commissioned not long after Eucharistic liturgy was introduced to Aragon, it fits neatly into the narrative established by Rubin, according to which growing devotion to the Eucharist went hand in hand with the increasing tendency to mark the Jew as the Eucharist's enemy. Rubin not only integrates an analysis of this altarpiece into her argument but also uses a detail from it on her book cover, thus clearly framing this painting as yet another example of the tale about the Jews told by Christians for Christians. Yet the last scene represented in the *banco* of this altarpiece may force us to nuance this sweeping narrative. Adjacent to the Serras' depiction of the tale of Jewish host profanation from Paris 1290 is another Eucharist miracle (fig. 2). This panel once again displays a narrative in two steps. In the first step, a Christian woman, depicted in almost exactly the same way as the Parisian woman procuring the host for the Jewish moneylender, engages in conversation with a man. Yet this man has none of the stereotypical attributes of Jews in Christian religious imagery. Instead, he is represented as dark-skinned, with a flat nose and a curly beard. He is dressed in lavish golden attire and wears a white turban. In short, the representation of this man clearly corresponds to the way premodern Iberians depicted Muslims. In the background, an infant lies inside a small crate. The subsequent scene portrays the same woman, who is now dressed in a more modest manner, taking communion from a priest. However, the host cuts through her throat in a way that we may imagine leads to her death.

The meaning of this peculiar image may be interpreted with the help of a literary work titled *The Mirror* (*Spill*, ca. 1460), which was written by the Valencian physician and author Jaume Roig (d. 1478). This rather misogynist book offers advice based on Roig's personal experiences about how to avoid the dangers posed by women.[22] In the *Mirror*, Roig narrates a case he claimed to have witnessed in Zaragoza in which a woman seeking to regain her husband's love turned to a Muslim sage (*un serrahy/ llur alfaqui*) for help.[23] The Muslim sage then said that he could help her in exchange for both monetary payment and a consecrated host. The woman followed the sage's request and went to the church of San Miguel in Zaragoza. She took communion falsely and, "as if she wanted to wipe her mouth," removed the consecrated wafer from her mouth and secretly placed it in a little case. When she brought the stolen host back to the Muslim sage and he, enthusiastically, opened the case, they both discovered that the consecrated wafer had been transformed into a "beautiful infant, all glowing and luminous." At this sight, the woman became "frightened, deranged, and out of her mind." The Muslim sage was first surprised. But then, this "morisco, an evil dog," as Roig calls him, suggested burning the case with the child-host. The woman, now called a "renegade" by Roig, followed the Muslim's advice and burned the case until it was charred. Yet the glowing child remained undamaged, despite the woman's insistent efforts. Not knowing what to do and "blinded by ire," the woman went in search of the sage, who was attending the Friday prayers at the local mosque. The Muslim sage was overwhelmed by fear and urged the woman to go with him to Zaragoza's cathedral and to confess their sins. If the Christian authorities spared both of them, he continued, he would "renounce Muhammad." The bishop found out about this incident. He gathered the city's ecclesiastical and secular notables in order to preach to them and explain how this "horrible" case was in fact a "confirmation of our faith." After a solemn

---

[22] I follow here Paulino Rodríguez Barral, who, to the best of my knowledge, is the first to propose this association. See idem, *La imagen del judío*, 200–201.

[23] For this and subsequent quotations, see María Celeste Delgado-Librero, *"The Mirror" of Jaume Roig: An Edition and an English Translation of MS. Vat. Lat. 4806* (Tempe, AZ, 2010), 109–13, verses 3500–3819; English translation, 304–6.

procession, the miraculous host-turned-into-a-child was taken and placed in the cathedral, at the altar of St Valerius, a patron saint of Zaragoza. When the priest celebrated the Eucharist, the "holy body" was transformed once again into the original form of the wafer. Roig concludes that this case "contradicted the evil infidels ... and it was shameful especially for women." And thus, while Roig did not specify the fate of the Muslim, this miraculous Eucharistic narrative terminates in the *Spill* with the death of the woman by lightning.

There are some problems in drawing too direct a line between the painted panel in the Altarpiece of the Virgin in Sigena and Roig's tale as it is told in the *Spill*. The first problem is the lack of complete correspondence between the narratives. The first scene depicted in the Sigena panel, which represents the woman and the Muslim sage anxiously discussing what to do with the host-child in the case, perfectly echoes Roig's narrative. However, the second scene, which displays the sinful woman's end, is clearly different from the closure of the narrative in the *Spill*. Another problem with the comparison between the Sigena Altarpiece and the *Spill* is the fact that the latter was written around a century after the painting and, additionally, refers to a miracle that allegedly happened in Zaragoza in 1427. Given that the Sigena Altarpiece was painted between 1365 and 1373, it is clear that it did not depict the same miraculous occurrence.

The possible solution to this conundrum is to assume that an earlier tradition circulated in the Iberian Peninsula. This tradition was either transmitted orally or through a written account that did not survive. This hypothetical earlier tradition could have been an adaptation of Cantiga 104 in Alfonso X's *Cantigas de Santa María*. This Cantiga begins with a squire's mistress who is saddened when her lover marries another. The Cantiga then tells how the woman sought the advice of her neighbors, without specifying whether they were non-Christians, and that the latter suggested she steal a host. This Cantiga clearly implies that the stolen host was intended for magical purposes, a well-known trope in medieval lore.[24] After procuring the host, the woman secretly placed it in her headscarf. There, the host started bleeding profusely. When other people reacted to seeing the blood flowing from her headscarf, the woman realized the miraculous nature of the incident, repented, and joined a convent as a nun. While the Cantiga neither refers to a Muslim sage nor ends with a divine punishment inflicted on the woman, its

---

[24] Alfonso X, el Sabio, *Cantigas de Santa María*, ed. Walter Mettmann, 3 vols. (Madrid, 1986–1989), Cantiga 104, 2:18–20; Jaime Ferreiro Alemparte, "Fuentes germánicas en las 'Cantigas de Santa María' de Alfonso X El Sabio," *Grial* 9, no. 31 (1971): 31–62, at 45–46, 48–49. See also Peter Browe, "Die Eucharistie als Zaubermittel im Mittelalter," *Archiv für Kulturgeschichte* 20 (1930): 134–54, at 135–37.

narrative structure strikingly resembles both the scene depicted in the Sigena Altarpiece and Roig's *Spill*.

It is possible, then, to postulate a precursor to the narratives in the Sigena Altarpiece and the *Spill* in which a Christian woman seeks to regain her lover's affection and turns for help to a certain sorcerer who can produce a love potion with a consecrated host. From this point the narrative can diverge in two directions. The more forgiving closing has the woman repenting and returning to the fold of the church. In the more vengeful resolution, the woman is put to death. In that analysis, the difference between the visual version of Sigena and the textual version of Roig is relatively minor. They are variations on the same theme: in both, the sinful, sacrilegious woman is receiving divine punishment.[25] As a matter of fact, in one of the later retellings of this Eucharistic miracle, the Muslim sage converted to Christianity and the woman asked for absolution.[26] We thus can see the story's ending as one of the more malleable elements of the narrative, open to at least two types of closure, each of which may involve variations of detail.

The appearance in the Sigena Altarpiece and in Roig's *Spill* of the figure of the Muslim sage poses a problem of a different order. Given the propensity of Christian Eucharistic tales to depict the person who obtains the consecrated host as a Jew who seeks to abuse it, as well as the long-standing association of Jews with magic in medieval Europe, the figure of the Muslim sage from Zaragoza may seem surprising. In her analysis of Roig's tale, Francesca Español Bertrán has argued that the reference to the Muslim sage resulted from "contamination" between the usual tale targeting the sacrilegious Jew, on the one hand, and contemporary Valencian preoccupations with Muslim coastal raids, in which churches were desecrated, on the other.[27] I believe, however, that the connections between Jew and Muslim in the medieval Iberian Christian imagination can be traced to an earlier period. In fact, the similar roles Jews and Muslims occupy in the Sigena Altarpiece show that the connections between the two run deeper than a particular fifteenth-century Valencian context.

Evidence for the similarities between Jews and Muslims in Eucharistic tales can be gleaned from the language employed by Roig. To begin with, Roig insultingly dubs the Muslim sage an "evil dog." This pejorative term

---

[25] Rodríguez Barral, *La imagen del judío*, 201 n. 200, gives several literary parallels.

[26] José Antonio Hebrera y Esmir, *Vida prodigiosa del ilustrissimo y venerable D. Martin García, obispo de Barcelona* (Zaragoza, 1700), 1:30. My thanks to Teresa Soto González for bringing this source to my attention.

[27] Francesca Español Bertrán, "Ecos del sentimiento antimusulmán en el 'Spill' de Jaume Roig," *Sharq al-Andalus* 10–11 (1993–1994): 325–45.

was repeatedly used in medieval and early modern Spanish sources with reference to Muslims.[28] At the same time, medieval Christian devotional works and religious art built on Ps 21:17 (*quoniam circumdederunt me canes multi*) in describing Christ's Jewish tormentors as dogs.[29] Another significantly ambiguous term is *alfaquí*, which Roig uses to describe the Muslim sage. The etymology of the term might be related to the Arabic Faqīh (فَقِيه), understood today mostly as an expert in Islamic jurisprudence. Medieval usage of the term, however, was looser. Most interestingly, perhaps, is the fact that the term did not refer exclusively to Muslims. For example, in 1220 Pope Honorius III granted protection to the Jewish physician of James I of Aragon, Isaac Benveniste, to whom he referred to as "alfakimo karissimi."[30] In other contemporary Aragonese documents, the term "alfaquín" or "our alfaquín" is widely used in reference to Jewish officials in the service of the Crown, whether physicians, advisors, ministers, or some combination thereof.[31] Finally, in the *Cantigas de Santa María*, the Alfonsine text employs the term "alfaquín" in reference to a blasphemous Jewish sage.[32] Thus, while Roig's alfaquí is clearly a Muslim, the term could also refer to Jews.

The issue here is not simply the shared designation as alfaquí but rather the association of both Jews and Muslims with potentially dangerous wisdom. The Christian association between Jews and magic is well known thanks to the seminal work of Joshua Trachtenberg, who argued that this belief led to the emergence of anti-Jewish libels such as the host desecration.[33] But in the Middle Ages, magic was not exclusively associated with Jews. Christian authors, especially from the twelfth century onwards, associated Muslims with

---

[28] For instance, Cantiga 192 refers to Prophet Muhammad as a dog (*Mafomete cão*); see Alfonso X, *Cantigas de Santa María*, 2:218–23, at 221, v. 104. Jaume Bleda, who is discussed below, refers to the moriscos as "rabid dogs" in his *Corónica de los moros de España* (Valencia, 1618), 882.

[29] Kenneth Stow, *Jewish Dogs: An Image and Its Interpreters; Continuity in the Catholic-Jewish Encounter* (Stanford, 2006); James Marrow, "Circumdederunt Me Canes Multi: Christ's Tormentors in Northern European Art of the Late Middle Ages and Early Renaissance," *Art Bulletin* 59 (1977): 167–81.

[30] Shlomo Simonsohn, *The Apostolic See and the Jews*, vol. 1, *Documents: 492–1404* (Toronto, 1988), 108–9 n. 105, and see also the other related documents which employ similar terminology in 109–10 nn. 106–7.

[31] See a short discussion in Jerome Lee Shneidman, "Jews in the Royal Administration of Thirteenth Century Aragon," *Historia Judaica* 21 (1959): 37–52, esp. 39–40, where he suggests that the etymology of alfaquí is derived from al-Hakim, that is, the "wise" or the "learned."

[32] Alfonso X, *Cantigas de Santa María*, 2:30–33, at 30, v. 9.

[33] Joshua Trachtenberg, *Jewish Magic and Superstition: A Study in Folk Religion* (New York, 1939). But see now Katelyn N. Mesler, "Legends of Jewish Sorcery: Reputations and Representations in Late Antiquity and Medieval Europe" (PhD diss., Northwestern University, 2012).

medicine, astrology, and magic, and Muhammad himself was described as a trickster who performed false miracles.[34] This common association of Jews and Muslims with magic led in some cases to striking conflations. An example of this may be found in one of the versions of the proto-Faustian legend, the Miracle of Theophile. In this legend, Theophile, a disappointed Christian, seeks the help of a Jewish sorcerer, who functions as an intermediary with the devil. Theophile makes a pact with the devil, only later to repent it and ask for the Virgin's help. He is eventually forgiven and his contract with the devil is annulled. For our purposes, it is significant that in the version written ca. 1260–1270 by the French poet Rutebeuf, the intermediary is called "Salatin," a name with evident Arab-Muslim connotations. As Gilbert Dahan has shown, Rutebeuf's text united the traditional Jewish enemy with the contemporary thirteenth-century Muslim enemy, both representing a religious Other who possesses dangerous wisdom.[35]

Ultimately, the Altarpiece of the Virgin in Sigena provides the most powerful evidence for the close association of, and even similitude between, Jews and Muslims in the premodern Iberian Christian imagination. While the sinful Christian woman who sacrilegiously procures the host is a constant in the different versions of the tale, the "infidel," who by mistreating the host eventually proves its power, may be either Jew or Muslim. Indeed, the close proximity in the Sigena Altarpiece of visual depictions of the Jewish host profanation of Paris and the Muslim host profanation of Zaragoza clearly indicates that to Christian eyes Jews and Muslims belonged to the same broader category and might even be prone to conflation. Admittedly, there are evident differences between the Jew and the Muslim in the Sigena Altarpiece. The former treated the host as an exchangeable good and thus fulfilled specific Christian stereotypes about Jewish materialism. In addition, it was only the Jew who was represented as directly and unabashedly attacking the host and thereby repeating the Passion. The Muslim, whose intended sorcery with the host can be contrasted with the priest and the true miracle of Eucharist, is depicted as distressed when his plot fails. These differences may be attributed to the unique place of the Jew in the premodern Christian imagination, from accused perpetrator of deicide to necessary element in salvation history. The

---

[34] See, for instance, John V. Tolan, *Saracens: Islam in the Medieval European Imagination* (New York, 2002), ch. 6, where the author compares this image of Muhammad as trickster to that of Jesus in the *Toledot Yeshu* narratives.

[35] Gilbert Dahan, "Salatin, du *Miracle de Théophile* de Rutebeuf," *Le Moyen Âge* 83 (1977): 445–68. For another case of literary conflation of Jews and Muslims, see the interesting essay by Michael Mark Chemers, "Anti-Semitism, Surrogacy, and the Invocation of Mohammed in the 'Play of the Sacrament'," *Comparative Drama* (2007): 25–55. Less substantial are Sheila Delany, "Chaucer's Prioress, the Jews, and the Muslims," *Medieval Encounters* 5 (1999): 198–213, and Sophia Rose Arjana, *Muslims in the Western Imagination* (Oxford, 2015), ch. 2.

figure of the Muslim cannot easily fulfill these functions. Perhaps for that reason, the visual representation of Muslims in Christian art is relatively scarce in comparison to that of Jews. But at least in the Sigena Altarpiece, both Jew and Muslim are represented as hostile to the salvific message of Christ. In the final analysis, these two "infidels" confirm—paradoxically, through their mistreatment of the host—the truth of the Church's teaching about the Eucharist.

Minorities under Christian Rule: Coalescence and Resemblance

The tendency to view both Jews and Muslims as potential enemies of the Eucharist is equally attested in medieval ecclesiastical and secular legislation. Here we are dealing not only with a fictional Jew or Muslim, but rather with flesh and blood ethnoreligious minorities who lived within Christian society. The legal sources discussed here reflect not so much the workings of the Christian imagination as late medieval and early modern sociopolitical issues. A case in point were Eucharistic processions, which gave rise across premodern Europe to anxieties about the possible contamination of the host. These concerns repeatedly targeted Jews, whose proximity to the Eucharistic wafers, the liturgical vessels, or the monstrance was considered a threat.[36] But here, again, there is ample evidence of parallel anxieties with regard to Muslims.

Canon 68 of the Fourth Lateran Council is an important starting point. The canon is usually cited because it decreed that "Jews and Saracens" ought to wear distinctive clothing throughout Christendom to distinguish them from Christians. The canon, however, also specified that on Easter Sunday and the last three days of the Holy Week, Jews and Muslims may not appear in public, specifically because they dress in rich attire while Christians are mourning in commemoration of the Passion.[37] Sentiments akin to those expressed in this canon also appear in Iberian ecclesiastical and secular legislation. Some late thirteenth- and fourteenth-century Iberian laws used broad categories to discuss the dangers Jews and Muslims posed to the Eucharist. For instance, in a Valencian synod held in 1278, Bishop Jazperto de Botonach forbade the selling of liturgical vessels, especially the Eucharistic chalice, to "infidels"

---

[36] Rubin, *Corpus Christi*, 35–49.

[37] *Decrees of the Ecumenical Councils: Nicaea I to Lateran V*, 266. On the increasing linking of Jews and Muslims in ecclesiastical legislation in the twelfth and thirteenth century, see Benjamin Z. Kedar, "*De iudeis et sarracenis*: On the Categorization of Muslims in Medieval Canon Law," in idem, *The Franks in the Levant, 11th to 14th Centuries* (Aldershot, UK, 1993), 207–13; James M. Powell, "The Papacy and the Muslim Frontier," in *Muslims under Latin Rule, 1100–1300*, ed. James M. Powell (Princeton, NJ, 1990), 175–203, esp. 186–93.

(*infidelibus*). The broad category used here was perhaps primarily a reference to Jews, but it might certainly also refer to Muslims, who constituted a significant population in Valencia. Indeed, less than forty years later in the same city, King James II of Aragon (d. 1327) ordered that Jews and Muslims ought to either genuflect or remove themselves when the host was carried in the city's streets.[38] Since the Feast of Corpus Christi was only introduced to Valencia in the 1320s, we can assume that the reference was to the ritual of the Viaticum, during which the Eucharist is taken to a person nearing his death. Be that as it may, it is clear that the tenor of this legislation reflects a concern about the disruption of the Eucharistic rituals by both Jews and Muslims.

Almost exactly the same legislation can be found in medieval Castile. Alfonso X's massive legal compendium, the *Siete Partidas* (composed around the mid-thirteenth century), declared that "Jews and Moors" ought to kneel down in front of the Eucharist like Christians, since "this is the truth and there is no other." If they choose not to do so, they should leave the street so that the clergy "could pass without any impediment."[39] About a century later, King Juan I promulgated a decree in the Cortes of Briviesca in 1387 which stated that "Jews and Moors should not dare to be in the street when Corpus Christi processions pass, and if one of them is caught he will be arrested by anyone and brought before a tribunal." This decree was later incorporated in Alfonso Díaz de Montalvo's *Ordenanzas Reales* (1484), one of the major legal compendia produced during the reign of the Catholic Kings; it thus informed secular legislation over the entire course of the early modern Spanish Monarchy.[40] Castilian synodal legislation of the later Middle Ages went beyond the special occasion of the Eucharistic processions to speak of the interiors of churches as endangered sites. For example, the Synod of Cuenca declared in 1446 that "no Jew or Moor should dare to be present in the Church when Mass is said, and any Christian who defends them will incur a sentence of excommunication."[41] Needless to say, these normative texts do not necessar-

---

[38]For Botonach's legislation, see Ignacio Pérez de Heredia y Valle, *Sínodos medievales de Valencia: Edición bilingüe* (Rome, 1994), 139–41. For Jaume II's legislation, see *Aureum opus regalium privilegiorum civitatis et regni Valentie: Cum historia cristianissimi Regis Jacobi* (Valencia, 1515), fol. 57r. Both are quoted in Mark Meyerson, *Jews in an Iberian Frontier Kingdom: Society, Economy, and Politics in Morvedre, 1248–1391* (Leiden, 2004), 90 n. 93 and 85 n. 76, respectively.

[39]Alfonso X, *Las Siete Partidas del Rey Don Alfonso el Sabio, cotejadas con varios códices antiguos por la Real Academia de la Historia* (Madrid, 1807), 1.4.119.

[40]Alfonso Díaz de Montalvo, *Ordenanzas Reales de Castilla o Libro de las Leyes* (Seville, 1495), 1.1.3.

[41]Antonio García y García, ed., *Synodicon hispanum. X: Cuenca y Toledo* (Madrid, 2011), 321 n. 191: "Que ningund judio nin moro non sea osado de estar en la iglesia en tanto que se dize la misa. E si algund christiano los defendiere, que por ese mesmo fecho incurra en sentencia descomunion." Cf. Rubin, *Gentile Tales*, 31 n. 120.

ily reflect enforcement in practice. Yet the coexistence of Jews and Muslims in the same legal clauses aiming to establish order during Eucharistic celebrations strongly indicates that the two ethnoreligious groups were viewed analogously in premodern Christian Iberia.

Admittedly, lumping together Jews and Muslims in laws dealing with the Eucharist was still far from accusing one group or the other of host profanation. Yet in particularly tense moments, Christians transformed what they saw as the potential danger to Christian society posed by Jews and Muslims into accusations that they had actually inflicted harm. During the second half of the fifteenth century, when Castile was immersed in civil strife, the opposition to the rule of Juan II (and later to Enrique IV) targeted the allegedly favorable attitudes of these monarchs to the Jewish and Muslim minorities. So, for instance, in a document known as the Sentence of Medina del Campo (1465), the noble faction rebelling against Enrique IV's rule demanded that all Jews and Muslims in the royal court should be thrown out of Castile and their property taken. They also declared that an Inquisition against the kingdom's "bad Christians" (probably referring to backsliding Jewish converts to Christianity) should be established. Most importantly for our purposes, the Sentence warned that "some Jews and Moors" were able to procure the consecrated host and other consecrated things for the sake of "performing some spells (*maleficios*) in injury to Our Lord and to His Holy Church and our faith." "Bad Christians" also participated in some of these host desecrations, the Sentence added. The nobles leading the rebellious faction demanded that such persons be judged heretics.[42]

The accusation of joint Jewish-Muslim host profanation conspiracy in the Sentence of Medina del Campo had clear political motives. Once again, however, it was not a unique case but rather part of a broader discourse. The host accusation in the Sentence clearly echoes other documents from the mid- and later-fifteenth century that criticize the Castilian government by attacking conversos. For example, Marcos García de Mora, one of the leaders of the 1449 Toledo Rebellion during which New Christians of Jewish origin were specifically targeted, included in his *memorial* a list of crimes committed by the conversos. Among them, he claimed that some clergymen of Jewish ancestry sold consecrated hosts and other liturgical objects to "Jews and other people and infidels."[43] Scholars are familiar with the tendency of Spaniards

---

[42]Fritz (Yitzhak) Baer, *Die Juden im Christlichen Spanien*, pt. 1, *Urkunden und Regesten*, vol. 2, *Kastilien, Inquisitionsakten* (Berlin, 1936), 331 n. 123.

[43]Eloy Benito Ruano, "El Memorial contra los Conversos del Bachiller García de Mora," *Sefarad* 17 (1957): 331. For a recent analysis of this important text, see Rosa Vidal Doval, "'Qui ex Iudeis sunt': Visigothic Law and the Discrimination against *Conversos* in Late Medieval Spain," in *Forced Conversion in Christianity, Judaism and Islam: Coercion and Faith in Premodern Iberia and Beyond*, ed. Mercedes García-Arenal and Yonatan Glazer-Eytan (Leiden, 2019), 60–85.

to scapegoat Jews and New Christians of Jewish origin during the tumultuous fifteenth century. Yet it is telling that Mora's *memorial*, when accusing Jews of sacrilege, lumped them together with other, unspecified accomplices, and that the Sentence of Medina del Campo explicitly named Muslims along with Jews as enemies of the Eucharist.

The dramatic events of the expulsion of the Jews in 1492 and the forcible conversion of Muslims to Christianity in the first decades of the sixteenth century created a new situation. As Jews and Muslims were no longer permitted in Iberia, Christian anxieties migrated from the problem of "infidelity" to the problem of the alleged heresy and apostasy of those New Christians of Jewish or Muslim origin. The yoking together of people of Jewish and Muslim origin that was prevalent in medieval legislation is rarely found in records of the Spanish Inquisition, which had the jurisdiction over baptized Christians suspected in crimes against the faith. This is partly due to the different chronology of inquisitorial prosecution of conversos and moriscos, respectively. Whereas the Spanish Inquisition began in 1481 its activity as a tribunal dedicated to the problem of "judaizing" Christians, around the third decade of the sixteenth century persecution of conversos waned and was replaced by concerns about "illuminists" (*alumbrados*) and "Lutherans." In contrast, the Inquisition did not operate intensely against the supposed danger of crypto-Islam until the second half of the sixteenth century. At this point, the number of inquisitorial trial records dealing with conversos diminished significantly. Indeed, only in the last few decades of the morisco presence in Spain did the Inquisition resume its operations against New Christians of Jewish origin, this time against conversos who had migrated from Portugal by the thousands after 1580. These changing patterns of inquisitorial persecution explain to some extent why inquisitors rarely refer to conversos and moriscos as companions in crime.

Nevertheless, there is evidence suggesting that Christian anxieties produced very similar accusations of acts of irreverence towards the Eucharist against both groups. In the first decades of inquisitorial activity in Spain, roughly between 1481 and 1520, we find numerous denunciations accusing New Christians of Jewish origin of avoiding, disrespecting, and even profaning the Eucharist. In some trial records, conversos were accused of spitting during Mass, refusing to kneel down, or making disrespectful gestures when the host was elevated. In others, conversos were reported to have refrained from swallowing the host and later spitting it out. Some were accused of placing the consecrated wafer in their shoes so that they would tread on it throughout the day. Conversos were also accused of making sacrilegious remarks about the Mass, to the effect that it was a joke, or that the host was a little white cake, or that the Eucharist was a fraud—for example, by reciting the ritual formula "bread and wine I see, in the Law of Moses I believe" (*pan y vino veo, en la Ley de Moisen creo*).[44]

Without entering into the thorny issue of the historical trustworthiness of these denunciations, it is evident that they reflect a widespread concern among "Old Christians": namely, that conversos were not only Jews in Christian garb but that they also were hostile to Christianity. Of course, Jews were accused in the past of hostility to Christianity, but it became more threatening when they entered Christian society. The accusations of sacrilegious statements about Catholic worship in general and the Eucharist in particular were thus a powerful weapon in the hands of those who wanted to harm New Christians of Jewish origin.[45] This was precisely what happened in one of the most infamous campaigns of the early days of the Inquisition against "judaizers," that of the inquisitor Diego Rodríguez Lucero in Córdoba between 1499 and 1507. This inquisitor reported to his superiors that the conversos of Córdoba were secretly congregating to hear anti-Christian sermons from a man named Alonso de Membreque. According to the inquisitorial report, Membreque, who was dressed ceremoniously in white, made an altar and performed rituals intended to negate the Mass (*hazia çiertas çerimonias contrafaziendo la Misa*).[46] On a different occasion, the conversos led by Membreque performed what the inquisitors considered to be a ritual of "Jewish cleansing." Membreque ordered the conversos to vomit the consecrated wafers they had been compelled to ingest, and to do so in the house's "dirtiest place." On yet another occasion, he produced a consecrated host. Then, states the report, Membreque and the assembled conversos took the host, tore it to pieces, threw it on the floor, and trampled it underfoot. Finally, they threw it into a latrine (*neçesaria*). While Lucero's anti-converso

---

[44]The quote is taken from Carlos Carrete Parrondo, "Melancholy among the Conversos of Castile and the Expulsion of 1492" [in Hebrew], in *Jews and Conversos at the Time of the Expulsion*, ed. Yom Tov Assis and Yosef Kaplan (Jerusalem, 1999), 184–85. For some further references see Haim Beinart, *Conversos on Trial: The Inquisition in Ciudad Real* [in Hebrew] (Tel Aviv, 1965), 196–97, 228–31; David M. Gitlitz, *Secrecy and Deceit: The Religion of the Crypto-Jews* (Albuquerque, NM, 1996), 148–52; Gretchen D. Starr-Lebeau, *In the Shadow of the Virgin: Inquisitors, Friars, and Conversos in Guadalupe, Spain* (Princeton, NJ, 2003), 63–64.

[45]For a broader discussion of this issue, see Yonatan Glazer-Eytan, "Incriminating the Judaizer: Inquisitors, Intentionality, and the Problem of Religious Ambiguity After Forced Conversion," in García-Arenal and Glazer-Eytan, *Forced Conversion in Christianity, Judaism and Islam*, 235–65.

[46]Archivo General de Simancas, Estado, 12, fols. 392–93. The document was transcribed by Rafael García y García de Castro, *Virtudes de la Reina Católica* (Madrid, 1961), 440–43, app. 18. A Hebrew translation and commentary is provided by Haim Beinart, "A Prophesying Movement in Cordova in 1499–1502," *Zion* 4 (Jerusalem, 1979), 190–200. See also John Edwards, "Elijah and the Inquisition: Messianic Prophecy among Conversos in Spain, c. 1500," *Nottingham Medieval Studies* 28 (1984): 79–94.

campaign met resistance and ultimately, in 1508, this inquisitor was deposed from his office, Christian concerns about conversos mistreating the Eucharist and the vulnerability of conversos to such denunciations persisted.

When the Inquisition finally began to fully operate against the converted Muslims in the second half of the sixteenth century, it made similar accusations of sacrilegious behavior towards the Eucharist against them. As in the case of the conversos, accusations of sacrilegious behavior towards the host almost never stood alone but were rather part of a long list of heterodox practices of which the New Christians of Muslim origin were accused. For example, when the Inquisition of Cuenca charged the morisco Luis Hernández with apostasy in 1569, it accused him of maintaining that he believed in Muhammad; that there was no Trinity; that the Virgin was not a virgin; and that the body of Christ was not present in the consecrated host—which he was reported to have called "just a little bread (*panete*) or a little bit of paper."[47] In 1601–1602, the morisca María de Talavera was tried by the Inquisition of Toledo for removing the consecrated wafer from her mouth and placing it inside a glove.[48] María claimed that she took the host out of her mouth because she had an urge to vomit but that she later ate it. The inquisitors accepted her version, and she received a relatively minor punishment, penitential in nature. All the same, the case, which echoes the Eucharistic tale of the sinful woman and the Muslim alfaquí discussed above, demonstrates the particular attention of inquisitors and early modern Spanish society to morisco contact with the Eucharist.

Some of the sacrilegious attitudes of which moriscos were accused reflected not only unbelief, but veritable mockery and ridicule. For instance, the Inquisition of Cuenca accused the morisco Gaspar Belbís in 1537 of having bought consecrated hosts stolen by a Christian thief from a local church. Belbís was then said to show complete and utter disrespect to the Eucharist: the inquisitors accused him of stringing together the hosts with a thread and hanging them with a nail in a "dishonest place," most probably a latrine—the same crime of which the so-called judaizers of Córdoba were accused (as mentioned above).[49] How can we account for these tacit yet evident resemblances between inquisitorial accusations against moriscos and conversos? Such similarities could be explained as the outcome of a common rejection of key Catholic doctrines among members of two religious groups who had been forced to convert to Christianity. Both Jewish and Muslim polemical literature against Christianity included strong criticism of the Eucharist, which

---

[47] Archivo Diocesano de Cuenca, Inquisición, 246: 3298, fol. 51v.

[48] Julio Sierra, *Procesos en la inquisición de Toledo (1575–1610): Manuscrito de Halle* (Madrid, 2005), 503 n. 970.

[49] ADC, Inq. 133: 1695A, fol. 66r.

may have informed some of the attitudes reported in inquisitorial trials.[50] But this resemblance also could be explained as a consequence of the fact that both groups were persecuted by the same institution, namely, the Inquisition. Whether inquisitors drew on methods used against conversos in their activities against moriscos is a question that goes beyond the scope of this present essay. But it is clear in both cases that as part of its working method the Inquisition actively looked for rejection of Catholic rituals as an indication of heresy and apostasy. In the Spain of the Inquisition, attitudes toward the Eucharist marked religious difference: they indicated that New Christians, whether they were of Jewish or Muslim origin, were in fact apostates and heretics.

From Profanation to Expulsion: Precedents and Links

While both conversos and moriscos were targets of inquisitorial persecution, it was only the latter who were expelled from Spain *after* their conversion to Christianity. The decision to expel baptized Christians was in many ways an unprecedented course of action and called for a significant campaign of justification. This campaign was undertaken through diplomatic efforts as well as by means of a proliferation of printed propaganda. These texts, published just after the beginning of the expulsion and seeking to legitimize it, accused the moriscos time and again of sacrilegious behavior towards the Eucharist. Significantly, these expulsion apologies also drew direct connections between Jewish and morisco host profanation.[51]

Among the apologists of the expulsion of the moriscos the Dominican Friar Jaime Bleda takes a prominent place. He was an inquisitor and a protégé of the all-powerful archbishop of Valencia, Juan de Ribera. In 1585, Ribera appointed Bleda as an acolyte in the town of Corbera, where a significant population of moriscos lived. As Bleda would later write, it was during mass in Corbera when he realized the extent to which the conversion of the moriscos was a complete and utter failure. Entering the church while the priest raised the host, Bleda knelt down near the door. From his concealed position, he saw how those "infidels," instead of venerating the host and the chalice, "scorned and mocked the Eucharist." The women pinched the toddlers so that they would cry, and there was not a single morisco who did not

---

[50] See Rubin, *Gentile Tales*, 93–103; Hava Lazarus-Yafeh, "Some Neglected Aspects of Medieval Muslim Polemics against Christianity," *Harvard Theological Review* 89 (1996): 61–84, at 78–79; Cardaillac, *Moriscos y cristianos*, 292–95.

[51] On the expulsion apologists, see Mercedes García-Arenal and Gerard Wiegers, eds., *The Expulsion of the Moriscos from Spain: A Mediterranean Diaspora*, trans. Consuelo López-Morillas and Martin Beagles (Leiden, 2014).

wiggle his lips or interfere with the mass, all in "manifest derision, insult, and outrage to the holy sacrament." Shocked by this heretical behavior, Bleda returned to Valencia and asked to be removed from office, but was denied his request. It was at this moment, he writes, that he decided to find the way to "liberate the holy sacrament from those injurious sacrileges."[52]

Bleda spent the following decades in total commitment to the anti-morisco cause, seeking to convince secular and ecclesiastical authorities of the urgency of the matter. During this time, Bleda published several works, among them a book dedicated to the Eucharist. This book describes various Eucharistic miracles, which prove, as usual in such narratives, that Christ was truly present in the Eucharist and that the host possessed or at least channeled divine powers. Among these tales appears the famous case of alleged Jewish host profanation known as the "*Billettes* affair," mentioned above, which Bleda dates to 1306, the year in which Philip IV the Fair expelled the Jews from France.[53] This was not a simple mistake. It is quite plausible that Bleda here followed the Franciscan Alonso de Espina, who claimed in his virulent polemical work, *The Fortress of the Faith* (composed between 1459–1561), that he had heard in Medina del Campo from Cluniac monks that the Jews were expelled from France because they profaned a host.[54]

Together with this and other anti-Jewish Eucharistic tales, Bleda's book included narratives in which Muslims and moriscos figured as enemies of the host. Most took place in the context of military struggles, yet among them we can also find the story about the sinful woman and the Muslim sage, which Bleda took directly from Jaume Roig.[55] Once again, Eucharistic tales of Jewish profaners appeared side by side with those of Muslim profaners. Bleda, however, not only placed narratives of Jewish and Muslim host desecration side by side but also made inferences from one to the other. This anti-morisco apologist emphasized one important aspect of the Paris 1290 host profanation libel, namely that it led to punishment of the entire Jewish community, not only of the accused Jewish profaner. For Bleda, this offered a model to emulate in the case of the moriscos. Just as Philip IV of France expelled the Jews after the "*Billettes* affair," Bleda argued, the moriscos should be expelled from "all of Spain" on account of the "injuries" they had committed against the holy sacrament.[56]

---

[52]Bleda, *Corónica de los moros de España*, 938.

[53]Jaime Bleda, *Libro de la cofradia de la Minerva: En el qual se escriuen mas de dozientos y cinquenta milagros del Santissimo Sacramento del Altar* (Valencia, 1600), 92–99 (milagro 20). Bleda published a shorter version of the same treatise in 1592.

[54]Alonso de Espina, *Fortalitium Fidei* (Lyon, 1487), II. IX, fol. 167.

[55]For Roig's tale, see Bleda, *Libro de la cofradia de la Minerva*, 181–83 (milagro 95). For other Eucharistic tales including Muslims, see 65–70 (milagro 7), 76–77 (milagro 11), 333–35 (milagro 223).

[56]Bleda, *Corónica*, 918.

While Bleda's book of Eucharistic miracles reflects aspects of his general anti-morisco campaign, it was another work, titled *Defense of the Faith on the Issue of the Neophytes or Moriscos of the Kingdom of Valencia and the Whole of Spain*, that proved to be his most influential work. This work circulated among secular and ecclesiastical notables in manuscript versions in the late 1590s and early 1600s, before it was finally published in Latin in 1610. The *Defense of the Faith*, which contained a list of ninety-one proofs demonstrating that the moriscos were heretics and apostates, including their sacrilegious behavior during mass, was Bleda's main weapon in his campaign against the moriscos.[57] References to Jews abound throughout this anti-morisco text, and they are not exclusively related to the Eucharist. For instance, Bleda argues that the moriscos are apostates because they mock the cross. Christians, therefore, should intervene to defend the faith. Bleda gives two examples of efforts to do so. In Lisbon in 1506, Old Christians killed over two thousand New Christians of Jewish origin after one of them mocked popular veneration of a miraculous crucifix. Bleda marshals this event, well known to Jewish historians thanks to the seminal study of Yosef Hayim Yerushalmi, as another precedent for collective action against moriscos.[58]

Bleda's second example cites a story told by Alonso de Espina about the expulsion of the Jews from England. The English king (unnamed by Espina and Bleda) forcibly converted all the Jews of his realm. After observing that the natural disasters that the Jews' infidelity had brought upon his kingdom did not then cease, the king decided to test the sincerity of these New Christians. He ordered the construction of two pavilions in a field near the port. In the first he placed the Torah and in the second the cross. He then told the newly converted to choose between them voluntarily. After the converts turned to the Torah, the king, saddened by this, ordered that their throats be slit and their bodies thrown into the sea. Bleda concludes: "There is no doubt that if a similar test was made with those New Christians [i.e., the moriscos], their perfidy would be proven since they deny the cross and the Crucified and embrace the beast Muhammad."[59] As in various other places throughout the vitriolic pages of the *Defense of the Faith*, Bleda draws on precedents from

---

[57] For the "proof" that moriscos were hostile to the Eucharist, see Jaime Bleda, *Defensio fidei in causa neophytorum, sive Morischorum Regno Valentiae totiusque Hispaniae* (Valencia, 1610), 39. For the ways in which Bleda used his prepublished book to convince dignitaries, see Manuel Ruiz Lagos, *Contra Moriscos: El sumario Bleda* (Huelva, 2009).

[58] See Yosef Hayim Yerushalmi, *The Lisbon Massacre of 1506 and the Royal Image in the "Shebet Yehudah"* (Cincinnati, 1976).

[59] Bleda, *Defensio fidei*, 44–45: "profecto istud esset efficacius argumentum omnibus, que ego hic scribo, ad probandam eorum perfidiam: interpide enim, & insolenter, non Christi Crucem, nec ipsum Dominum crucifixum, sed bestiam illam, Mahometum inquam, amplecterentur."

anti-Jewish literature to make his case that the moriscos were all apostates and should be expelled.

Given the fundamental influence of the *Defense of the Faith* on other expulsion apologies, it is hardly surprising to find in the latter similar allegations and arguments. A case in point is the anti-morisco book titled *Justified Expulsion of the Spanish Moriscos* composed by the Aragonese friar Jerónimo Aznar and his nephew, the *licenciado* Pedro Aznar y Cardona (who signed the work).[60] The general thrust of this malicious work is an attempt to substantiate Bleda's arguments with details that give a sense of historicity— details that are sometimes missing from other expulsion apologies. In a long and very detailed discussion of moriscos' animosity towards the host, the authors of the *Justified Expulsion* described moriscos not only as secretly ridiculing the Eucharist, but also as brazenly desecrating it. In one incident, for example, a morisco throws a cloth dirtied with feces on the chalice as the priest is raising the host.[61] But it is not only the detail included in this work that is of interest. As a matter of fact, the treatment of morisco sacrilege in this work goes beyond formally echoing the accusations of host profanation leveled against Jews and conversos or seeing anti-Jewish policies as model for the morisco problem. The book takes a step further and establishes a direct link between the two groups. If the moriscos accepted the truth of Catholic sacraments, argue the authors of the book,

> They would not deny what they ought to admit, nor would they accept things according to their capricious whim, as do the obstinate Jews, [who] deny the real and true presence of the most sacred body of Christ in the holy sacrament of the altar under the accidents of bread and wine. And the moriscos expelled from Spain have always followed those harshly incredulous Jews.[62]

This is not an isolated statement in the *Justified Expulsion*. While arguing that the moriscos were apostates and rejected and ridiculed the Eucharist, the book offers a long discussion which, quite astonishingly, focuses on the Jews. This not always systematic argument draws on classical Christian polemic

---

[60] Pedro Aznar Cardona, *Expulsion justificada de los Moriscos españoles, y suma de las excelencias Christianas de nuestro Rey Don Felipe el Catholico Tercero* (Huesca, 1612). On the book and its authors, see Julio Caro Baroja, "Los Moriscos aragoneses según un autor de comienzos del siglo XVII," in idem, *Razas, pueblos y linajes* (Madrid, 1957), 81–98.

[61] Aznar Cardona, *Expulsion justificada*, fol. 63v.

[62] Aznar Cardona, *Expulsion justificada*, fol. 62r: "y assi fundandose en la verdad, no negarian, lo que deuen conceder, ni solo aceptarian lo que les dita su antojo boltario, como los Iudios obstinados, niegan la presencia real y verdadera, del cuerpo sacratissimo de Christo en el Santo Sacramento del altar, debaxo de los acidentes de pan y de vino: y a estos Iudios duramente incredulos, han seguido siempre en este error heretico, los Moriscos expellidos de España."

against Judaism by comparing Scriptural traditions and pointing to the "falsifications of the Talmudists." Towards the end, however, it surveys Eucharistic miracles—most prominently, that of the alleged Jewish host profanation in Paris, 1290, but also some that involve Muslims—with which it proves the truth of the Eucharist. At the end of this rather inconsistent argument, the final conclusion of the *Justified Explusion* is nevertheless unequivocal: "the moriscos followed the error that Muhammad took from the Jews."[63]

Intersecting Histories

The evidence presented above complicates the exceptionalist historiographical narrative that sees accusations of host profanation only within the framework of increasingly deteriorating Christian-Jewish relations. At the very least, it shows that in premodern Iberia, Christians considered both Jews and Muslims as potential enemies of the Eucharist. It might be tempting to see this argument along the lines of R. I. Moore's thesis about the "persecuting society."[64] According to Moore, the rise of centralizing state power in medieval Europe was tied to the emergence of scapegoating discourses that legitimized violence against minorities, be they Jews, heretics, women, homosexuals, or lepers (Muslims are not mentioned in the work). Moore's thesis may therefore provide a general model with which we can understand the accusations of host profanation leveled against Iberia's "Others." This much-discussed thesis, however, cannot replace the close analysis of the particular realities of late medieval and early modern Iberia, which also included cohabitation and exchange between religious groups. Nor can it equip us with a lens powerful enough to look at the specifities of anti-Judaism and anti-Islam. It equally does not account for the reciprocal ties between accusations of Jewish/converso and Muslim/morisco host profanation.

In that final respect, not only should the exceptionalist historiographical narrative of Jewish host profanation be revised but also any neat division between Jews as "theological enemies" and Muslims as "political enemies"

---

[63]Connecting Jews and Muslims in Christian polemic has a long tradition. See Norman Daniel, *Islam and the West: The Making of an Image* (Oxford, 2009), 105–6, and the references there in n. 21; Sidney H. Griffith, "Jews and Muslims in Christian Syriac and Arabic Texts of the Ninth Century," *Jewish History* 3, no. 1 (1988): 65–94; John C. Lamoreaux, "Early Eastern Christian Responses to Islam" in *Medieval Christian Perceptions of Islam: A Book of Essays*, ed. John V. Tolan (New York, 1996), 3–31, at 14.

[64]Robert I. Moore, *The Formation of a Persecuting Society: Authority and Deviance in Western Europe, 950–1250* (Malden, MA, 2007).

must be nuanced.[65] Instead, the complex relations between the two in Christian imagination and policy should be explored further. True, there can be no doubt that Jews and Judaism hold a unique, perhaps incomparable place in Christian thought.[66] Yet in some specific contexts, Christians thought about their sacred order through two, interrelated "objects" rather than one. This was frequently the case in premodern Iberia, yet there may be comparable cases elsewhere. I do not want to belabor the argument. There are crucial differences between the histories of Jews and Muslims in Iberia, as well as between the histories of the conversos and the moriscos. But these histories are not necessarily two parallel paths that never intersect. At times they overlap and inform one another. Christian polemical literature, inquisitorial inquiries, law codes, and Eucharistic tales and art might draw direct connections between these groups, lump them together, and even regard them as interchangeable. As a matter of fact, in some of the religious plays celebrating the miracle of the Sacred Forms of Alcalá with which this essay opened, it was not moriscos who committed the sacrilege, but Jews.[67]

Acknowledgments The author would like to thank Miriam Bodian, Yanay Israeli, and Cloe Cavero de Carondelet for their valuable comments and suggestions.

Publisher's Note Springer Nature remains neutral with regard to jurisdictional claims in published maps and institutional affiliations.

---

[65] See, for example, Dwayne E. Carpenter, "Minorities in Medieval Spain: The Legal Status of Jews and Muslims in the Siete Partidas," *Romance Quarterly* 33 (1986): 275–87, at 276. The division is a subject of an insightful critique by Gil Anidjar, *The Jew, the Arab: A History of the Enemy* (Stanford, 2003).

[66] The literature on the subject is vast. For an ambitious recent analysis, see David Nirenberg, *Anti-Judaism: The Western Tradition* (New York, 2013).

[67] Juan Carlos Garrot Zambrana, "El Auto de las formas de Alcalá y el antijudaísmo de los años 1630," *eHumanista* 3 (2015): 246–66.

Jewish History (2021) 35: 293–328
https://doi.org/10.1007/s10835-021-09426-y

The Conflation of Judaism and Islam in Hernando de Talavera's Conversion Plan

DAVIDE SCOTTO

University of Naples L'Orientale, Naples, Italy
E-mail: dscotto@unior.it

Accepted: 17 July 2021 / Published online: 2 December 2021

Abstract This article aims to show that Hernando de Talavera's evangelization strategies toward Muslims and Muslim converts in Granada (1492–1507) cannot be fully understood without investigating his previous preaching activities from the late 1470s aimed at a group of Jewish converts in Seville whom he considered "judaizers." By closely comparing the arguments against Jewish practices which Talavera outlined in his polemical work *Católica impugnación* to a series of instructions on Christian and Muslim practices that he issued as archbishop of Granada, it will be argued that in his reformist view of a society modeled on Paul's theology of the two Laws, Judaism and Islam are closely associated. The article seeks to determine to what extent Judaism, as a well-defined set of cultural and religious practices, shaped Talavera's strategies toward Muslims within the broader conversion plan, with its universalistic character, that was promoted by the Spanish Crown in the late fifteenth-century Mediterranean. At the same time, it will demonstrate how specific aspects of both religions, such as the language (Arabic, Hebrew) or the theological view of Law (the Qur'ān, Jewish law), challenged a simplistic conception of the Abrahamic faiths as interchangeable. Finally, the study will raise the question of how Talavera adapted the apostle Paul's universalistic call for conversion.

Keywords Hernando de Talavera · Evangelization · Polemics · Judaizing · Conversos · Muslims · Moriscos · Paul · Spain

> Does this mean universalism? ... One should not surrender himself in any case to the panic which this word seems to spread abroad, before informing himself exactly concerning its possible sense or non-sense.
> —Karl Barth, *The Humanity of God*, 1960

In popular media as well as scholarship, Hernando de Talavera has often been regarded as a champion of tolerance ahead of his time: a strenuous defender of Christians of Jewish origins and a Muslim-friendly thinker who aroused opposition among his contemporaries.[1] A Hieronymite monk, the confessor of Queen Isabella of Castile, and the first archbishop of Granada after

---

Chapter 4 was originally published as Scotto, D. Jewish History (2021) 35: 293–328. https://doi.org/10.1007/s10835-021-09426-y.

---

[1] In media see, for instance, http://www.cardenalbelluga.es/milenio1/fray-hernando-de-talavera.html, where Talavera is presented as an "ejemplo de respeto y tolerancia." Regarding Talavera's attitude towards Muslims see, for example, https://www.granadaporelmundo.com/fray-hernando-de-talavera: "Allí procedió a aplicar a la población musulmana una

the Christian conquest of 1492, Talavera continues to evoke the image of a nonconformist churchman, cast in opposition to the Franciscan cardinal and inquisitor Jiménez de Cisneros.[2] It is surprising that the scholars supporting this apologetic image of the first archbishop of Granada—which Francisco Javier Martínez Medina has labelled "the myth of Talavera"—have barely bothered to scrutinize Talavera's theological and pastoral writings, where he articulates his attitude towards Judaism and Islam in unambiguous terms.[3] Scholars accentuating Talavera's tolerance have mainly limited themselves to repeating tropes drawn from the archbishop's hagiographies, which were written in the early sixteenth century by his Hieronymite pupils.[4] There is no need to underscore how an uncritical approach to hagiographic sources, written with implicit apologetic aims, can lead to serious distortions.[5] A critical examination of Talavera's writings demonstrates that his ideas on conversion and assimilation echoed contemporary policies, and that they were more theologically interesting and less straightforward than his hagiographic representation would suggest.

Besides contributing to complicating the sterile binary of "tolerance" and "intolerance," a critical, comparative examination of Talavera's writings

---

política de conversión muy suave, evitando amenazas y coacciones. De hecho, impidió que la Inquisición se estableciera en Granada. Aprendió árabe y se ganó la consideración de los musulmanes, que le apodaron alfaquí santo." There are echoes of this theme in popular culture. In a recent television series on the Catholic Monarchs ("Isabel," 2012–2014, directed by Jordi Frades), Talavera plays a pivotal role as the tolerant confessor of Queen Isabella. In scholarship see, among others, the otherwise excellent book by David Coleman, *Creating Christian Granada: Society & Religious Culture in an Old–World Frontier City, 1492–1600* (Ithaca, NY, 2003), 84.

[2]Paradigmatic of this view are the studies of Tarsicio Herrero del Collado, *Talavera y Cisneros: Dos vivencias socio–religiosas en la conversión de los moros de Granada* (Madrid, 2001), and Jesús R. Folgado García, "Fray Francisco Jiménez de Cisneros y fray Hernando de Talavera: Dos religiosos, arzobispos y confesores regios en el Reino de Granada," *Toletana* 34 (2016): 51–77.

[3]Francisco Javier Martínez Medina, *Cristianos y musulmanes en la Granada del XVI, una ciudad intercultural: Invenciones de reliquias y libros plúmbeos; El Sacromonte* (Granada, 2016), 73.

[4]On the development of the hagiographic narrative on Talavera among Muslims, see Davide Scotto, "'Como en un resplandeciente y terso espejo': Hernando de Talavera tra i musulmani nelle vite della prima età moderna," in *Esperienza e rappresentazione dell'islam nell'Europa mediterranea (secoli XVI–XVIII)*, ed. Andrea Celli and Davide Scotto, monographic issue of *Rivista di Storia e Letteratura Religiosa* 51 (2015): 431–64.

[5]See Jesús R. Folgado García, "Un instrumento usado en la evangelización de la Granada Nazarí: La 'Breve Doctrina' de Hernando de Talavera," *Toletana* 24 (2011): 291–307, esp. 307, where the author states as a conclusion: "Tras el estudio de este texto, debemos afirmar que las enseñanzas de Fray Hernando, siguen vigentes en nuestros días; sobre todo porque intentan que nuestro creer y nuestro orar se plasmen en nuestro actuar."

opens up new perspectives on the close association of Judaism and Islam in the history of Spanish-Catholic evangelization.[6] In so doing, it contributes to the broader debate on the entangled history of the Abrahamic religions in the physical and symbolic Mediterranean context.[7] Although exceptions do exist and should be taken as a guide for further research, scholarship on interfaith encounters in the premodern Mediterranean has as yet thrown little light on the connections and mutual influences among Jews, Muslims, and Christians in shaping the strategies and expectations of Christian evangelization and expansionism.[8] The case of Talavera clearly shows that an approach dealing with both Jews and Muslims in Christian evangelization strategies offers a correction to the prevalent focus on either Jewish-Christian or Muslim-Christian relations, as if the two were distinct, parallel, and mutually exclusive phenomena.[9]

This study of Talavera and his attitude towards Jewish and Islamic religious practices should be situated within this research framework. I aim to show that Talavera's attitude towards the Muslim converts of Granada can

---

[6]Recent research has served to warn against the projection of contemporary conceptions of tolerance and intolerance onto medieval and early modern times. Relying on studies by Benjamin Kaplan, Sarah Mortimer, and John Robertson, Carlos Cañete has observed that toleration "did not always follow a principle of parity and frequently resulted in a practice of exclusion. The practice of tolerance in early modern Europe was never absolute, but rather embedded in conflicts and the affirmation of identities." See Carlos Cañete, "Ambivalent Origins: Isaac La Peyrère and the Politics of Historical Certainty in Seventeenth Century Europe," in *The Quest for Certainty in Early Modern Europe: From Inquisition to Inquiry, 1550–1700*, ed. Barbara Fuchs and Mercedes García-Arenal (Toronto, 2020), 242–72.

[7]A fruitful research approach can be found in Garth Fowden, *Abraham or Aristotle? First Millennium Empires and Exegetical Traditions* (Cambridge, UK, 2015); and see Adam Silverstein, Guy G. Stroumsa, and Moshe Blidstein, eds., *The Oxford Handbook of the Abrahamic Religions* (Oxford, 2015).

[8]Among the exceptions, see Steven F. Kruger, "Medieval Christian (Dis)identifications: Muslims and Jews in Guibert of Nogent," *New Literary History* 28 (1997): 185–203; Jeremy Cohen, "The Muslim Connection or On the Changing Role of the Jew in High Medieval Theology," in *From Witness to Witchcraft: Jews and Judaism in Medieval Christian Thought*, ed. Jeremy Cohen (Wiesbaden, 1996): 141–62; Suzanne Conklin Akbari, *Idols in the East: European Representations of Islam and the Orient, 1100–1450* (Ithaca, NY, 2009), 112–54; David Nirenberg, *Neighboring Faiths: Christianity, Islam, and Judaism in the Middle Ages and Today* (Chicago, 2014), 1–13.

[9]See, for example, the eighteen-volume series *Christian–Muslim Relations: A Bibliographical History*, ed. David Thomas et al. (Leiden, 2009–2021), 6:60–66. Talavera is mentioned only for having issued his first list of instructions addressed to Muslim converts, while his second list of instructions is not mentioned; also not mentioned is his liturgical *Office for the Conquest of Granada*, which is equally relevant to his thinking on Islam. In compliance with the editorial program of the book series, there is no mention of Talavera's *Católica impugnación*, which although mainly devoted to Judaism, however, includes many references to Islam.

be better understood in light of his previous preaching to a group of Christians of Jewish origins in Seville. I analyze the arguments Talavera made against the practice of Jewish rites and ceremonies in his 1487 polemical treatise *Católica impugnación*, and compare his arguments there with two lists of instructions about Islamic and Christian religious practices that he issued as the archbishop of Granada soon after the forced conversions of Muslims by royal decree in February 1502. Considering Talavera's writings on moral theology as well, I argue that in his evangelization plan Judaism and Islam are closely associated and, hence, that his effort to replace non-Christian religious practices among converts with Christian ones implies a strong universalistic claim. However, I also suggest that Talavera's understanding of two key aspects of the non-Christian religions—the language of the revelation and the concept of religious law—challenges any simple notion of the conflation of Judaism and Islam in his evangelization strategies. To do so, I compare Talavera's understanding of Hebrew and Arabic as well as his conceptions of the Jewish Law and the Qur'ān. Finally, the study raises the question of Talavera's recourse to the apostle Paul's universalistic call for conversion. Naturally, the reception of Paul's theology of the Laws was deeply affected by the subjective and context-bound perspectives of his later readers. From the time of the exegetical writings of the Church Fathers, Paul's thinking about the relationship between the new faith in Christ and the Jewish Law has been subject to a variety of interpretations, both anti- and pro-Jewish, ranging from those stressing continuity between Judaism and Christ's followers to those that are radically supersessionist. Wherever located along the spectrum, through interpretation Paul's ideas were adapted and necessarily distorted. To what extent, in terms of religious practices, did Talavera faithfully implement Paul's call in the interreligious context of late medieval Castile? To what extent did he misrepresent or even twist it?

Interiority vs Exteriority: Anti-Jewish Tropes Underlying Christian Evangelization

In 1478, Queen Isabella sent Talavera to preach to Seville's Old and New Christian communities about the obligation to engage in Christian devotional practices. Local Christian churchmen had loudly denounced the persistence of Jewish practices among a group of reluctant converts regarded as judaizers and had asked for the Monarchs' intervention. Sponsored by the powerful archbishop of Seville, Cardinal Pedro González de Mendoza, Talavera's preaching aimed to eliminate the supposed observance of Jewish rites and ceremonies among converts and replace it with the veneration of Christian images and, more broadly, the strict observance of Christian rituals and obligations.

Talavera gave an account of his mission to Seville in his work *Católica impugnación*, a harsh anti-judaizing polemic written in Castilian and dedicated to the Catholic Monarchs. The book was a reaction to a provocative pamphlet, today considered lost, composed by an anonymous author from Seville whom Talavera regarded as either a judaizer (and thus a heretic) or an unbaptized Jew who was hiding his true identity. While scholars have long held that Talavera composed his polemic as early as 1478–80, there is reason to believe that it may in fact have been completed only shortly before its publication in 1487.[10] First, on the work's title page Talavera is referred to as bishop of Ávila, a role he assumed no earlier than 1485. Moreover, his piercing anti-judaizing arguments can be better understood in light of allegations of judaizing raised against the Hieronymite friars in 1486, just months before the *Católica impugnación* was published in Salamanca. The Hieronymites were accused of adopting Jewish rites, including circumcision, as well as concealing the presence of judaizing monks inside their religious houses. The case of the Hieronymite Monastery of Santa María de Guadalupe, near Cáceres, has been carefully investigated.[11] Talavera might have conceived the *Católica impugnación* as a defensive response to the inquisitorial accusations against his own Order.

The first part of the *Católica impugnación* (chs. 1–26 and 31–33) provides a refined exegetical reflection on the relationship between Jewish and Christian Law, based on Paul's supersessionist arguments on the "Old Law." The second and most extensive part (chs. 27–30 and 34–70) consists of a systematic attack on Jewish customs and rituals, from Shabbat to the dietary laws and from ritual slaughter to burial practices. In the third and shortest part (chs. 71–77), Talavera examines the role of Scripture in Judaism and Christianity, respectively, in particular the role of the prophetic books, and calls for the final, true conversion of the anonymous author of the pamphlet from Seville.

Talavera's explicit aim is to prevent the formation of a syncretic practice combining elements of Christian and Jewish Law. He warns Christians of Jewish origins against the continued observance of Jewish practices; at the same time, he warns Old Christians against yielding to a fascination with Judaism. In his opinion, the persistence of Jewish practices was endangering the peaceful coexistence of converts and Old Christians in Seville. Moreover, it was preventing reluctant converts from achieving salvation. Written for a Christian readership made up of both ecclesiastics and laymen, the *Católica*

---

[10]The only extant copy of the *Católica impugnación* is kept at the Biblioteca Vallicelliana of Rome and was printed in Salamanca in 1487.

[11]See Gretchen D. Starr-LeBeau, *In the Shadow of the Virgin: Inquisitors, Friars and Conversos in Guadalupe, Spain* (Princeton, NJ, 2003).

impugnación presents a model of evangelization, one that relies on Paul's theology of the two Laws, on the one hand, and Greek moral philosophy, on the other—especially Aristotle's *Nicomachean Ethics*.[12] Talavera elaborates on both Aristotle's and Paul's arguments in an effort to uproot what Castilian chronicles, in the wake of the anti-Jewish riots and concomitant forced conversions of 1391, had labeled "the judaizing heresy" (*la herejía judaizante*).[13] With recourse to the age-old Christian confrontation with Judaism dating back to early Christian literature, Talavera attempts to achieve conformity to the Church's teaching by means of persuasion and legal measures. His thinking about heresy and his theology of sin are accompanied by the threat of the harsh punishments, including death, available to the civil and ecclesiastical authorities who supervised relations among Jews, Christians, and Muslims in postconquest Castile.

Close analysis of the second part of the *Católica impugnación* reveals exactly which anti-Jewish tropes are at the core of Talavera's plans for evangelization. Here, Talavera discusses in detail the devotional, ritualistic, and liturgical aspects of daily life among Jews and Christians, respectively. These include sacramental confession, forms of prayer, food habits, religious holidays (especially the Christian replacement of Shabbat with Sunday rest), the veneration of devotional images, and burial practices. Turning to rites and sacraments, in chapter 25 Talavera examines the distinction between Christian and Jewish confession. He highlights the sacramental character of Christian confession, which delves into believers' inner existence to unearth and address the Christian's "hidden sins" (*pecados ocultos*) and "wicked thoughts" (*malos pensamientos*), ultimately leading to reconciliation through the mediation of a priest. Jewish confession, in contrast, is described as all outward, "like penitence or a public compensation for a public sin that was committed in the public sphere,"[14] and originally conducted in the Temple through animal sacrifice. Moreover, since it predated Christian redemption (*no era abierta la puerta del paraíso por aquel Redentor nuestro*), it

---

[12]On Talavera's use of Paul and Aristotle to condemn the persistence of Jewish practices among converts, see Davide Scotto, "Theology of the Laws and Anti-Judaizing Polemics in Hernando de Talavera's *Católica impugnación*," in *Polemical Encounters: Polemics between Christians, Jews and Muslims in Iberia and Beyond*, ed. Mercedes García–Arenal and Gerard Wiegers (Philadelphia, 2018), 117–53.

[13]See Rosa Vidal Doval, "La matriz medieval de la disidencia en Castilla: La herejía judaizante y la controversia sobre los conversos," in *Disidencia religiosa en Castilla la Nueva en el siglo XVI*, ed. Ignacio J. García Pinilla (Toledo, 2013), 13–28.

[14]Here and later in this article, I am referencing the 1961 edition: Hernando de Talavera, *Católica impugnación*, ed. Francisco Márquez Villanueva and Francisco Martín Hernández (Barcelona, 1961), ch. 25, 134.

could in fact offer no reconciliation with God.[15] Talavera's focus on animal sacrifice, the Temple, and public ceremony in Judaism is based not on the daily practices of atonement in contemporary Jewish communities in late fifteenth-century Castile, but rather on the Jewish conception of repentance and forgiveness as expressed in the so-called Old Testament,[16] especially in Jeremiah (2:5), Nehemiah (9:2), and Psalms (50). This seems to be a conscious choice, in order to theologically highlight all the more the carnality of Judaism in contrast to the spirituality of the Christian faith.[17]

A further issue Talavera discusses (ch. 52) is prayer. Talavera defends the Christian practice of praying on the doorstep in the street or in other places that the Jewishly-oriented author of the Seville pamphlet asserts to be profane. Talavera's discussion of prayer ultimately makes the same point as his interpretation of Jewish and Christian confession: no place is profane when a Christian is praying there, as the inward-oriented content of prayer outweighs the external character of place, which has no bearing on faith.

Talavera addresses dietary habits in chapters 30 and 34, where he states that Christians are allowed to eat pork and pig's blood even though those foods are forbidden to Jews. Talavera evidently suspected that Christians of Jewish origins continued to feel obligated, or were even eager, to observe the laws of kashrut. In chapter 70, he explains why it is illicit for Christians to eat meat which has been butchered according to Jewish ritual slaughtering practices.[18] The result is paradoxical: through a process of confrontation and differentiation, a well-established dietary norm peculiar to Judaism is inverted into a (previously unbinding) reverse norm for Christians. On the one

---

[15]Talavera, *Católica impugnación*, ch. 25, 134–35.

[16]I am aware—and do agree with—the recommendations on the replacement of "Old" and "New Testament" with "First" and "Second Testament" offered by James Sanders (1987) and Erich Zenger (1991), and adopted by the *Biblical Theology Bulletin* as well as individual scholars: see James Sanders, "First Testament and Second," *Biblical Theology Bulletin* 17 (1987): 47–49; Erich Zenger, *Das Erste Testament: Die jüdische Bibel und die Christen* (Düsseldorf, 1991). This usage avoids the hermeutical implications of the label "Old Testament," which has played such a major role in Christian anti-Jewish polemics. In this essay, however, I will stick to the expression "Old Testament," which was systematically employed by Talavera, to highlight his typological understanding of the relation between the two parts of the Christian Bible.

[17]For a list of biblical loci reflecting the development of "public" practices of penitence and confession in the Hebrew Bible, see *Dizionario teologico interdisciplinare*, 3 vols. (Genoa, 1977), s.v. "Penitenza," 2:708–9. For the soteriological implications of repentance in the Book of Judges, see Serge Frolov and Mikhail Stetckevich, "Repentance in Judges," *Hebrew Studies* 60 (2019): 129–40. For the Jewish conception of repentance among Christians of Jewish origins in early modern Iberia, see Pier Cesare Ioly Zorattini, "Derekh Teshuvah: La via del ritorno," in *L'identità dissimulata: Giudaizzanti iberici nell'Europa cristiana dell'età moderna*, ed. Pier Cesare Ioly Zorattini (Florence, 2000), 195–248.

[18]Talavera, *Católica impugnación*, respectively, 145–46, 151–52, 222–25.

---

hand, Christians can eat and are even encouraged to eat that very food which Jews are not allowed to eat; on the other hand, they cannot eat the foods that Jews must eat according to Jewish slaughtering practice and rules. Evidently, this prohibition for Christians did not concern food in its own right but rather, as Talavera suggests between the lines, the symbolic adherence to Judaism expressed through physical contact with food prepared according to the Jewish rite. This clearly echoes his persistent concern with sins and punishments, in both a Christian and a pluralistic religious context. In his *Breve forma de confesar*—a handbook conveying a reformist view of confession written in the 1470s[19]—Talavera distinguishes Christians and "infidels" in terms of the cultural habits by which they were identified religiously in the public sphere. Conceived in 1478 and printed in 1487, his *Católica impugnación* follows the same pattern, though it deals almost exclusively with Jewish practices. It reinforces Talavera's previous recommendations about such practices using theological arguments based on biblical exegesis. The stigmatization of Jewish practices within the framework of theological polemics mirrors the way in which, throughout the sixteenth century, the Spanish Inquisition traced the origins of suspicious food habits among Christians of Muslim ancestry back to Islamic sources.[20]

The importance of the outward expression of religious identity in a politically christianized society becomes increasingly apparent as, in eight consecutive chapters (38–45), Talavera addresses the issue of religious holidays, and in particular Shabbat and Sunday rest. He refutes the pamphlet author's claim that early Christians rested from work and recited special prayers on Saturday, arguing that although the practice of Saturday rest was unevenly adopted by Christians in the past (and persisted, in part through the practice of praying to the Virgin on that day), the day of rest was eventually moved to "the first or eighth day" of the week, "which is the day called Sunday, or the day of the Lord."[21] Following the teachings of the Church

---

[19] See Hernando de Talavera, *Breve forma de confesar*, in *Escritores místicos españoles*, vol. 1, *Hernando de Talavera, Alejo Venegas, Francisco de Osuna, Alfonso de Madrid, con un discurso preliminar de Don Miguel Mir* (Madrid, 1911), 3–35.

[20] Ana Echevarría Arsuaga, "Food as a Custom among Spanish Muslims: From Islamic Sources to Inquisitorial Material," in *Essen und Fasten: Interreligiöse Abgrenzung, Konkurrenz und Austauschprozesse*, ed. Dorothea Weltecke (Köln, 2017), 89–110. A broader overview is provided in David M. Freidenreich, *Foreigners and Their Food: Constructing Otherness in Jewish, Christian, and Islamic Law* (Berkeley, 2011).

[21] Talavera, *Católica impugnación*, ch. 12b, 88: "Innovó el tercero mandamiento, que era guardar el día septeno, que vulgarmente es llamado sábado, mandando guardar, como adelante parecerá, el día primero o el octavo, que es día llamado domingo, que quiere decir, del Señor."

Fathers—Ambrose's typological interpretation in particular[22]—Talavera defines Sunday as "the first" or "the eighth" day of the week in the first part of *Católica impugnación*, where he justifies the abrogation of the Jewish Law using Paul's arguments.[23] The injunction to celebrate Mass on Sunday is legitimized through a traditional theological argument: since Christ rose on a Sunday, it is on that day that Christians must celebrate an event that is pivotal to achieving salvation. In terms of Sunday-related prohibitions, Talavera firmly states that no one must work on Sunday, especially Jewish converts and their descendants. The latter remark suggests that converts had to prove themselves to be Christians not just inwardly, but outwardly, in the eyes of the Old Christian community. While Talavera holds that Jews are allowed to observe their own law regarding the day of rest—according to the Castilian model of religious coexistence adhered to since the thirteenth century[24]—he asserts that, by contrast, any Christians caught observing Shabbat should be put to death.[25]

Talavera's theological perspective on public displays of religious identity is reflected in his treatment of two further aspects of ritual, namely images and burial. He discusses these in response to the Seville judaizer's harsh accusations against Old Christian devotional images and funerary rites. The pamphlet author went so far as to state that Christians themselves should refrain from entering churches, which he termed "houses of idols and ossuaries for the dead" (*casas de idolos y osuarios de muertos*). Issues around images and burial practices represented key challenges to Christian evangelization in late medieval Castile; indeed, Talavera dedicates nine chapters to promoting the veneration of images. In the first three (27–29) he legitimizes the use of images by showing that both the Law of Moses and the Gospels entail the use of images and that their worship is allowed only if one does not search for their material meaning, but for the inner or spiritual one.

First, Talavera clarifies the reasons Christians adhere to some of the rites (*cerimonias*) and concepts (*juicios*) conveyed by the Old Law. They do so not because these rites are still mandatory, as they were before Christ's advent, "but because in the present they are reasonable and expedient in order

---

[22] See Garry Wills, *Font of Life: Ambrose, Augustine, and the Mystery of Baptism* (Oxford, 2012), 9–10.

[23] Talavera's typological interpretation of the Gospels leads him to claim, following the Church Fathers, that Christ was resurrected the day after Shabbat by elaborating on John 20:1, Luke 24:1, Matt 28:1, and Mark 16:2. See also several passages in chapters 38–41, where he repeatedly (and intentionally) defines Sunday as "the eighth day."

[24] Ángel Galán Sánchez, *Una sociedad en transición: Los granadinos de mudéjares a moriscos* (Granada, 2010), 56–58.

[25] See Talavera, *Católica impugnación*, chs. 38–45, 159–74.

to serve Our Lord in the way that he wants us to serve Him in our times."[26] He maintains that Christians do not worship images in the way "idolatrous pagans" and "wicked gentiles" did before them. Those peoples, in fact, were attached to the matter of images (wood, stone, metal) and to the figures they represented, thus making of them idols (*las tenían por dioses*). In contrast, Christians "so to speak worship them or, better to say, keep and worship images because they bind one to memory, and they represent those persons and things, of which they are images, reminding us of them."[27] Talavera thus reiterates that Christians do not worship images for their intrinsic value, like idolaters in ancient times; rather they worship the "persons" those images represent. Being angels or holy men, the "persons" on the images hark ultimately back to God: they are worshiped because they are "respectable and very faithful creatures and servants of Our God"; as such, they work as "mediators and intercessors between Him and us."[28]

Second, Talavera shows that venerating saints' images and attending places of worship is consistent with the religious practices adopted by the Jews in ancient times. And this is so despite the fact that God had forbidden the Jews to worship elements of the natural world or animals, in order to avoid idolatry, which was still a widespread practice at the time. For, Talavera argues, in the time of the Old Law God himself ordered the Jews to worship holy objects. These objects included the holy tabernacle with the seven-lamp candelabrum (menorah) and the Ark of the Covenant (*arca del testamento*) within it, representing the entire world ruled by God and its cosmological structure (Exodus 24); so too the bronze serpent which God ordered men to raise toward the sky on a wooden pole to ward off snakes during the exile of His people in the desert (Numbers 21). Following a typological interpretation of the Old Testament, Talavera suggests that the Ark be viewed as the prefiguration of the Virgin Mary and the bronze serpent as the prefiguration of Christ's death and resurrection. In this way, he justifies their use in worship.[29]

In the following six chapters (53–58) Talavera rebuts the claims of his adversary against the backdrop of contemporary events and existing places of worship. In Seville in 1478 Christian authorities had issued an injunction requiring the use of devotional images in public and private spaces. They required all Christians, including converts and their descendants, to keep painted images of the crucifix, the Virgin, and Christian saints in the home so as to arouse (*provocar*) or awaken (*despertar*) their faith. Opposing this decision, the pamphlet's author had held that the veneration of images was "clear

---

[26] Ibid., ch. 27, 137.

[27] Ibid., ch. 27, 137.

[28] Ibid., ch. 27, 138. See also 139, where Talavera further rejects the charge of idolatry made in the anonymous pamphlet against Christians.

[29] Cf. ibid., ch. 28–29, 140–45.

idolatry" (*clara idolatría*), arguing that it was inadmissible for Christians to pray in front of finely painted and decorated images. He had also mocked Christians who not only distinguished between the "Elder" and "Younger" Virgin, but who even debated which of the Virgins was the most spiritually powerful.[30]

Talavera defends the Seville injunction, urging Old and New Christians to venerate devotional images and encouraging them to choose ones that were well painted and richly adorned. He assures believers that instances of images actually laughing, crying, or sweating were real phenomena that should not be doubted, and moreover that the veneration of images had nothing to do with idolatry. On the contrary, Christians were allowed and even enjoined to hang images in their homes, in the street, and in churches, as well as to undertake pilgrimages to sanctuaries where important images were safeguarded, such as the Sanctuary of Peña de Francia, known as Our Lady of the Rock, as well as in the cult of Our Lady of the Pilar of Zaragoza, which was widespread across Castile—the miracles attributed to the Virgin were collected in a fifteenth-century *Libro de los milagros* which deeply influenced the cult of the Pilar up to the seventeenth century.[31] Talavera ultimately aims to reject the radical iconoclastic inclination of his adversary, contesting the claim that rulers old and new, from Alexander the Great to the Ottoman Turks, had sought to destroy religious images.[32]

The second part of the judaizer's accusation—that the church is an "ossuary for the dead"—reflected the ecclesiastical topography of late medieval Seville, with particular reference to the monasteries of Saint Bernard and Saint Augustine located in the city's suburbs. The Seville injunction had prevented Christians of Jewish origins from burying their dead in the courtyards of these monasteries, contrary to longstanding practice. Rather, such corpses had to be buried either inside urban churches or in their adjoining cemeteries. In contrast, the pamphlet's author feared the proximity of the dead and the living resulting from burial of corpses inside churches or in their close surroundings. In his opinion, the enactment of burial rites in places that were far away from the city's space protected the living from contamination by the dead. This concern underlying the discussion of burial is reflected also in the author's repugnance for touching corpses, a practice that likewise entwined the living and the dead, thus entailing the implicit risk of incurring

---

[30]On the dispute over devotion to the *Virgen de la Antigua*, her oriental origins, and her relevance to evangelization, see Felipe Pereda, *Las imágenes de la discordia: Política y poética de la imagen sagrada en la España del cuatrocientos* (Madrid, 2007), 145–248.

[31]See Eliseo Serrano Martín, "Milagros, devoción y política a propósito de la virgen del Pilar en la edad moderna," *e-Spania* 21 (June 2015), https://doi.org/10.4000/e-spania.24814.

[32]See Talavera, *Católica impugnación*, ch. 53–58, 186–202.

ritual impurity. In his view, corpses by their very nature evoked abomination, horror, and pollution.[33] Claiming to be a better Christian than Talavera himself, the pamphlet's author pointed to the Gospels to reinforce his arguments: he asserted that Christ, whom he regarded as an ethnically pure Jew, urged Christians who had touched the dead to avoid contamination by observing purification rites that included soaking and washing their clothes in water. The today self-evident notion that Christ was a Jew, whether religiously or ethnically, polemically resurfaced later in Inquisition trials, when Christians of Jewish origins were accused of spreading a judaizing, and thus heretical, understanding of Christ's identity.[34]

In response, Talavera states that all "new converts," without exception, are obliged to bury their dead within their respective parish churches to prove they truly belong to the Church. If for whatever reason they absolutely must bury them in rural monasteries, the bodies are to be buried inside the main building rather than in the outer courtyard. This reflects the concerns of Old Christians in Seville, who worried that New Christians would continue to follow Jewish or pagan funeral rites if they were allowed to use open spaces for burials. Talavera also refutes his adversary's interpretation of the Gospels, pointing to Christ's recommendations concerning burial and the body's passage into the afterlife. He does so using the same hermeneutical device, distinguishing between interiority and exteriority, that he employs in his discussions of confession, prayer, and food habits. He maintains that Christ exhorted his believers to beware of touching corpses not out of a disdain for corpses themselves, since corpses are not repugnant until they start decomposing, but rather to avoid attachment to mortal and perishable things (*cosas mortales y perecederas, cuales son todas las cosas temporales y traspasaderas*). Again, the interior or spiritual implication of a religious practice is given priority over the external or ritualistic one. Echoing late antique exegetical and heresiological writings, Talavera goes so far as to assert that in Christ's time idolaters would interact with or even eat corpses, committing sinful acts of necromancy that Christ abhorred. Rather than clinging to the physical dead, Christ offered a spiritualized vision focused on the afterlife, with the aim of warning believers against idolatry and delivering them from eternal death.[35]

Talavera insists that corpses must be buried as close as possible to parish churches, as it is there that the process of redemption bridges the gap between worldly death and eternal life for those free of mortal sins. In contrast,

---

[33] Ibid., ch. 68, 220–21.

[34] I am grateful for this information to Marco Volpato, who is preparing a chapter on this topic as part of his PhD dissertation (Scuola Normale Superiore, Pisa / CORPI Project, CSIC, Madrid) focusing on the early modern theory of the Jewish origins of the Amerindians.

[35] See Talavera, *Católica impugnación*, ch. 64, 211–12.

pagans, heretics, Muslims, and Jews were buried in fields located far from churches, where salvation was not granted.[36] According to Christian anthropological thinking, human bodies had as much spiritual significance as human souls. Since Paul had claimed that the "psychical bodies" of the dead would be gathered and resurrected together as a united "spiritual body" (1 Cor 15:35–49),[37] to the eyes of medieval ecclesiastics they had to be buried either inside churches or in cemeteries annexed to them, even if their foul smell proved to be a nuisance. From late antiquity to Talavera's time, the degree of proximity between buried corpses and the church's space depended on the social or ecclesiastical rank of the dead and was justified in soteriological terms. The bodies of churchmen belonging to major or minor orders, as well as those of distinguished laymen, were always required to be buried inside churches, since their holiness would hasten the second coming of Christ and hence the enactment of the Final Judgment, "because this corporeal and palpable [thing] that we see here on the ground, corresponds to the spiritual and intelligible, which we believe and hope for in heaven."[38]

Harking back to the ancient times, Talavera pinpoints why—before "the gleam and the clarity of Christian doctrine came to light"[39]—renowned or holy figures belonging to the Jewish, pagan, and Christian traditions were buried in sacred or symbolic places outside urban spaces: in the first century, Jesus Christ in Joseph of Arimathea's garden, close to the Hill of Calvary (Golgotha), and the Virgin Mary in the Valley of Josaphat, where the Final Judgement would commence; in the fourth century, Saint Catherine, buried by angels on Mount Sinai, where "our God" delivered the Law to Moses; and, finally, in the first century before Christ, Julius Caesar and other Roman military leaders, buried "in very high towers called pyramids" or in monumental arks to prevent the smell of decomposition from spreading over the city. Talavera lists these examples in order to counteract his adversary's

---

[36]On the presence and influence of what were regarded as deviant and parallel cultures of burials (paganism, heresy, reformation) in medieval Christianity, see Mia Korpiola and Anu Lahtinen, "Cultures of Death and Dying in Medieval and Early Modern Europe: An Introduction," in *Cultures of Death and Dying in Medieval and Early Modern Europe*, ed. Mia Korpiola and Anu Lahtinen (Helsinki, 2015), 1–31.

[37]Paul's controversial claim on the "psychical body" was soon discussed by early Christian writers such as Origen and Philoponus to prove that resurrection regards only the spiritual body. See Antonia S. Kakavelaki, "The Resurrected Body, Will It Be of Flesh or Spiritual? Theological Discussions from the Time of the Apostle Paul up to the Sixth Century AD," *Scrinium* 11 (2015): 225–41.

[38]See Talavera, *Católica impugnación*, ch. 61, 206. On the connection between theological conceptions of the afterlife and late medieval burial practices, see Deirdre O'Sullivan, "Burial of the Christian Dead in the Later Middle Ages," in *The Oxford Handbook of the Archaeology of Death and Burial*, ed. Liv Nilsson Stutz and Sarah Tarlow (Oxford, 2013), 259–80.

[39]Talavera, *Católica impugnación*, ch. 60, 204–5, esp. 205.

claim that Christian burials in open spaces were known to have habitually and indiscriminately occurred in the past. In Talavera's opinion, in contrast, these cases were exceptions to the general rule established in principle by the Gospels, issued by the Holy Spirit, and progressively implemented within Christianity, according to which Christians of all backgrounds have to be buried either in churches or in adjacent graveyards so as not to risk jeopardizing their prospects of salvation.[40]

Talavera cites these examples to chasten his adversary for his ideas and, on a broader level, to warn his readers against improper burial practices. In this regard, he explicitly mentions four types of transgressors side by side, calling all of them "infidels" as if they were a single group, together belonging to the trans-confessional category of infidelity. He had already systematically resorted to the category of infidelity in his moral treatises, written when he was prior of the Prado monastery in Valladolid, especially in the *Breve forma de confesar*, in reference to the regulation of daily interactions between Christians and non-Christians.[41] Printed ten years later, the *Católica impugnación* further reveals Talavera's universalistic understanding of proper Christian practices by including judaizing rites in the all-embracing category of infidelity.

Forcing Muslims to Abandon Islamic Habits and Rites

Talavera's meticulous discussion of religious practices, with its underlying reliance on Paul's theology of the Laws, was to resurface several years later when he was put in charge of the christianization of postconquest Granada. As the archbishop of a former Islamic kingdom, he ruled over a territory with a heavily Muslim-majority population, into which Old Christians from all over Castile proceeded to move and settle at the behest of Christian authorities.[42] After a few years of relatively positive relations between Muslims and Christians under the terms of Granada's November 1491 treaty of surrender (the much-debated *capitulaciones*[43]), the situation rapidly deteriorated as the

---

[40]Ibid., ch. 61, 205.

[41]Talavera, *Breve forma de confesar*, 3–35. On the role of non-Christians in this treatise, preliminary observations are provided in Davide Scotto, "'Neither through Habits, nor Solely through Will, but through Infused Faith': Hernando de Talavera's Understanding of Conversion," in *Forced Conversion in Christianity, Judaism and Islam: Coercion and Faith in Premodern Iberia and Beyond*, ed. Mercedes García-Arenal and Yonatan Glazer-Eytan (Leiden, 2019), 291–327, at 308, 312.

[42]See Coleman, *Creating Christian Granada*, 13–31.

[43]Edition and study by Miguel Garrido Atienza, *Las capitulaciones para la entrega de Granada* (Granada, 1910; repr. 1992). Among the extensive literature analyzing the *ca-*

Christian population grew. In 1498, the Chapter of the Cathedral of Granada issued an injunction regulating everyday interactions between Christians and Muslims, and forced the Muslim community to live segregated in the Albaicín. Sometime afterwards, Archbishop Talavera issued two sets of instructions aimed at coercing Muslim converts to thoroughly abandon their Islamic customs and religious rites. Both sets of instructions fostered the assimilation of converts into a politically and socially christianized society through the imposition of strict norms of conduct.

The first set of instructions, whose title refers to Muslim converts as "the newly converted," was allegedly issued shortly after the forced conversions of the Granada Muslims in fulfillment of a royal decree of February 1502, either just after February 1502, as a consequence of the decree, or after Queen Isabella's death in 1504, when the religious freedom of Muslim converts was further restricted.[44] The first part of the document consists of eight general obligations for Muslim converts, including attending Mass, learning Christian prayers, baptizing newborn children and, for pregnant women, mandatory confession. The final regulation bars Islamic scholars (*fuqahā'*) and their wives from entering the homes of pregnant Christian women who are close to their delivery date. The second part of the document details twenty-three further obligations, with respective punishments and fines for violators. While some of the obligations deal with the same issues covered in the first part of the document, others are aimed at regulating everyday interactions that could compromise the success of the evangelization campaign. As the archbishop of Granada, Talavera sought to establish neat boundaries between the Christian community made up of both Old and New Christians, on the one hand, and those who rejected belonging to it by resisting the imposition of Christian cultural practices and religious rites, on the other. This aim, felt to be urgent, was to be achieved by replacing the Islamic rites and beliefs observed by the

---

pitulaciones, see Miguel Ángel Ladero Quesada, *Granada: Historia de un país islámico (1232–1571)* (Madrid, 1969); idem, *Granada después de la conquista: Repobladores y mudéjares* (Granada, 1988); idem, *Los mudéjares del Reino de Granada* (Granada, 1991); Sánchez, *Una sociedad en transición*, esp. 75–84; Isabelle Poutrin, "Los derechos de los vencidos: Las capitulaciones de Granada (1491)," *Sharq Al–Andalus* 19 (2008–2010): 11–34; eadem, *Convertir les musulmans: Espagne, 1491–1609* (Paris, 2012), 33–48.

[44] *La horden que se tiene en el arçobispado de Granada para enseñar la doctrina cristiana a los nuevamente convertidos*, Toledo, Archivo Histórico Nacional, Sección Nobleza, Osuna, 1897–1898; transcribed in Francisco Javier Martínez Medina and Martin Biersack, *Fray Hernando de Talavera: Primer arzobispo de Granada; Hombre de iglesia, estado y letras* (Granada, 2011), 352–57 (for the full transcription of the document) and 348–51 (for discussion of its dating).

former Muslims with a whole new system of practices which were anchored in Christian theology yet served the same religious and social functions as the Islamic ones.

It is no coincidence that in the document, the Castilian word *dotrina*, referring to the Gospels as a collection of mandatory norms, is also used to refer to Islamic beliefs and rites, which were singled out for systematic erasure. Talavera's first set of instructions implicitly addresses Muslim converts as well as Christian clergy involved in the education of converts after the mass baptisms. The twenty-three obligations he lays out include the following: the requirement to observe Sunday rest; the prohibition of Muslim dietary and slaughtering practices; the requirement to observe Christian marriage rites and refrain from all Muslim ones; and the prohibition of Islamic cultural and legal practices (dancing, singing, coloring the body, religious attire, Muslim names, oaths, and baths). Further, they include the obligation of attending Mass, observing all the Christian sacraments, following Christian funerary and burial practices and refraining from Muslim ones, and residing in assigned villages. Finally, the converts were instructed on what to do if captured by Muslims.

Talavera's instructions, when compared to the *capitulaciones* governing Muslims after 1491, clearly reflect a radical shift in Christian attitudes in late medieval Castile towards Islam as a religion and towards Muslims as a community of faith (albeit a minority one). It is clear that after the campaign to convert Muslims began in 1499, Christian authorities—including Talavera—knew that forcibly converted Muslims were still as attached to their faith as they had been as unbaptized Muslims, when Sultan Boabdil negotiated a treaty (the *capitulaciones* of 1491) granting Muslims the use of mosques, minarets, and public spaces, the right to practice their dietary laws and rites, and both social rights and economic benefits. However, by 1499 the conversion of all Muslims to the Christian faith had become an urgent aim for Christian authorities, leading them—Talavera included—to disregard the accepted view that, according to a biased reception of Augustine's saying on the relation between faith and will, conversion must take place as an act of free will.[45]

As envisioned by Talavera in this period, the role and the attitude of Christian clergy (preachers, instructors, etc.) towards Islam as a religion and to-

---

[45]Peter Brown has written important studies on Augustine's shift from the defense of willing conversion to the justification of forced conversion, while Jeremy Cohen and Sarah Stroumsa have discussed Augustine's theological view of the role of the Jews in medieval Christian theological thinking. I cannot linger here on the thorny issue of Augustine's opinion on forced conversion nor on its reception in the Middle Ages. For a critical assessment of this debate, which needs to be updated, see John R. Bowlin, "Augustine on Justifying Coercion," *Annual of the Society of Christian Ethics* 17 (1997): 49–70.

wards Muslims as a community of faith was totally at odds with those laid out in the *capitulaciones* of November 1491. In contrast to the religious and social rights of (unbaptized) Muslims laid out in the *capitulaciones*, Talavera's instructions call for an urgent change in Christian attitudes towards the former Islamic community. While the *capitulaciones*, which were legally still in force in 1502, did not forbid Muslims to practice Islam in private and in public, thus allowing for mosques and minarets to coexist with Christian churches,[46] Talavera's instructions aimed to eliminate Islam altogether, not only through the sacrament of baptism but by transforming the converts' inner and outward existence.

Talavera issued a further list of instructions that explicitly addressed the community of Muslim converts in Granada.[47] The contents of these instructions, in particular the tightening of restrictions on the use of Arabic, suggest that they date from the last years of Talavera's tenure as archbishop, between 1502 and 1507. As such, they might well reflect the continuous and rapid shifts taking place in the former Islamic community in the wake of the forced conversions, along with the Christian authorities' effort to quickly assimilate massive numbers of Muslim converts at any cost. In this second set of regulations, Talavera displays a benevolent, fatherly attitude towards Muslim converts—whether sincere or rhetorical it is hard to say—defining them as "Much beloved in Our Lord, good men, inhabitants of the Albaicín," the new Islamic quarter of the city to which they had been confined since 1498. Aiming to provide converts with "full information and reminders" (*conplida avisaçion y memoria*) of what they are supposed to do, he never mentions the forced conversions that took place just a few months or possibly years be-

---

[46] On the debate over mosque building in late medieval Castile, see Ana Echevarría Arsuaga, "Neue Moscheen in christlichen Ländern: Die Debatte im Mittelalter," in *Transfer and Religion: Interactions between Judaism, Christianity, and Islam from the Middle Ages to the Twentieth Century*, ed. Alexander A. Dubrau, Davide Scotto, and Ruggero Vimercati Sanseverino (Tübingen, 2020), 103–28.

[47] Hernando de Talavera, *Memorial y tabla de ordenaciones dirigidas por Talavera para la comunidad morisca de Granada. Se les reglamenta taxativamente la vida religiosa que debían llevar y se les adelantan diversas exigencias para la buena convivencia con los cristianos*, Archivo General de Simancas, *Diversos de Castilla*, libro 8, fol. 114, transcribed by Tarcisio de Azcona, *Isabel la Católica: Estudio crítico de su vida y su reinado* (Madrid, 1964), 761–63. (Azcona dated the document to "after January 1492," but a number of clues suggest that it must in fact date from after February 1502.) The same document, published under the title *Instrucción y carta para los vecinos del Albaicín escrita por el obispo fray Hernando de Talavera, en que les amonesta lo que deben hacer*, was also transcribed by Ladero Quesada, *Granada después de la conquista*, 464–66; Ladero Quesada rightly noticed that the document is undated. Talavera's second list of instructions was listed as the first in a series of sixteenth-century handbooks for the evangelization of Muslims by Jesús Framiñán de Miguel, "Manuales para el adoctrinamiento de neoconversos en el siglo XVI," *Criticón* 93 (2005): 27–28.

---

fore, and takes for granted that former Muslims are now Christians who fully belong to the Christian Church. In the preface, in order to justify delivering the new rules in writing rather than orally, he also apologizes for not having "recently" visited the Albaicín in person, for which he provides several reasons.[48]

Talavera's cordial tone masks the stern reminder at the heart of the instructions: Islamic rites have been banned, and the adoption of Christian practices is mandatory. Indeed, "the first and most important thing is that you forget all Moorish ceremony (*çerimonia*) and practice (*cosa*) regarding prayers, fasting, Easters and festivals, childbirth and marriages, baths, burials, and all the rest." As is often attested in Christian sources discussing Islamic rites, by "Easters" (*pascuas*, in the plural) Talavera is referring to the most important fasting rite of the Islamic year, Ramadan, which was to be replaced by the fast for Lent.[49] The document goes on to review one by one all the Christian customs and rites converts must now adopt.[50] It consists of eighteen regulations, ranging from detailed instructions on the observance of Christian sacraments and religious practices (fasting, marriage, and burial), to the recommendation of founding religious institutions aimed at assisting the ill and the poor, following the model of medieval brotherhoods and hospitals. There are careful stipulations about how often and where to attend Mass, as well as about Sunday rest and participation in communion processions. Talavera also mentions the obligation to hang devotional images in private and public spaces, as well as regulations concerning the use of Arabic as a spoken language and the owning and use of religious books in Arabic.

When juxtaposed, the contents and aims of the first and the second sets of instructions prove to be coherent and even complementary. Both oblige converts to break radically with a set of deeply-rooted Islamic customs and rites, and to replace them with the corresponding Christian ones. What is more, the contents and underlying intentions of these two sets of instructions clearly resemble the evangelization plan Talavera directed towards Christians of Jewish origins that he launched through the injunction of 1478 and later outlined in polemical terms in the *Católica impugnación*.

A comparison of the three texts—Talavera's *Católica impugnación* and the two lists of instructions he issued as the archbishop of Granada—exposes a common roadmap of evangelization, one that was based on six pillars governing the everyday religious life of "good Christians," whether of Jewish or Muslim origins:

---

[48] Talavera, *Memorial y tabla de ordenaciones*, 761–62.

[49] Ibid., 762.

[50] Ibid., 762–63.

Pillar of evangelization	Católica impugnación	Two lists of instructions
1 Sacramental confession	Ch. 25	List 1: Part 1, point 5; part 2, point 16 List 2: Point 2
2 Detailed mandatory prayers	Ch. 52	List 1: Part 1, point 3 List 2: Point 1
3 The day of rest and religious festivals	Chs. 38–45	List 1: Part 2, points 1 to 3 List 2: Point 9
4 Dietary habits, fasting, and slaughtering	Chs. 30–34 and 70	List 1: Part 2, points 4 to 6 List 2: Point 13
5 Burial and funerary rites	Chs. 59–67	List 1: Part 2, points 17 to 19 List 2: Points 6 and 15
6 Veneration of devotional images	Chs. 27–29 and 53–58	List 2: Points 1 and 17

The comparison of the contents of Talavera's instructions for Muslim converts with those of his polemics against the judaizers suggests that neither the religious identity nor the cultural characteristics of the targeted audience require adjustments in a single cogent, preconceived strategy of evangelization, one based on the dynamic of rejection and systematic replacement. While the tone (polemical or pastoral), the literary genre employed (confutation or catechism), and the target audience (descendants of Jewish converts or recently baptized Muslims) of the two assimilation campaigns differ, the underlying conversion strategy is the same, one that is based on a moral and legal view of the Gospels as a "new law" (*nueva ley*) that is universally valid, that entails specific religious practices, and that is mutually exclusive to other Laws.

The religious identity of Talavera's audience may shift, as may the language and strategy he adopts, but the underlying intellectual scheme remains unchanged. In the *Católica impugnación* he calls for the elimination of Jewish practices using a sophisticated exegesis aimed at an educated readership. In Granada, instead, he writes in his role of archbishop addressing his new believers, enlisting the pastoral language befitting his office to make clear to Muslim converts the need to abandon Islamic practices. At the same time, some of the instructions touch on practices specific to Muslim life in post-conquest Castile, with no parallel in Castilian Jewish life. They include such things as discussion of the status of Islamic song and dance (*moçafara*, *zujul*, and the much-debated *zambra*), as well as the prohibitions of wearing medallions and jewelry bearing the name of Muhammad or Fatima, of painting the hands or other parts of the body with henna, and of speaking Arabic in the home. Yet the vast majority of the instructions for converted Muslims reveal close similarities to Talavera's directives concerning the religious habits and rites of Seville's Christians of Jewish origins. It is precisely the deep-seated quality of these practices, with all their specificity, that made it difficult for the converts of either background to abandon them and adhere to the increasingly inflexible set of Christian rules of conduct.

83

Many of these aspects of religious and cultural practice can be traced back to the centuries-long history of the Abrahamic religions in the Mediterranean. In late medieval Castile, such practices regulated the basic daily functions of religious and social life among Jews, Christians, and Muslims alike, and their observance was believed by all believers to have repercussions for redemption and, hence, for salvation. Talavera's extensive discussion of salvation dynamics and ways to attain the afterlife, in the chapters of the *Católica impugnación* that condemn Jewish burial practices, clearly demonstrates his anxiety about the continued soteriological relevance of such religious rites. In the new conditions created by the forced conversions, the theological meanings behind Jewish and Muslim customs underwent systematic transformation, as Christian authorities emphasized their material nature, viewing them in contrast to Christian customs. From a hermeneutical point of view, Jewish and Muslim practices were to be fully deprived of their salvific meanings by applying Paul's supersessionist thinking. This reinterpretation of non-Christian practices went far beyond a purely theoretical discussion. Changes in the theological meanings of customs implied that customs themselves were to be forcibly changed. This was true for all practices mentioned in Talavera's writings, but it was especially urgent in the case of those practices affecting doctrine and thus salvation—as in the case of burials. Another such practice was the wearing of medallions and jewelry bearing the name of Muhammad or Fatima: the use of these aesthetic ornaments was to be strictly forbidden because, more than with other practices, it evoked for both Old Christians and converts of the essence of Islam as a religion.

In a time of rapid christianization, it was felt that the suppression of Islam could be delayed no further. Talavera committed himself to achieving this aim both in public spaces and in the minds of new believers, a task at which, as a preacher and former royal confessor, he was expert. His writings bring evidence of the urgency with which he felt his evangelization plan had to be undertaken. His instructions for the Muslim converts of Granada mirror the *Católica impugnación* in terms of the moral and legal consequences for violating the new rules, including harsh punitive measures. While in the early years after the conquest of Granada the *capitulaciones* granted extensive religious rights to Muslims, during the riots of Seville (1478) and the mass conversions of Granada (1502) Talavera's call for a conversion that was to be both interior and exterior became mandatory and irreversible. Both his *Católica impugnación* and his two sets of instructions reiterate the firm belief that transgressors shall be punished adequately.

Towards a Universalistic Evangelization Plan

Talavera's plan for evangelization was pursued from the late 1470s to the early 1500s, affecting communities of converts from Seville to Granada. In this period, he developed an approach to the christianization of religious practice that he applied to converts of both Jewish and Muslim origins. Does this imply that in Talavera's mind, Judaism and Islam could be subsumed into a single undifferentiated religious category? Judging from his writings, Talavera considered converts from both non-Christian religions as being amenable in the same way to the inculcation of Christian beliefs and practices. This conviction would have had significance not only for the final stage of the christianization of Iberia, but also, in the same period, for the exportation of Christian evangelization strategies beyond the European borders, to North Africa and the New Word. Around 1502, when Talavera was seeking to eliminate Islamic practices and instill Christian practices among Muslim converts, the Catholic Monarchs' expansionist and evangelization plan was advancing. One of the leading architects of the transfer of this evangelization plan from Iberia to Africa and the Americas was the supposed antagonist of Talavera, namely Cardinal Jiménez de Cisneros, who spent foundational years with him in Granada during the Islamic rebellions and the mass conversion of 1499–1502.[51] Talavera's catechism offers substantial evidence of this trans-confessional and trans-European trajectory. Originally conceived for Old Christian adults and children, the catechism was apparently used among Muslim converts and their children in Granada and was later printed in thousands of copies and taken to the Americas for the evangelization of Amerindians. In fact, from the very beginning of his mandate as archbishop of Granada, Talavera was aware of the global potential of an evangelization plan with a universalistic and multilinguistic character. It was with the aim of promoting his program that he personally helped organize the meeting between Queen Isabella and Christopher Columbus in Salamanca, where they discussed the terms of his first expedition.[52] It was with this same aim that he promoted Antonio de Nebrija's prominent Castilian grammar, given its value as a linguistic tool for spreading the faith.[53]

We can see a reflection of such an outlook in the first edition of Talavera's moral and doctrinal writings, which were printed in Granada in 1496, at least six years before he issued his instructions for Muslim converts.[54] Talavera composed his moral writings in the 1470s and 1480s, when he was

---

[51] See Beatriz Alonso Acero, *Cisneros y la conquista española del norte de África: Cruzada, política y arte de la guerra* (Madrid, 2006).

[52] See Miguel Molina Martínez, "Fray Hernando de Talavera y Colón," *Naveg@mérica: Revista electrónica de la Asociación Española de Americanistas* 1, no. 1 (2008), https://revistas.um.es/navegamerica/article/view/44001/42121.

[53] See Isabella Iannuzzi, "Talavera y Nebrija: Lenguaje para convencer, gramática para pensar," *Revista Española de Historia* 68, no. 228 (2008): 37–62.

[54] A list of contents is provided by Mark D. Johnston, "Hernando de Talavera on Conduct: Cultural Hegemony in Post-Conquest Granada," *Confluencia: Revista Hispánica de Cultura y Literatura* 30 (2015): 11–22, at 12.

prior of the monastery of Valladolid and confessor to Queen Isabella, and as such they were originally addressed to Old Christian women, children, and men. The various writings cover all sorts of cultural and religious aspects of the daily life of a "good Christian": from how to dress and put on shoes to time management; from the prohibition on whispering and gossiping to the practice of confession; from warnings about overeating and gluttony to the symbolic meanings of each liturgical act of the Mass.[55]

Talavera's moral writings have recently drawn scholarly attention because they are a rich reflection of the social and cultural shifts underway in fifteenth-century Castile—e.g., the new regulations regarding sumptuary laws, or the reforms affecting monastic life, which provide special insight into the role of Christian nuns and noble women.[56] However, his recurring references to "the infidels" in these writings reflect the new reality of an entirely Christian society in which Jewish and Muslim practices nevertheless persisted. As Mark Johnston has demonstrated with regard to Talavera's interest in dietary rules,[57] the relevance of his moral writings for a society with mixed religious loyalties is evident in the decision to publish them in the 1496 collection. In this new iteration, they were intended for use in postconquest Granada, where around 1495–98, during the three years preceding the first Islamic rebellion in the Albaicín, the confrontation between Christian authorities and the leaders of the Muslim community was rapidly escalating. There was a need to christianize both Muslim converts and Old Christians who, having moved to the city, were required to instruct their relatives and children. This provided a new, "mixed" readership for Talavera's moral works.

One of Talavera's most significant writings is the *Breve y muy provechosa doctrina christiana*, a short catechism that, significantly, was placed at the beginning of the 1496 collection. As I mentioned, in the early sixteenth century, this catechism apparently achieved a certain degree of popularity and was even used by missionaries for the evangelization of the Amerindians, especially in New Spain.[58] Victor Infantes has claimed that it was originally

---

[55] Three copies of the 1496 Granada edition—one of which had belonged to Queen Isabella—are presently kept at the library of the Royal Monastery of San Lorenzo de El Escorial and were acquired by Philip II in the context of his interest in the early history of Christian Granada.

[56] See Cécile Codet, "Hablar de la mujer o hablar a la mujer en tiempos de los Reyes Católicos: visiones contrastadas en tres tratados de Hernando de Talavera," *La Clé des Langues* 2 (2010–11): 1–18, http://cle.ens-lyon.fr/espagnol/fichiers/codet_1273045731229.pdf.

[57] Mark D. Johnston, "Gluttony and *Convivencia*: Hernando de Talavera's Warning to the Muslims of Granada in 1496," in *Mens et mensa: Thinking of Food in Medieval Cultures (1000–1600 CE)*, ed. Piera Montserrat, monographic issue of *eHumanista*, 25 (2013): 107–26.

[58] The transcription of the text is provided in Luis Resines, *La "Breve doctrina" de Hernando de Talavera* (Granada, 1993), 111–18. On the place of the *Breve doctrina* in Castilian pedagogical literature, see Framiñán de Miguel, "Manuales para el adoctrinamiento," 26.

employed as a basic handbook for the primary education of Christian children.[59] As Jesús R. Folgado García recently observed, however, the publication of the catechism in Granada in 1496 must be seen as part of Talavera's evangelization strategies directed towards Muslims and Muslim converts.[60] Originally conceived as a pedagogical tool for the education of Christian pupils during Talavera's years as prior in Valladolid, the *Breve doctrina* was apparently reworked at the end of the century as a manifesto of the Catholic faith intended for an audience of both young and adult Muslims.

The *Breve doctrina* provides norms regarding Christian religious practices, rites, and sacraments (from crossing oneself to the observance of Christian holidays), as well as brief instructions concerning moral conduct inspired by the basic principles of moral theology (the practice of confession, the commandments, the seven deadly sins).[61] The topics covered in this short treatise, and the order in which they appear, exhibit clear parallels both with the arguments about Jewish practices provided in the *Católica impugnación* and with the instructions for Muslim converts issued in Granada fifteen years later. The six pillars of the life of a "good Christian" that I have highlighted above also underpin Talavera's catechism, with one exception: burial practices are not discussed, although there is a general reference to the anointing of the sick and deathbed confession.[62]

Talavera's attempt to reform religious practices was not new to the pastoral strategies adopted by the Spanish Church during the final stage of the conquest. Religious practices, in addition to doctrine, had been accorded salvific value in a 1322 canonical decree of the National Council of Valladolid, which oriented the decisions of later Castilian synods and produced a reformist catechism that would prove influential into the sixteenth century. The Valladolid decree stated that knowing the Christian sacraments, commandments, practices, virtues and sins—in fact, all aspects of moral theology—was essential for the salvation of the soul.[63] Talavera's catechetical program thus was inspired by a long process of the Church's reassessment of the significance of moral behaviors, cultural habits, and religious

---

[59]Victor Infantes, *De las primeras letras: Cartillas españolas para ... enseñar a leer de los siglos XV y XVI; Preliminar y edición facsímil de 34 obras* (Salamanca, 1998), 68–83. On Talavera's pedagogical writings and their relationship to the *Breve doctrina*, see Isabella Iannuzzi, "Educar a los cristianos: Fray Hernando de Talavera y su labor catequética dentro de la estructura familiar para homogeneizar la sociedad de los Reyes Católicos," *Nuevo Mundo Mundos Nuevos* (20 January 2008), http://journals.openedition.org/nuevomundo/19122.

[60]See Folgado García, "Un instrumento usado en la evangelización de la Granada Nazarí," 291.

[61]A description of the work's contents is provided in Resines, *La «Breve doctrina» de Hernando de Talavera*, 67–78.

[62]See Hernando de Talavera, *Breve y muy provechosa doctrina*, transcribed in Resines, 115.

[63]See *Colección de cánones de la Iglesia española*, 7 vols. (Madrid, 1849–1862), 3:509–10.

rites, a reassessment that reached its peak at the end of the fifteenth century with the Church's full-blown confrontation with Jewish and Muslim practices. Drawing on a sophisticated exegesis of the New Testament, especially Paul's letters, Talavera adopted this model first among the Christians of Jewish origins of Seville, using polemical language, and later in Granada, using it in a more pastoral vein, as a tool for the education of Muslims after their forced conversion.

It is difficult to draw conclusions about the extent to which Talavera's earlier confrontation with Judaism influenced his later approach to the conversion and education of Muslims. The universalistic character of his pastoral plan allows us to infer that it was originally conceived for Christians with the assumption that it could be applied across time, space, and cultural boundaries. A confirmation of this comes from Felipe Pereda's groundbreaking monograph on fifteenth-century controversies over religious images, where he has shown that, at Talavera's time, devotional images played a pivotal role in the Christian evangelization of both Jewish converts and their descendants, on the one hand, and Muslims and Muslim converts, on the other. It is also true that in the late Middle Ages, as Ana Echavarría has suggested, funerary rites and burial practices were simultaneously debated within the communities of the three Abrahamic religions throughout the Mediterranean. Christian leaders like Talavera and, later, the Inquisition—though with different methods—tried to replace Jewish and Muslim burial practices with Christian ones, without making any great effort to study and assess the practices of either religion in terms of rituals and their related theological meanings.[64] The Christian use of devotional images for evangelization and the hegemonic attempt to replace non-Christian with Christian burials across time and space suggest that the concerns of ecclesiastical authorities regarding the christianization of Jewish practices, on the one hand, and Muslim practices, on the other, overlapped significantly. This evangelization program employed Paul's supersessionist thinking and the banner of orthodoxy against heresy to impose a Christian system that overrode Judaism and Islam, ignoring the intrinsic value they had for their adherents.

My comparative analysis of Talavera's polemical and pastoral writings leads to the conclusion that, at least regarding religious practices, it was not his earlier experience with Christians of Jewish origins that shaped his later thinking about Muslims. Rather, Judaism and Islam were conflated within a broader, morally-oriented evangelization plan that Talavera had probably begun to devise well before his mission to Seville in 1478. Certainly Talavera's

---

[64] See, respectively, Pereda, *Las imágenes de la discordia*, 254–92, and Ana Echevarría Arsuaga, "Funerary Practices in a Multi–Religious Context from the Iberian Peninsula to the Eastern Mediterranean," in *Das Mittelmeer und der Tod: Mediterrane Mobilität und Sepulkralkultur*, ed. Alexander Berner et al. (Paderborn, 2016), 179–94.

spiritual formation as a monk of the Hieronymite Order oriented his ecclesiological view and his assimilationist policies for non-Christians within a broader attempt to reform Spain's Church. His universalistic call for conversion, in fact, echoes Alonso de Oropesa's *Lumen ad revelationem gentium et gloria plebis Dei Israel*,[65] a pro-converso treatise written by an eminent Hieronymite monk and a mentor of Talavera in the aftermath of the Toledo anti-Jewish riots of 1449.[66] Both Oropesa's and Talavera's writings have recourse to Paul's conception of conversion as they seek to define the role of Christians of Jewish origins within Christianity, reflecting a general phenomenon in fifteenth-century Castile. Regarding religious practices, Talavera uses the term "Christians" to refer without distinction to both Old and New Christians, following the inclusivist ecclesiological model that had been outlined by his predecessor and mentor.[67] It is no coincidence that in the *Católica impugnación*, Judaism and Islam are explicitly regarded as two unruly branches of a common Abrahamic trunk in need of pruning. Elaborating upon Paul's olive tree metaphor and the underlying concept of roots (Romans 11:16–24), Talavera himself polemically employs this image of the trunk and branches when arguing for the common genealogical roots of all Christians, Old and New, whether of Jewish or Muslim origin.[68]

Perceived Distinctions between Judaism and Islam

Nevertheless, in two areas—namely, religious law and the language of revelation—Talavera's otherwise common evangelizing strategy does take into consideration differences between Judaism and Islam. Obviously, Christian denial of the salvific value of Jewish Law and its undermining of the authority of Jewish practices predates Christianity's engagement with Islam. The Christian theological confrontation with Judaism regarding the nature of the Law as a means for salvation served for Christians as a model of interaction with another faith. This model tended to shape how medieval Christians understood Islamic doctrine and practices, as they coped with the problem of the coexistence of different revelations and the underlying risk of syncretism.

---

[65] Fray Alonso de Oropesa, *Luz para el conocimiento de los gentiles*, ed. and trans. Luis A. Díaz y Díaz (Madrid: 1979). On the link between this work and the Toledo riots, see Starr–LeBeau, *In the Shadow of the Virgin*, 46–49.

[66] See Tomás González Rolán and Pilar Saquero Suárez–Somonte, *De la sentencia–estatuto de Pero Sarmiento a la instrucción del relator* (Madrid, 2012), and bibliography there.

[67] See Maurice Kriegel, "Alonso de Oropesa devant la question des conversos; une stratégie d'intégration hiéronymite?," in *"Qu'un sang impur...": Les conversos et le pouvoir en Espagne à la fin du Moyen Âge*, ed. Jeanne Battesti Pelegrin (Aix–en–Provence, 1997), 9–18.

[68] Hernando de Talavera, *Católica impugnación*, ch. 31, 148.

89
 Springer

Talavera's work offers a paradigmatic example of the effort to comprehend the reality of three religious systems within the same Abrahamic trajectory: Paul's arguments on the replacement of the observance of Jewish Law with faith in the resurrection of Christ were readily enlisted by Talavera to legitimize the suppression of Islamic practices in christianized Castile.

Yet while Talavera expanded at length upon Paul's rejection of Jewish Law, filling the pages of the *Católica impugnación* with creative anti-judaizing imagery and typological metaphors, he has not a single word to say against the Qur'ān. In fact, the holy book of Islam is never mentioned in his writings, neither in his letters to the Catholic Monarchs concerning the christianization of Granada, nor in his instructions, which were expressly addressed to Muslim converts. The Qur'ān is not cast as the religious law of Islam, and Talavera avoids using the concepts of *lex Mahumeti* or *lex Sarracenorum*—concepts that are extensively employed and discussed in Christian polemical literature (both anti-Muslim and anti-Jewish) from the twelfth to sixteenth centuries.[69] Talavera's writings give the impression that the Qur'ān does not exist at all, as if Islam were just a set of habits and rites with no legal or theological basis, a religion without a book. In the *Católica impugnación*, he confines himself to defining Muslims as members of a sect (*secta mahomética*) echoing a widespread concept extensively debated in the twelfth century (*secta Sarracenorum*),[70] whereas at the same time he always refers to Judaism and the Jews in terms of "Jewish Law."[71]

This should not be taken, however, as a reflection of the reality on the ground, where the Qur'ān was the most important doctrinal book within the *mudéjar* communities prior to the forced conversions and Christians of Muslim origins who dissimulated in later periods. While the Qur'ān was mainly read in Arabic, it was also translated into the Romance vernacular, as attested by multiple *aljamiado* manuscripts dating from the fifteenth to seventeenth centuries. Manuscript collections of religious writings used by Spanish Muslim converts who secretly practiced Islam contain transcriptions of suras and *'āyāt* made for liturgical or devotional purposes. Although after the conversions Christian authorities forbade the reading of the Qur'ān, it continued to

---

[69] For an overview of the recurrence of this concept in the High Middle Ages, see Matthias M. Tischler, "'Lex Mahometi': The Authority of a Pattern of Religious Polemics," *Journal of Transcultural Medieval Studies* 2 (2015): 3–62.

[70] In his *Liber contra sectam Sarracenorum* (ca. 1155), Peter the Venerable provides reasons and doubts regarding the doctrinal nature of "the sect of the Saracens," oscillating between classifying them as "heretics" or "pagans." Cf. Peter the Venerable, *Writings Against the Saracens*, trans. Irven M. Resnick (Washington, DC, 2016), 67–69.

[71] See, for example, Hernando de Talavera, *Católica impugnación*, ch. 50, 180, where he provides a definition of apostasy suitable for converts from both Judaism and Islam: "y digo que son apóstatas, si dejan del todo la santa ley evangélica y determinadamente creen siguen y guardan la ley mosaica o la secta mahomética."

circulate among converts, as shown by recent research into the morisco book corpus.[72]

In Talavera's time, the Qur'ān was also easily available to learned Christian readers.[73] Latin translations of the Qur'ān, especially that of Robert of Ketton (1143), were well known in late medieval Iberia, especially after the Second Council of Lyon (1274), where the methods of Christian missions to Muslims in North Africa and the Near East were openly discussed.[74] Moreover, it seems that at least partial translations of the Qur'ān into Catalan and Castilian were available between the fourteenth and the fifteenth century. The glaring absence of any reflection on the Qur'ān in Talavera's writings, or even a single explicit mention of it, is even more surprising if one considers that, according to the *donatio inter vivos* of his private library, he owned at least three copies of it, one of which, as far as we know, was written in Castilian.[75] It has been maintained that this translation is a copy of the Castilian translation based on the trilingual edition of the Qur'ān composed in Savoy in 1456 by Juan de Segovia and the eminent Islamic *faqīh*, Iça Gidelli.[76] However, philologists have questioned whether there is any connection between

---

[72] The case of eleven *aljamiado* manuscripts of the Qur'ān kept at the CSIC's Tomás Navarro Tomás Library in Madrid, which Nuria Martínez de Castilla Muñoz has studied, is telling in this regard. See Nuria Martínez de Castilla Muñoz, "The Copyists and their Texts: The Morisco Translations of the Qur'ān in the Tomás Navarro Tomás Library (CSIC, Madrid)," *Al-Qanṭara* 35 (2014): 493–525; Nuria Martínez de Castilla Muñoz, "Qur'ānic Manuscripts from Late Muslim Spain: The Collection of Almonacid de la Sierra," *Journal of Qur'ānic Studies* 16, no. 2 (2014): 89–138.

[73] See Thomas E. Burman, *Reading the Qur'ān in Latin Christendom, 1140–1560* (Philadelphia, 2007).

[74] Anthony John Lappin, "Riccoldo's View of the Qur'ān in the Context of its Translation and Annotation," paper presented at *Riccoldo da Monte di Croce (†1320): Missionary to the Middle East and Expert on Islam*, a conference organized by Kurt Villads Jensen, Davide Scotto and Mohammad Fazlhashemi, Royal Swedish Academy of Letters, History and Antiquities, Stockholm, 7–8 September 2017. The proceedings of the conference will be published as a book in 2022.

[75] See Quintín Aldea, "Hernando de Talavera, su testamento y su biblioteca," in *Homenaje a Fray Justo Pérez de Urbel OSB*, 2 vols. (Santo Domingo de Silos, 1976–1977), 1:513–47.

[76] For this claim, see Isabella Iannuzzi, *El poder de la palabra en el siglo XV: Fray Hernando de Talavera* (Valladolid, 2009), 424. Iça Gidelli is the author also of the *Breviario Sunni*, a compendium of Islamic doctrine that was widely used by the Inquisition in Spain and disseminated in both Iberia and its overseas territories, as the discovery of a copy of it in New Spain shows. See María Judith Feliciano Chaves, "Yça Gidelli y la Nueva España: Un manuscrito del 'Breviario Sunní' en el Archivo General de la Nación (México, D.F.)," *Aljamía* 13 (2001): 48–51. On the interfaith implications and the ultimate aims behind the trilingual edition of the Qur'ān, see Davide Scotto, "'De pe a pa': Il Corano trilingue di Juan de Segovia (1456) e la conversione pacifica dei musulmani," *Rivista di Storia e Letteratura Religiosa*, 48 (2012): 515–78.

Segovia's translation and the dissemination of the first Castilian version of the Qur'ān in Iberia.[77] In any event, Talavera's library and his long-standing experience with Muslims suggest that he was among the fifteenth-century readers of the Qur'ān. Unless he failed to mention the Qur'ān for purely political reasons, his silence on this point indicates an area of differentiation in his theological understanding of Judaism and Islam.

Talavera maintained that in Judaism, detailed instructions on religious habits and rites were part of a religious law that could not bring salvation, one that should not mingle with Christian laws and norms of conduct inspired by the Gospels. According to Talavera, access to Jewish Law should thus be prohibited among Christians, especially recent converts from Judaism. Drawing on Paul's theology of the Laws, Talavera understood Judaism as a religion inspired by "a law that kills," one that—according to the later development of Christian moral theology—was incompatible with "the new Christian law" and that threatened the desired assimilation of Old and New Christians in Castile. In contrast, Islam emerges from the little Talavera wrote about it as a religion based on moral, religious, and cultural practices that lacked a scriptural foundation. Before the mass conversions of 1502, he never expressed any need for converted Muslims to abandon Islamic practices; and even after 1502, at least according to his first set of instructions, converts were entitled to retain some cultural practices associated with Islam. In Talavera's eyes—other Christian churchmen coping with Islam had a different view—Islamic beliefs are of no importance compared to the challenge of Jewish beliefs, primarily because the fundamental teachings of Christianity rely on the Hebrew Bible. Although Talavera maintains that the names of Muhammad and Fatimah—implicitly regarded as dangerously seductive—are to be erased from memory, he makes no mention of the Qur'ān or of a threat posed by its existence.

A second distinction Talavera makes between Judaism and Islam concerns the language in which religious laws or revelations are codified and transmitted. Talavera was most likely not conversant in Hebrew. Although he was knowledgeable about Catalan, translated a Latin work by Petrarch into Castilian, imported the German movable-type printing press to Valladolid and Granada, and promoted the translation and printing of grammars and dictionaries,[78] he cannot be considered a humanist. Nor can he be regarded as a

---

[77] See Consuelo López–Morillas, *El Corán de Toled:. Edición y estudio del manuscrito 235 de la Biblioteca de Castilla–La Mancha* (Gijón, 2011); Ulli Roth, "Juan of Segovia's Translation of the Qur'ān," *Al–Qanṭara* 35 (2014): 555–78, 559–60.

[78] See Andrea Baldissera, "Petrarca ispanizzato: Le 'Invectivas' o 'Reprehensiones contra el médico' di Hernando de Talavera," *Revista de poética medieval* 18 (2007): 53–73; Carlos Romero de Lecea, "Hernando de Talavera y el tránsito en España del manuscrito al impreso," in *Studia Hieronymiana*, 2 vols. (Madrid, 1973), 1:317–77.

Christian Hebraist along the lines of Pico della Mirandola in Italy, Johannes Reuchlin in Germany or, later on, the Bible scholar Benito Arias Montano in Spain.[79] Trained at the prestigious University of Salamanca, Talavera can best be described as a pastoral writer who served as a trustworthy officer and experienced diplomat in the service of the Crown. Moreover, throughout his life he was a committed evangelizer driven by the spiritual concerns peculiar to the Hieronymite Order, that is to say, ecclesiological universalism and centrality of the Bible in the study and pastoral practice. Although it is true that Talavera, in response to his judaizing adversary's insistence on Christ's Jewish origins, lingers on the meanings of certain Hebrew words,[80] he undoubtedly draws his knowledge from patristic exegetical discussions of the Old Testament Hebrew lexicon.[81] Among the Church Fathers he arguably read was Jerome, the patron of his own religious order, whom Talavera characterizes as an exemplary "hammer" in the fight against heretics (*martillo de los herejes*).[82]

In the *Católica impugnación*, Talavera never criticizes or discusses the Hebrew language in its own right, but rather treats it as a cultural artifact of the past. In his view, Hebrew has little to do with contemporary Jewish identity, but rather belongs to the realm of the Israelites of the Bible, that is, the so-called "living letters of the Law" dealt with in Christian exegesis ever since Augustine's interpretation of Ps 58:12.[83] There are two possible reasons for this. For one thing, Hebrew was the language of the Hebrew Bible, which medieval Christians accepted as part of the Christian canon and, especially in the fifteenth cenutry, promoted as a purely symbolic proof of the *hebraica veritas*. Deemed to be misunderstood by the Jews, the Hebrew Bible was to be retained as Scripture, but transformed by the centuries-long practice of typological interpretation. For another, the population of Spanish

---

[79]For the Iberian context, see Jonathan Decter and Arturo Prats, eds., *The Hebrew Bible in Fifteenth–Century Spain: Exegesis, Literature, Philosophy, and the Arts* (Leiden, 2012).

[80]Hernando de Talavera, *Católica impugnación*, ch. 11, 84–86.

[81]In Talavera's time the typical ecclesiastic education, including the monastic one, did not entail any teaching of Hebrew, or Greek, or Arabic. At the University of Salamanca, chairs of Oriental languages formally existed after the decree of the Council of Vienne of 1311, but they were vacant, as the Spanish theologian Juan de Segovia, who taught there between 1421 and 1431, reported about the Arabic chair. Nor is there any evidence—despite what scholars have inferred or insisted for decades—that Talavera had Jewish ancestry (at least it is not traceable in his recent ancestry) and, hence, that he knew Hebrew for communication or liturgical purposes.

[82]Hernando de Talavera, *Católica impugnación*, dedication letter to the Catholic Monarchs, 69.

[83]See Anna Sapir Abulafia, *Christians and Jews in Dispute: Disputational Literature and the Rise of Anti–Judaism in the West (c. 1000–1150)* (Aldershot, UK, 1998); Jeremy Cohen, *Living Letters of the Law: Ideas of the Jew in Medieval Christianity* (Berkeley, 1999).

Jews, Jewish converts, and Christians of Jewish origins did not speak Hebrew in everyday life, even if Jews and reluctant converts did use it as a liturgical language. Since Hebrew was not closely linked to contemporary Jewish belief and practice, it was not perceived as a doctrinal challenge to the Christian faith nor as an obstacle to the progressive development of evangelization.

Arabic, on the other hand, was regarded as a living language, used by the community of Arabic-speaking New Christians in postconquest Granada to speak and, less commonly, to write, and thus to disseminate their religious beliefs. This must be at least one of the reasons why the use of Arabic among converts was among the most pressing concerns in Talavera's second set of instructions. Talavera's opposition to the use of Arabic flatly belies the sixteenth-century hagiographies focused on his pastoral deeds, which, despite their blatantly biased narrative, have led scholars to consider the archbishop of Granada as a passionate Arabist and even a Muslim-friendly thinker.[84] This is far from having been the case, as Talavera's second set of instructions shows. He treats Arabic by turns either polemically, in order to claim that it is as dangerous as the beliefs it conveys, or instrumentally, in order to exploit it as a further means of evangelization. Either way, he regards Arabic as a language closely associated with Islam, and thus as a language that must be carefully monitored. When, then, he encourages Muslim converts to read Christian books in Arabic, he views that language purely as a vehicle for evangelization. Towards the end of the second set of instructions, he states, "so that your behavior may be without scandal to the Christians of the nation and that they may not think that you still have the sect of Mohammed in your heart," adult Muslim converts should cease to use Arabic for everyday communication, because of its inextricable association with Islamic doctrine.[85] The same acceptance of Arabic for instrumental purposes can be detected in the innovative *Vocabulista aravigo en letra castellana* and the *Arte para ligeramente saber la lengua araviga*, both of which Talavera commissioned from the Arabic expert Pedro de Alcalá, and both of which were printed in Granada in 1505.[86]

In his fear that the Arabic language had the potential to facilitate the survival and spread of Islamic doctrine, Talavera is not as far removed from Cardinal Cisneros, as historians have long maintained. On closer inspection, Talavera's concerns proved to be the same as those that prompted Cisneros

---

[84] See Scotto, "'Como en un resplandeciente y terso espejo'," 449–52, 457.

[85] Hernando de Talavera, *Memorial y tabla de ordenaciones*, 763.

[86] See Jesús R. Folgado García, "Las lenguas romances y la evangelización granadina. La aportación de Hernando de Talavera y la liturgia en arábigo de Pedro de Alcalá," *Espacio, tiempo y forma*, ser. 3, *Historia medieval* 27 (2014): 229–38; Jesús R. Folgado García, "Un intento de diálogo en la Granada nazarí: *El arte para ligeramente saber la lengua aráviga* de Pedro de Alcalá," *Hispania Sacra* 67, no. 135 (2015): 49–59.

to order the burning of all copies of the Qur'ān and other religious books.[87] As I have shown elsewhere,[88] both Talavera's acceptance of coercion in the evangelization of non-Christians and Cisneros' letter to Talavera—in which the Cardinal shows gratitude to the Archbishop for having facilitated the conversions—suggest that the two ecclesiastics shared a common view of the mass baptisms of 1499–1502. Altogether it would seem that, at least after 1498, when the measures taken by Christian authorities to regulate Muslims in Granada had already become more severe, Archbishop Talavera shared with Cisneros the aim of eliminating Islam as a religion, or at the very least did not attempt to stand in his way.

A Normative Interpretation of Paul's Call for Conversion

Despite the way in which Talavera differentiated between Judaism and Islam when dealing with issues of religious law and language, he does not appear to have behaved differently towards those he was evangelizing, whether they were Christians of Jewish ancestry or Muslim converts. On the contrary, he treats the Abrahamic religions as if they were one, inviting both baptized and unbaptized people to adopt proper Christian practices. In his writings, he addresses Old Christians, Christians of Jewish or Muslim origins, and unbaptized Muslims indistinguishably, and at times explicitly glosses over the differences between their religious origins. They must all be equally scrupulous in complying with a well-defined array of Christian practices. Reforming the behaviors and religious habits of Christians and non-Christians alike was one of Talavera's main concerns, from his earlier mission to Seville (1478–80) to his later years in Granada (1492–1507). Shaped by his university education and Hieronymite worldview, his call for moral and spiritual reform must be considered part of a broader current of pre-Reformation reformist thought, in which the confrontation with Judaism and Islam played an instrumental role in debates about how to shape and expand Christian society.[89]

It is only recently that scholars have begun to turn their focus from the doctrinal and literary tropes of medieval Christian anti-Islamic polemics—first examined by Norman Daniel in his influential *Islam and the West*[90]—to

---

[87] See Daniel Eisenberg, "Cisneros y la quema de los manuscritos granadinos," *Journal of Hispanic Philology* 16 (1992): 107–24.

[88] Scotto, "Neither through Habits, nor Solely through Will," 318–20.

[89] On the role of Islam in debates revolving around the Catholic Reformation, see Bernard Heyberger et al., eds., *L'Islam visto da Occidente: Cultura e religione del Seicento europeo di fronte all'islam* (Milan, 2009); and Andrea Celli and Davide Scotto, "Breve storia di un titolo, a modo d'introduzione," *Rivista di Storia e Letteratura Religiosa* 51 (2015): 395–409.

[90] Norman Daniel, *Islam and the West: The Making of an Image* (Edinburgh, 1960).

the role and relevance of religious practices in medieval polemics between the three Abrahamic religions.[91] In this light, a final word can be said about Talavera's theological understanding of religious practices and their role in the conversion of Jews and Muslims within his universalist evangelization plan. The priority given to religious practices over doctrine in Talavera's methods of conversion and assimilation raises broader questions about the impact of Judaism and Islam on the history of Christian evangelization throughout the Mediterranean and beyond. Scholars of Christian theology, medieval history, and Judaism have increasingly acknowledged that for a number of fifteenth-century churchmen who were involved in interreligious disputations and evangelization campaigns, Paul's arguments on the relationship between the Old Law and the new faith in Christ were essential in order to make sense of the presence and role of non-Christians in newly christianized territories.[92] Talavera's intellectual preconceptions, the exegetical devices he employed, and the final outcomes of his pastoral action should be understood within the broader history of recourse to Paul's theology of the Laws in the Middle Ages and beyond.

Talavera's focus on the convert's transitioning from Jewish or Muslim practices to generically parallel Christian practices seems a far cry from the original spirit of Paul's arguments and expectations about conversion. As is well known, the universalistic nature of Paul's conception of conversion is mainly expressed in his First Letter to the Corinthians (15:20–28) and his Letter to the Galatians (3:28), both of which address the relationship between Jewish Law and Christian faith at a theological level.[93] In contrast to the opinion symbolically summarized by the apostle Peter that emerged at the First Council of Jerusalem, Paul's appeal implied no distinction between Jew or Gentile, slave or freeman, male or female; he denied that the

---

[91] See the meaningful cases discussed in José Martinez Gázquez and John Victor Tolan, eds., *Ritus infidelium: Miradas interconfesionales sobre las prácticas religiosas en la Edad Media* (Madrid, 2013).

[92] For a short but stimulating study of Jewish–Christian disputes drawing on Paul's letters in fifteenth–century Castile, see Bruce Rosenstock, *New Men: "Conversos," Christian Theology, and Society in Fifteenth–Century Castile* (London, 2002). For two case studies involving Christian–Muslim relations, see Ryan Szpiech, "Preaching Paul to the Moriscos: The *Confusión o confutación de la secta mahomética y del Alcorán* (1515) of 'Juan Andrés'," *La Corónica* 41 (2012): 317–43; and François Soyer, "'All One in Christ Jesus'? Spiritual Closeness, Genealogical Determinism and the Conversion of Jews in Alonso de Espina's *Fortalitium Fidei*," *Journal of Spanish Cultural Studies* 17 (201): 239–54. For an overview of diverse use of Paul in the medieval times, see Steven R. Cartwright, ed., *A Companion to St. Paul in the Middle Ages* (Leiden, 2013).

[93] On Paul's soteriological thinking, see among other studies George M. Wieland, *The Significance of Salvation: A Study of Salvation Language in the Pastoral Epistles* (Bletchley, UK, 2006).

believer's cultural habits and religious rites (i.e., Jewish Law or natural law) had any bearing on a path to salvation guided only by adherence to the living Christ. From this point of view, previous cultural habits could be preserved or abandoned insofar as they were irrelevant to salvation, a principle that can easily be read as a declaration of theological indifference towards religious practices.[94]

Against this background, the assumption that the Gospels ought to be regarded as a set of binding rules or norms to be imposed on others—*nueva ley del Evangelio*: an expression that emerges as the backbone of Talavera's polemics and pastoral instructions—clashes in many respects with the aims of Christ's message as it is understood in both Paul's letters and other writings of the New Testament. While Paul's writings indicate soteriological indifference to cultural practices and focus on baptism as a transformational act of death and rebirth, Talavera's conception of conversion focuses on a complete substitution of Christian for non-Christian practices and calls for the instruction of non-Christians and converts in these practices both before and after baptism. Unlike Paul, who belittled practices because they were soteriologically meaningless compared to faith, Talavera viewed believers' habits and rites as an obstacle to the success of conversion. For him, prior religious practices, whether Jewish or Islamic, should systematically be abandoned after baptism and replaced with proper Christian practices. Talavera's fervent warnings against converts' observance of Jewish and Muslim practices were rooted in moral and legal arguments that he claimed to derive from the Gospels. The "new law" of the Gospels was deemed to be a corpus of examples and norms with a binding character, with which all new believers should comply. Legitimising this understanding of the Gospels through a radicalized interpretation of Paul's reflection on the Jewish Law, Talavera develops an increasingly extreme christianization scheme, leaving no room within the Christian community for the coexistence of different religious or cultural practices, and no option for the convert to continue observing non-Christian practices.

As suggested by David Nirenberg, the main concern of the theological dispute between representatives of the three Abrahamic religions in medieval Iberia, prior to mass conversions and expulsions, was to define religious identity through a continuous process involving the acknowledgment of common origins, mutual borrowings, assimilation, and ultimately separation from the

---

[94] See, among an extensive bibliography, M. Eugene Boring, "The Language of Universal Salvation in Paul," *Journal of Biblical Literature* 105 (1986): 269–92; Andrew Wilson, "The Strongest Argument for Universalism in 1 Corinthians 15:20–28," *Journal of the Evangelical Theological Society* 59 (2016): 805–12.

other religion, resulting in what he has defined as the "coproduction of religious communities."[95] This process required drawing theological boundaries on the basis of sacred texts in order to create and redefine religious identity. Talavera's recourse to Paul's letters to the Galatians, the Romans, and the Hebrews—all of them tackling with different nuances the issue of the Old Law—is just one example, though an important one,[96] of the extensive use of these texts in medieval interfaith controversies.[97] Sometimes, however, intellectual efforts were not sufficient: conflicts that broke out between the different communities were essentially desperate attempts to safeguard group identity in the face of threats to their existence. Talavera was aware of the risk of conflict and made every possible effort to prevent it. On the one hand, he emphasized that unbaptized Jews and Muslims in Castile were allowed to observe their own law within their respective *juderías* and *morerías*, according to the model of coexistence and segregation established after the Fourth Lateran Council (1215) and reiterated several times in late medieval Castilian legislation. On the other hand, he underscored that once baptized Jews entered the Christian community, those who observed Jewish practices were to be punished harshly; those who clung to Jewish funerary practices and Shabbat were even to be sentenced to death.[98]

According to ecclesiastics like Talavera and Oropesa, the Church's womb was universally open to new believers of Jewish and Muslim origins. Therefore, establishing boundaries within the Christian community based on the religion or culture of those who embraced the true faith through baptism was to be avoided. Once new believers had entered the Church, however, they had to comply rigorously with its set of beliefs (inwardly) and its system of practices (outwardly). Imbued with this exclusivist conception of the universality of Christianity, Talavera saw an intrinsic potential threat of disaggregation and violence in Christian communities that absorbed converts. This is why he had no interest in forcing Jews to convert, yet called for the harsh punishment of converts who did not maintain strict adherence to Christian practice and continued to engage in former, now extrinsic, practices. The regulation

---

[95]Nirenberg, *Neighboring Faiths*, 5, 9, 27.

[96]See Scotto, "Theology of the Laws and Anti-Judaizing Polemics," esp. 128–35.

[97]See Hava Lazarus–Yafeh, *Intertwined Worlds: Medieval Islam and Bible Criticism* (Princeton, NJ, 1992); Kathleen Biddick, *The Typological Imaginary: Circumcision, Technology, History* (Philadelphia, 2003); Thomas J. Heffernan and Thomas E. Burman, eds., *Scripture and Pluralism: Reading the Bible in the Religiously Plural Worlds of the Middle Ages and Renaissance* (Leiden, 2005); Burman, *Reading the Qur'ān*; Ryan Szpiech, ed., *Medieval Exegesis and Religious Difference: Commentary, Conflict, and Community in the Premodern Mediterranean* (New York, 2015).

[98]On the combination of freedom of religion and segregation in Talavera's thinking, see Scotto, "Neither through Habits, nor Solely through Will," 302–7.

of religious practices was the most effective means to maintain the boundary between erroneous faiths and the true faith.

The apostle Paul showed total indifference to religious practices, as long as believers who came from different religious or cultural backgrounds did not claim that these practices had significance for salvation: the case of his letter to the Galatians, which Talavera read and used in his *Católica impugnación*, is the most radical and, at the same time, the most telling example of Paul's reaction to this claim. As exegetical research has abundantly showed in the last decades, Paul was not against the Old Law itself, but was extremely careful, and harshly firm when needed, regarding the exact meaning attributed to it. Along this line, Paul's anti-law polemic in the Letter to the Galatians has been recently reassessed, showing how his antipathy was addressed towards pagan practices taken by Galatian converts as Jewish practices, rather than against Jewish pratices themselves.[99] Talavera, in contrast, would never have accepted the continued observance of non-Christian religious practices—such as Shabbat or circumcision, but also Islamic way of dressing or burial practices, as showed by his second list of instructions—within the community of Old and New Christians once they were baptized.

Fifteen centuries after Paul's mission to the Galatians, Talavera enforced a theological device that inextricably connect faith and practice along a well-established exegetical tradition harking back to the Church Fathers and elaborated in the medieval scholastic debate. This articulated exegetical tradition forged the moral and catechetical thinking of which Talavera himself, as a former student and a professor of moral theology at the University of Salamanca, was deeply imbued. When Talavera had to cope with Jewish and Muslim converts in late fifteenth-century Granada, a binding legal system based on an interpretation of Paul as the liquidator of all non-Christian laws was ready to be enacted. In calling for the enforcement of Christian religious practices as a moral and legal obligation, Talavera's evangelization plan proves to be a complete inversion of the anti-law stance underlying Paul's conception of conversion. Rather than releasing mankind from the chains of "a Law of sin and death," as Paul intended to do (Romans 8:2), Talavera substantially contributed to shaping an understanding of Christianity as a normative system. As a consequence—contrary to Paul's focus on the inner transformation of the "new man" through baptism according to Christ's example—in Talavera's times the act of conversion to Christianity was increasingly understood as something that took place not primarily in the spiritual realm, but rather in the terrestrial realm of stifling moral and legal norms.

---

[99] See Neil Martin, *Regression in Galatians: Paul and the Gentile Response to Jewish Law* (Tübingen, 2020).

Acknowledgments The research leading to this study was funded by the ERC under the European Union's Seventh Framework Programme [(FP7/2007–2013)/ERC Grant Agreement #323316], for the project CORPI: "Conversion, Overlapping Religiosities, Polemics, Interaction: Early Modern Iberia and Beyond," PI: Mercedes García-Arenal. I presented the results of this research at the 64th annual meeting of the RSA, New Orleans, 2018, and at the biannual lecture series *Aktuelle Forschungen zur Geschichte der Vormoderne* organized by the Department of History of the University of Basel in March 2019. I am grateful to all of the colleagues who have helped me improve my findings with their stimulating questions and suggestions. I wish to express my gratitude to Mercedes García-Arenal and Yonatan Glazer-Eytan for having encouraged my research proposal, to Miriam Bodian for the invaluable discussion of the research outcomes, and to Nicholas Callaway for his help in editing this article.

Jewish History (2021) 35: 329–349
https://doi.org/10.1007/s10835-021-09422-2

Entangled Discourses of Dissent in Early Modern Spain

MIRIAM BODIAN

University of Texas at Austin, Austin, TX, USA
E-mail: bodian@austin.utexas.edu

Accepted: 14 July 2021 / Published online: 17 December 2021

Abstract For more than a century, scholars of early modern Spanish heterodoxy accepted the Inquisition's categories of heresy as their own. The various types of heretics the Inquisition identified—*judaizantes* (judaizers), crypto-Muslims, *alumbrados* (illuminists), and *luteranos* (Protestant-leaning persons)—appeared in their research to have had little to do with one another, or with the broader population of orthodox Catholics. Since the 1980s, this conceptualization has been challenged from several angles. Scholars have uncovered crosscurrents among supposedly distinct groups and have shown that doubts about the authority and sanctity of the Catholic Church knew no clear bounds. This essay analyzes the development of scholarly revision of the long-standing conception. It then examines the findings of more recent research and explores some of the difficulties and unresolved issues in that research.

Keywords Conversos · Inquisition · Heresy · Atheism · Spain · Portugal · Judaizers

The Iberian inquisitions, like all judicial systems, could not operate without establishing categories of crime. The inquisitions required a fixed taxonomy of heretical practices, among other things, to facilitate the identification of suspects. But in creating such a taxonomy, inquisitors unwittingly put their imprint on historical conceptualizations of Iberian society for generations to come. A glance at bibliographies and tables of contents of works dealing with heterodoxy in early modern Iberian lands demonstrates just how closely scholars have adhered to inquisitorial typology in their research. They have often limited entire works to one or another of these types: *judaizantes*, crypto-Muslims, *alumbrados*, *luteranos*, witches, or blasphemers.

Even when scholars have dealt with more than one of these types in a single work, they have routinely segregated them into separate chapters. Two early cases in point are Marcelino Menéndez y Pelayo's *Los heterodoxos españoles* (1880–1882), with its separate sets of chapters dealing with *erasmistas*, *luteranos*, *alumbrados*, *judaizantes*, and *moriscos*, and Henry Charles Lea's classic *History of the Inquisition of Spain* (1906–1907), with chapters on "Jews," "Moriscos," and "Protestantism."[1] Gustav Henningsen and Jaime

---

Chapter 5 was originally published as Bodian, M. Jewish History (2021) 35: 329–349. https://doi.org/10.1007/s10835-021-09422-2.

[1] Marcelino Menéndez de Pelayo, *Historia de los heterodoxos españoles* (Alicante: Biblioteca Virtual Miguel de Cervantes), http://www.cervantesvirtual.com/obra/historia-de-los-heterodoxos-espanoles, Table of Contents for Books 4 and 5; Henry Charles Lea, *A History of the Inquisition of Spain*, 4 vols. (New York, 1906–1907), vol. 3, bk. 8, chs. 1, 2, and 3.

Contreras, in their important study of forty-four thousand Inquisition trials (1986), relied entirely on the Inquisition's categories in their analysis. This approach cannot be faulted given their aims, but it also served to reinforce the conventional mapping of Iberian heresy.[2] Likewise, in their important anthologies of documents about Spanish inquisitions, both Lu Ann Homza and John Chuchiak organized their material using the Inquisition's typology of crimes.[3] The picture that emerges is one of a system of repression arrayed against a set of disconnected heresies.

To be sure, if we want to understand the Inquisition, it is important to think about how that institution deployed and elaborated its criminal categories. But if our aim is to understand the religious and cultural contours of Iberian society, the compartmentalized treatment of heterodox thinking that has emerged over time—one that tends to assume a distinct socioethnic "base" for each crime—has distorted and simplified a complex reality.

Challenging the Assumption

As early as the 1980s scholars began to challenge the assumption of separate heresies moving separately through time. In 1984, José María Monsalvo Antón, analyzing 444 denunciations by witnesses who appeared before the Soria tribunal between 1490 and 1502, observed that in many cases there was no clear difference between "Old Christian" blasphemy and certain "New Christian" statements that the tribunal classified as "judaizing." Among other things, Monsalvo Antón noted that the blasphemous expressions he studied did not necessarily reflect a truly heretical posture. That is, expletives deriding this or that Church doctrine, uttered in a moment of exasperation, did not necessarily represent genuine skepticism about the Church and its teachings.[4]

---

[2] The categories: *judíos, moros, luteranos, alumbrados, proposiciones, bigamos, confesores solicitantes.* See Jaime Contreras and Gustav Henningsen, "Forty-four Thousand Cases of the Spanish Inquisition (1540–1700): Analysis of a Historical Data Bank," in *The Inquisition in Early Modern Europe: Studies on Sources and Methods*, ed. Gustav Henningsen and John Tedeschi (Dekalb, IL, 1986), 100–29.

[3] Lu Ann Homza, ed., *The Spanish Inquisition, 1478–1614: An Anthology of Sources* (Indianapolis, IN, 2006); John F. Chuchiak IV, ed., *The Inquisition in New Spain, 1536–1820: A Documentary History* (Baltimore, 2012).

[4] Such expressions could belong to "a type of ritual, transgressive language," one that might be triggered by quarrels or games of chance. Monsalvo Antón saw in these expressions "unmistakable traces of a [certain] popular culture—... irreverent, antipathetic to the solemnity of religion, skeptical in the face of grandiose words." José María Monsalvo Antón, "Herejía conversa y contestación religiosa a fines de la Edad Media: Las denuncias a la Inquisición en el obispado de Osma," *Studia historica: Historia medieval* (1984): 118.

Yet some of the statements in the Soria documents *were* clearly heterodox theological claims—the claim that the soul died with the body, for example, or that the world was eternal, or that "there is nothing but being born and dying."[5] Earlier scholars had done little to examine the sources of such "*proposiciones*" (a classification the Inquisition used frequently only some decades after the period studied by Monsalvo Antón). Relying on Yitzhak Baer's assessment of the late medieval Jewish courtier class, Monsalvo Antón hypothesized that the heterodox opinions he encountered in the Soria documents had their origins in rationalistic, skeptical Averroist currents that had taken root among educated late medieval Spanish Jews. When such Jews converted (and according to Baer, Jews who harbored Averroist views were more *likely* to accept conversion), they became the conduit through which Jewish skepticism entered the Christian orbit. In Monsalvo Antón's words, "an entire current of philosophical and moral thought … that existed within Judaism passed through the sieve of false conversion and established itself in Christianity."[6] The rupture and disorientation of conversion reinforced existing skeptical attitudes by enhancing the converts' sense of religious autonomy and interiority.[7] And the latter's heterodox ideas inevitably made their way into Old Christian minds.

John Edwards challenged this position in a 1988 essay that made use of the same Soria documents.[8] Edwards was struck by the possibility that Old Christians were developing positions of unbelief on their own. He argued that the heterodox expressions in the Soria files reflected a socioreligious phenomenon that could be found not only in Iberian lands but throughout Europe, both in the medieval and early modern periods. In effect, he implied that even if there had been no conversos in Spain, the kind of heterodox thoughts the Inquisition was documenting would have been present in medieval and early modern Spanish towns and villages. In support of this claim, he cited

---

[5]Nicholas Griffiths has pointed out the possibility of the coexistence of credulous anger and skepticism. See Nicholas Griffiths, "Popular Religious Scepticism and Idiosyncrasy in Post-Tridentine Cuenca," in *Faith and Fanaticism: Religious Fervour in Early Modern Spain*, ed. Lesley Twomey (Aldershot, UK, 1997), 102 n. 19.

[6]Monsalvo Antón, "Herejía conversa," 133.

[7]Ibid., 133–34.

[8]John Edwards, "Religious Faith and Doubt in Late Medieval Spain: Soria circa 1450–1500," *Past and Present* 120 (1988): 3–25. By this time the Soria documents had been published by Carlos Carrete Parrondo, *Fontes iudaeorum Regni Castellae*, vol. 2, *El Tribunal de la Inquisición en el Obispado de Soria (1486–1502)* (Salamanca, 1985). Edwards somewhat misleadingly maintained that Monsalvo Antón failed to see the Soria documents as anything other than "a converso source, displaying as its most conspicuous features nostalgia and reverence for Judaism as a faith" (Edwards, "Religious Faith," 6), but he qualified that remark later in the same article (18).

research on thirteenth-century inquisitorial tribunals in France, which documented expressions that were very close to those being reported by witnesses in sixteenth-century Spain—for example, that the host was nothing but baked dough, or that the purported holiness of saints and shrines was a fraud.[9] Edwards quoted Walter Wakefield's comment that such opinions "may well have arisen spontaneously from the cogitations of men and women searching for explanations that accorded with the realities of the life in which they were enmeshed."[10] Carlo Ginzburg previously speculated similarly about the genesis of such thinking. He found in his sixteenth-century subject Menocchio "the elemental, instinctive materialism of generation after generation of peasants," a frame of mind that was "intolerant of dogma and ritual, tied to the cycles of nature, and fundamentally pre-Christian."[11] Edwards underscored his view that the Soria statements were not in essence particular to Iberia by noting the similarity between the eccentric views of the sixteenth-century Castilian wool carder Bartolomé Sánchez, who had contact with conversos, and Ginzburg's Menocchio who did not.[12]

Nicholas Griffiths articulated a different view in 1997 using testimony recorded by the Cuenca tribunal. He located the catalyst for Spanish expressions of skepticism about aspects of Church teaching not in Old Christian exposure to Jewish/converso nonconformism but, ironically, in the very program of post-Tridentine confessionalism whose purpose was to inculcate Catholic orthodoxy.[13] "Increased exposure to the official teachings of the Church," Griffiths wrote, "seems only to have fueled rather than eradicated" the expression of popular skepticism and idiosyncratic beliefs.[14] That is, when ordinary people were confronted with Church teachings they had previously never had to consider or of which they may have been entirely unaware, their subliminal doubts were brought to the surface. Among these teachings were the doctrine of the "real presence" in the consecrated host and the teaching that Christ was conceived without the participation of a human male.[15] While his key causal factor was new, Griffiths seems to have viewed

---

[9]Edwards relied on Walter L. Wakefield, "Some Unorthodox Popular Ideas of the Thirteenth Century," *Medievalia et Humanistica*, n.s., 4 (1973), 25–35, esp. 27, 29.

[10]Edwards, "Religious Faith," 21; Wakefield, "Unorthodox Popular Ideas," 33.

[11]Carlo Ginzburg, *The Cheese and the Worms: The Cosmos of a Sixteenth-Century Miller* (New York, 1989), 61, 112. The Italian original, *Il formaggio e i vermi*, was published in 1976.

[12]Edwards, "Religious Faith," 120–21. On Menocchio, see Ginzburg, *Cheese and Worms*; on Bartolomé Sanchez see Sara Tilghman Nalle, *Mad for God: Bartolomé Sánchez, the Secret Messiah of Cardenete* (Charlottesville, VA, 2001).

[13]Nicholas Griffiths, "Popular Religious Skepticism and Idiosyncrasy in Post-Tridentine Cuenca," in Twomey, *Faith and Fanaticism*, 95–128.

[14]Ibid., 99.

[15]Ibid., 102–3.

the problem posed by post-Tridentine education as arising, ultimately, from what Ginzburg referred to as the "elemental, instinctive materialism" of simple people who were baffled by doctrines that, to them, seemed detached from reality.

Griffith's argumentation is problematic. He suggests at the outset that he is interested in "popular religious deviance among Old Christians."[16] Yet he never offers clear evidence that his subjects *were* Old Christians. Rather, he seems to assume that "*proposiciones*" were by definition uttered only by Old Christians and that conversos were only ever tried for judaizing.[17] Since a judaizer disparaging the doctrines of the real presence and the virgin birth was presumably affirming his or her faith, rather than expressing an absence of faith, lack of clarity on this point is a significant flaw and suggests that Griffiths was relying on the very scholarly assumptions this article questions.

Moreover, Griffiths seems to have ignored the implications of evidence he himself cited. He presented the important 1609 case of the Old Christian Latin scholar Francisco de Marcilla who, beset by doubts about core aspects of Christian teaching, argued that one could only be certain of things that could be apprehended through natural reason.[18] He believed that on many points the pope and councils might well be in error. Griffiths argued that Marcilla's radical doubts "were directly related to his detailed knowledge of Christian doctrine."[19] Yet this is far from convincing. There had always been scholars in the Catholic world with a "detailed knowledge of Christian doctrine," and while this had often produced disagreements on the fine points of theology, it had rarely led to heresy. Moreover, Griffiths' explanation contradicts Marcilla's own richly suggestive explanation for how he became riddled with doubt, namely as a result of the "contemplation of the existence of so many religious sects."[20]

It was precisely to the reality of "so many religious sects" that Stuart Schwartz pointed in order to explain the proliferation of a certain cluster of heterodox ideas in Iberia. In his 2008 work, he narrowed his lens to focus on statements making the claim that all persons, whether Christians, Jews, or Muslims, could be saved in their respective faiths.[21] While others had included statements to this effect in their discussions of skepticism, Schwartz

---

[16]Ibid., 96, and see 115.

[17]Ibid., 114.

[18]This case has also been analyzed by Mercedes García-Arenal, "Mi padre moro, yo moro: The Inheritance of Belief in Early Modern Iberia," in *After Conversion: Iberia and the Emergence of Modernity*, ed. Mercedes García-Arenal (Leiden, 2016), 304–35.

[19]Griffiths, "Popular Religious Skepticism," 112.

[20]Ibid., 111.

[21]Stuart B. Schwartz, *All Can Be Saved: Religious Tolerance and Salvation in the Iberian Atlantic World* (New Haven, CN, 2008). Schwartz opened the book with recollection of his own

methodically amassed material from a wide variety of sources, emphasizing positive expressions of tolerance as well as vexed expressions of doubt. He underscored the fact that the discovery of "hundreds of cases of people who expressed some kind of attitude of religious tolerance, relativism, universalism, or skepticism" challenged existing scholarship on the history of toleration, which generally excluded early modern Spain and Portugal altogether.[22] Pointing once more to the Soria documents, which dated from the very early period of the Inquisition's activity, Schwartz suggested that the sentiments they contained, uttered by Old and New Christians alike, had their roots in "the long intimacy of medieval convivencia" during which the interaction of different religious cultures in Iberia, sometimes violent, produced notions of toleration.[23] "Multiple and competing claims to religious truth," he suggested, "might lead not to the fervor of the convert or the dissimulation of the forced adherent, but to skepticism and doubt about all faiths."[24] This echoes the remarks of the Latin scholar Francisco de Marcilla mentioned above, when he explained the origins of his own heterodox ideas, which incidentally included the idea that all could be saved.

Schwartz cited an additional possible stimulus to heterodox thinking in Iberia in the wake of the mass conversions. According to Schwartz, skeptical thinking might be aroused by competing religious claims, but it might also be aroused by disapproval of the persecutions perpetrated by Church and state—persecutions that, he argues, ran counter to the fundamental sense of justice and fairness of some Old Christians.[25] Schwartz explicitly dismissed the claim of scholars that skeptical and relativistic ideas about religion were an exclusive proclivity of conversos[26] and demonstrated that an Iberian current of tolerationist, skeptical, universalistic ideas—a consequence of long-term interactions among people of different faiths—cut across religioethnic boundaries.

Recently, Stefania Pastore, enriching the discussion, called for a revision of long-held ideas about the arc of skeptical and tolerationist thinking in European history as a whole. Pastore claimed that "long before Jean Bodin and Michel de Montaigne's Europe was ravaged by religious war, the paths of doubt and comparativism had already been trodden in a multiconfessional

---

surprise and delight years earlier when he first encountered in Ginzburg's famous account the opinion of Menocchio that salvation was possible in any religion; this led him to be alert later, as he worked in the archives of the Spanish Inquisition, to expressions similar to Menocchio's, expressed not only by "simple folk" but by clerics and educated laypersons as well. Ibid., 1.

[22] Schwartz, *All Can Be Saved*, 6.

[23] Ibid., 54.

[24] Ibid., 68.

[25] Ibid., 78–79, 84.

[26] Ibid., 60, 269 n. 63.

and multicultural Iberian world, which had had no other choice than to come to terms with the fact of multiple faiths and revelations."[27] Pastore argues that even before the burst of skeptical and tolerationist thinking in sixteenth-century Europe north of the Pyrenees, a phenomenon that scholars have routinely taken as a starting point in discussions of skepticism and toleration, such thinking had taken root in Iberia and could be found in educated Averroist circles in Italy. Eventually, conversos fleeing Spain introduced more popular forms of skepticism to Italy. Pastore argues that the multireligious climate of late medieval Iberia, with its rival religious traditions and its forced conversions, served as a veritable catalyst for doubt, raising troublesome questions for people across the social spectrum about the validity of competing faith claims. Pastore refers to this neglected story as "a 'southern way', an Iberian-Italian route that is still completely undiscovered."[28]

This is a bold claim, one complicated by the fact that Pastore sees in early Iberian expressions of religious skepticism and relativism the seeds of modernity, a term she uses in the sense of a sensibility or an outlook that emerged in the modern period. Pastore acknowledges that certain scholars *have* explored the Iberian roots of modern European thought. These are the scholars of "marranism" who have identified Iberian conversos as being the first bearers of a distinctly subjective, skeptical, conflicted consciousness.[29] Yet for such scholars, Pastore argues, Spain and Portugal are mainly the lands from which converso innovators *fled*; they do not figure as sites where native skeptical ideas were disseminated and cultivated.[30] However, the problem is not that the phenomenon of converso skepticism in Iberia has not been recognized by scholars of "marranism"—Stephen Gilman's *Spain of Fernando de Rojas*, for example, illuminates an entirely Spanish context[31]—but rather that this specialized field, focusing solely on conversos, has failed to address the phenomenon of cross-ethnic heterodox discourse in Iberia and, partly as a

---

[27]Stefania Pastore, "Doubt in Fifteenth-Century Iberia," in García-Arenal, *After Conversion*, 285.

[28]Pastore, "Doubt," 303.

[29]On the literature of "marranism," especially as it relates to subjectivity, see Miriam Bodian, "Américo Castro's Conversos and the Question of Subjectivity," *Culture & History Digital Journal* 6, no. 2 (2017): 2–3.

[30]Pastore, "Doubt," 284 n. 7. Here, Pastore is perhaps not entirely justified. Since the publication of Américo Castro's work, several scholars have taken an interest in currents of thinking among conversos that anticipate modernity both on Iberian soil and elsewhere. Probably the best-known work dealing with this phenomenon is Yirmiyahu Yovel, *The Other Within: The Marranos; Split Identity and Emerging Modernity* (Princeton, NJ, 2009), which deals quite extensively with Spain.

[31]Stephen Gilman, *The Spain of Fernando de Rojas: The Intellectual and Social Landscape of "La Celestina"* (Princeton, NJ, 1972).

      Springer

result of this, has not been integrated into the broader field of early modern Iberian religious history.

What Pastore and other scholars have shown with great clarity is that currents of belief and unbelief that were far more widely diffused than once thought converged and diverged in Iberian cultural space, oblivious to religioethnic boundaries or inquisitorial classifications. To be sure, Pastore too relies heavily on sources that bring to light Jewish/converso heterodoxy in particular, whether Averroism among late medieval Jews or skepticism among forced converts in fifteenth-century Castile. But her overall argument is that the very fact of living in a multireligious environment engendered doubt among Christians and Jews alike. "Doubt emerged," she writes, "in a mixed environment, where two religious confessions confronted one another and exchanged views." Expressions of doubt were not a *judeoconverso*/Jewish phenomenon but "a phenomenon that is heavily Spanish."[32]

While Pastore argues persuasively that converso skepticism colored the perceptions of some Old Christians, the impression she conveys of a Spanish society in which doubt was pervasive in all sectors is overly sweeping. Pastore here tends to cloud the important differences between the experience of conversos (and, later, moriscos) and the experience of Old Christians. "The traumas of fifteenth-century Spain," she writes, "the passage from the old law to the new, the forced conversions, and the breakup of a core identity based on community and religious membership, gave rise to a new way of living the phenomenon of faith, one which was unwittingly modern."[33]

One might think from this quotation that all Iberians experienced the "passage from the old law to the new" or the "breakup of a core identity." From a sociological, psychological, and religious perspective, however, the experience of the Jewish and Muslim converts differed radically from that of Old Christians. If we could return to the late fourteenth- and early fifteenth-century towns where forced conversions took place, we would be able to locate the sites of trauma rather specifically in the *juderías* and *morerías* of those towns. Elsewhere, men and women would have participated in civic and parish life much as they had before. Certainly the malaise and confusion among newly-converted Jews and Muslims had repercussions for Spanish Old Christians as well, especially as the converts began sitting in church pews alongside Old Christians, intermarrying with Old Christian families, and moving into occupations previously closed to them. But their discomfort was the mild discomfort of the hegemonic population. Conversos and moriscos were far more likely than Old Christians to engage in heterodox practices generally, since they were likely to remain attached to the traditions

---

[32]Pastore, "Doubt," 296.

[33]Ibid., 302.

they had been expected to abandon. This had to do not only with their ancestral loyalties, but also with the need to preserve self-esteem in the face of hostile Old Christian rhetoric and the statutes of *limpieza de sangre*. Surely it is important to acknowledge the experiential differences among converts and their descendants, on the one hand, and Old Christians, on the other, if we want to understand accurately the contours and dimensions of cross-ethnic heterodox discourse.

The notion that Iberian expressions of skepticism anticipated "modernity" is also problematic. Pastore suggests that the catalyst for the earliest expressions of a modern sensibility was the Iberian experience of facing competing and incompatible truth claims, coerced conversion, and religious persecution. But late medieval Iberia was not the first cultural space to witness such rupture and conflict. Might we not expect similar confusions and vacillations among, say, populations conquered by Islam in the seventh and eighth centuries, or among the forcibly baptized pagans of Kievan Rus' at the end of the tenth century? Might not people in those historical contexts have made witticisms about aspects of Muslim or Christian traditions they found absurd? That is, must doubt and confusion be modern? We will return to this issue further on.

In two wide-ranging and multifaceted contributions to this discussion, Mercedes García-Arenal sees the primary stimulus for Iberian expressions of religious skepticism (and indeed, utter unbelief) not in the mere reality of a multireligious environment, but in the forced conversions that came later.[34] Paradoxically, she notes, the attempt to eliminate religious difference through conversion served to create conditions that encouraged some people to view other faiths as genuine options. Not only did judaizing conversos and islamizing moriscos raise doubts about which faith was the "true" one; they triggered doubts about the truth of *any* sect. García-Arenal concluded:

> I have tried to show that an argument about conversion as engendering unbelief or irreligion was pertinent in Iberia at the end of the fifteenth century and throughout the sixteenth. The documents that have been examined here show how the contemporary concept of atheism as used by [Jerónimo] Gracián, which deals with people who are doubtful, perplexed or detached from religion and follow their own opinion (who verge, in fact, on "libertinism"), also included a more modern understanding of atheism, the absence of faith in any religion.[35]

---

[34] García-Arenal, "'Mi padre moro," 304–35; eadem, "What Faith to Believe? Vacillation, Comparativism, and Doubt," in *From Doubt to Unbelief: Forms of Scepticism in the Iberian World*, ed. Mercedes García-Arenal and Stefania Pastore (Cambridge, UK, 2019), 53–72.

[35] García-Arenal, "What Faith to Believe?" 56.

García-Arenal's marshalling of examples is impressive, especially as she brings moriscos into a scholarly conversation from which they have been mostly absent. Given the accumulation of evidence, the relationship between forced conversion and religious doubt in early modern Iberia now seems indisputable. Yet some of the material García-Arenal adduces raises an important question. Are we dealing in all of the instances cited with a single phenomenon that can accurately be termed "doubt" or "unbelief"?

In general, when dealing with statements reported to or elicited by the Inquisition, interpretation can be tricky. For example, García-Arenal describes the case of a morisco from Granada who in 1575 found himself engaged in conversation with Old Christians who sought to convince him of the benefits of papal bulls and indulgences for souls in Purgatory. This effort at indoctrination made the morisco angry and, according to an Inquisition witness, he responded "that he did not believe in God or in Saint Mary ... nor did he believe in the articles of faith; he believed in nothing, nothing, nothing."[36] Perhaps this was an expression of religious nihilism, as García-Arenal interpreted it. But perhaps what the morisco intended to say, if indeed the remark was reported accurately, was that he believed nothing *of what the Church taught*. Perhaps an overeager witness embellished the statement by adding unbelief in God to unbelief in Saint Mary. Or perhaps this was just an impulsive, defiant remark. As Monsalvo Antón and others have pointed out, angry blasphemous statements about the existence of God were common and might simply reflect momentary rage, rather than a condition of nagging existential doubt. We simply do not know enough about this morisco's thinking to draw conclusions.

Another example of such apparent ambiguity is the report of a dinner conversation in 1459 among four conversos in Calatayud. After a long debate about Christian versus Jewish law, these men were reported to have said, "We know not which of them is better; let us do what is right, for he who does right will do well."[37] Given that the men had been debating at length, it seems unlikely that they had no stake in the doctrinal differences between Christianity and Judaism. Perhaps at the end of the evening they *did* conclude that they were left suspended in a state of doubt. But perhaps they wanted to end the evening on a conciliatory note and set aside doctrine to stress a common shared notion of practical morality—an irenic approach that, then

---

[36]"El Reo había respondido con enojo que no creya en Dios ni en Santa María ... ni creya en los artículos de la fee ni en nada, nada, nada." AHN, Inquisición, leg. 2022, caja 1, exp. 20.

[37]"No sabemos qual dellas es la mejor; fagamos bien que quien bien fará bien habrá." See Encarnación Marín Padilla, *Relación judeoconversa durante la segunda mitad del siglo XV en Aragón: La Ley* (Madrid, 1988), 85. (The source: Archivo de la Real Audiencia Territorial de Zaragoza, leg. 12, no. 2, fol. 26: Bartolomé de Cetina, January 18, 1489, Calatayud.)

as now, was one way of dealing with religious difference. Such an approach did not entail unbelief, but rather a more capacious belief.

The common saying that "each can be saved in his own law" is equally ambiguous. Clearly this remark has meaning only in an environment in which multiple religious traditions are present. But it cannot be assumed automatically that a remark of this kind "contains a dose of relativism and detachment from established religion," or that it "had an impact on the very concept of religion because of the skepticism it entails."[38] To be sure, any such statement contradicts the Catholic doctrine "*extra Ecclesiam nulla salus.*" Yet it need not reflect generalized skepticism or relativism about Catholicism or religion. It might be no more than a repudiation of this *particular* Church doctrine (and its cruel consequences)—heretical, to be sure, but not radical.

That tolerationist discourse need not imply a relativistic perspective can be illustrated by the classic rabbinic view that non-Jews could be saved in their own law, as long as they fulfilled certain basic precepts.[39] Might this have informed the opinion of conversos who echoed the saying that "each can be saved"? For moriscos, too, the fact that Islam recognized both the Hebrew Bible and the New Testament as semi-sacred books might have rendered Judaism and Christianity semi-legitimate, so to speak. This might have encouraged some moriscos to adhere to one of the "Muhammadan errors" cited by the Valencian ecclesiastic Gaspar de Escolano, namely, "believing that although our law is good and holy, so is theirs and that of the Jews, and that all are saved who keep to them."[40]

In general, we cannot assume that people in early modern Iberia were either entirely orthodox believers or radical religious skeptics. There is enormous territory between the two. The efforts of men and women to deal with cognitive dissonance in their complex religious environments have historically taken manifold forms. In general, however, people tend not to be overly fastidious about what they believe. They brush off fine points of theology and arrive at patterns of thought they can live with. If tolerationist beliefs look like relativism or skepticism to us, that may have to do with the lens we are using, especially if we are in search of the roots of modernity. This is not to say that doubt and alienation from the Church had no place in Iberian life. They clearly did, as the now-copious documentation surely demonstrates. But it is hard to squeeze nuance out of Inquisition documents, and interpretive caution seems in order.

---

[38] García-Arenal, "Mi padre moro," 312–13.

[39] On these precepts, known as the Noahide Laws, see the two somewhat contrasting views of David Novak, *Natural Law in Judaism* (Cambridge, UK, 1998), 149–64, and Christine Hayes, *What's Divine About Divine Law? Early Perspectives* (Princeton, NJ, 2015), 328–70.

[40] García-Arenal, "Mi padre moro," 313–14.

Unanswered Questions

Even if we take a cautious approach to the sources scholars have unearthed, the discovery of popular religious heterodoxy among significant numbers of Iberians of *all* religioethnic backgrounds has fundamentally altered our perception of the religious landscape of early modern Spain and Portugal. It is simply no longer possible to view the post-Tridentine Iberian Peninsula as a stronghold of orthodoxy except in isolated pockets of judaizers, moriscos, and *alumbrados*. A plausible argument has been made that the long conflictual history of three faiths in the Iberian Peninsula generated religious questioning of a kind not found anywhere else in Europe before the sixteenth century. Yet even if it is only at a later point—after the mass conversions of Jews and Muslims and after the establishment of the Inquisition—that we have satisfactory evidence about popular heterodoxy, this evidence tells us something important. In fact, religious confusion, vacillation, and heterodoxy were not an exclusively New Christian phenomenon; they crossed religious and ethnic boundaries and were part of a more fluid discourse critical of Church teachings than could once have been imagined.

Yet as with any new direction of scholarly exploration, the current state of research leaves many questions unanswered. In my view, five issues in particular need to be addressed further. First is the question of Iberian exceptionalism. Does the evidence support the argument that Iberian lands were a singular breeding ground for religious skepticism of a kind that would appear only later, with the onset of the Reformation, elsewhere in Europe? One of the problems with this argument is that the bulk of the evidence for popular heterodox beliefs in Spain and Portugal comes from Inquisition files. These files constitute an unparalleled source of material about what ordinary men and women were thinking—rural agricultural workers, urban artisans, sailors, and servants, as well as scholars, merchants, nuns, and nobles. No such mother lode of evidence exists for non-Iberian lands in early modern Europe—with the partial exception of Italy.

Italy did not have a history of interreligious contact and conflict comparable to that in Spain and Portugal, nor did it ever have a large population of forcibly converted Jews or Muslims. Yet it *did* produce a wide array of radical skeptics and other religious heretics.[41] One might argue that Italy, as a Mediterranean land with a population of Jews (including ex-conversos) and

---

[41] On heterodox thought in early modern Italy see, inter alia, Ronald K. Delph, Michelle Fontaine, and John Jeffries Martin, eds., *Heresy, Culture, and Religion in Early Modern Italy: Contexts and Contestations* (Kirksville, MO, 2006); for bibliography, see William Hudon's review article, "Religion and Society in Early Modern Italy: Old Questions, New Insights," *American Historical Review* 101 (1996): 797–801.

with deep connections to North Africa and the Ottoman Empire, was "exceptional" in the same way Iberian lands were. As mentioned above, John Edwards noted the similarity of the heresies of the miller Menocchio in Italy, on the one hand, and Bartolomé Sánchez in Castile, on the other.[42] Scholars seem in agreement that these two cultural spaces each had distinct sources of skepticism: in Spain, the profoundly conflictual religious environment; in Italy, the engagement (at least of an intellectual elite) with Greek and Latin sources. Yet the lively intellectual traffic between Spain and Italy eroded the differences. That is to say, the tangled web of heterodoxy in Iberia and the tangled web of heterodoxy in Italy were themselves entangled with one another. It is no accident that the Castilian author and Catholic reformer Juan de Valdés (ca. 1490–1541) found such fertile soil for his unorthodox ideas in Naples.

At the same time, it is evident that Spain and Italy were penetrated by heretical ideas (both Erasmian and Protestant) coming from the north, as the case of Juan de Valdés also demonstrates.[43] Marcel Bataillon's magisterial work *Érasme et l'Espagne* (1937) long ago shattered any notion that the Reformation stopped at the Pyrenees and Italian Alps.[44] The question remains, however, whether it is at all possible to draw conclusions about the prevalence (or lack thereof) of popular heterodoxy in the "north," since we lack the kind of evidence about popular religious ideas in that region that we have for Italy and Iberia. This absence of evidence alone renders claims about Iberian exceptionalism problematic.

The second issue is the question of Iberian skepticism and modernity. For various reasons—including the dissemination of the so-called "Black Legend"—Iberian lands have long been regarded as a backwater that lacked the creative ferment of other early modern European societies. That view has been somewhat corrected by the work of scholars, including some scholars discussed in this essay. Yet there is a problem, I think, in seeing an equivalence between the pithy, often slogan-like statements recorded by the Inquisition and the elaborate, systematic, and sophisticated texts that were disseminated elsewhere in print or manuscript. Let us consider this sweeping passage

---

[42]Edwards, "Religious Faith," 22.

[43]As Massimo Firpo put it in his evaluation of Juan de Valdés, "Italian Valdesianism, the heir of a complex religious tradition in which Erasmianism, *alumbradismo*, and Lutheranism come together in a subtle doctrinal synthesis, constitutes, also through the northern emigration of certain of its adherents, a fundamental element for understanding the religious crisis of the sixteenth century." See Massimo Firpo, "The Italian Reformation and Juan de Valdés," *Sixteenth Century Journal* 27 (1996): 353. On this topic see also, idem, *Juan de Valdés and the Italian Reformation* (London, 2016).

[44]Marcel Bataillon, *Érasme et l'Espagne: Recherches sur l'histoire spirituelle du XVIe siècle; Recherches sur l'histoire spirituelle du XVIe siècle* (Paris, 1937). An expanded edition appeared in 1966 in Spanish.

by Stefania Pastore, suggesting the possible need for a revision of the way we imagine modernity to have come into being:

> We are used to seeing in Montaigne, in the reflections of Sébastien Castellion or in the drastic solution put into practice by Bodin, the roots of the history of doubt and tolerance, of the path to modernity taken by a West that is faced for the first time with a divided Christianity and a multi-confessional society.... Long before Jean Bodin and Michel de Montaigne's Europe was ravaged by religious war, the paths of doubt and comparativism had already been trodden in a multi-confessional and multi-cultural Iberian world, which had had no other choice than to come to terms with the fact of multiple faiths and revelations.[45]

It is true that scholars have often seemed to ignore the rich lode of heterodox and skeptical thinking in late medieval and early modern Iberia. But while Iberians lived in a religiously conflictive world long before northern Europeans experienced irresolvable religious conflict, this does not necessarily mean that Iberians were developing recognizably "modern" ideas or ideas that were equivalent in their scope and intellectual power to those of Castellio, Montaigne, or Bodin. It is undoubtedly true that a religiously fractured late medieval Iberian environment stimulated new ways of thinking about religious truth. But by the early modern period, radical or heterodox ideas could circulate in Iberian lands only in rudimentary oral form; they could not be elaborated in learned essays, disseminated in manuscript, contested, revised, and built on. This is not to say that prohibited books were never smuggled into Spain and Portugal or that visitors to Madrid or Lisbon from northern lands never discussed with local residents what was happening in Paris or Amsterdam. But those who lived in the orbit of the Inquisition had little chance of engaging with radical new conceptions in a free and sustained way.

Does it matter that heterodox currents in Spain and Italy probably nourished the early careers of complex thinkers like Miguel Servetus and Giordano Bruno? From a biographical perspective, yes. But these men could not have developed and spread their beliefs if they had lived out their lives in Spain, Portugal, or Italy. Likewise, the young Amsterdam Jew Isaac de Castro Tartas would not have been able to make his rather sophisticated arguments for religious toleration before the Lisbon tribunal in the 1640s had his parents not left their native Bragança and had he not been raised and educated in France and the Netherlands.[46] As with other emigres of converso origin,

---

[45] Pastore, "Doubt," 283–85.

[46] See Miriam Bodian, "The Geography of Conscience: A Seventeenth-Century Atlantic Jew and the Inquisition," *Journal of Modern History* 89 (2017): 247–81.

Castro's ideas matured in an environment where tolerationist ideas were debated rather openly and where the sustained intellectual enterprise that we associate with modernity was being launched.

This is not to minimize the importance of the various currents and crosscurrents of Iberian heterodox thought that have been explored so fruitfully in recent decades. The unearthing of bold, dissenting voices south of the Pyrenees has without question brought the Iberian story into deeper conversation with that in the rest of Europe. Further exploration and analysis hopefully will integrate Spain and Portugal more fully into ongoing debate about the emergence of modernity.

Third, there is the question of causation. The discussion continues today about the constellation of factors that generated so much doubt about Church teaching or the truth of Christianity itself. What role did Averroistic notions with origins in the Muslim world play? While the dimensions of late medieval Averroistic currents in the Iberian Peninsula are difficult to assess, vestiges of Averroism are quite evident in certain popular expressions of unbelief well into the early modern period. Was the simple existence of competing truth claims in the Iberian environment the major trigger for religious doubts? To be sure, there were Jews elsewhere in Europe, if not Muslims; but their numbers were smaller than in Spain and Portugal, and their social segregation far greater. Or was the key factor the mass conversions of Jews and Muslims in Spain and Portugal? These conversions created conditions in Iberia so different from anything earlier, with countless people experiencing profound psychic and spiritual disorder, that they seem a likely catalyst for religious doubts of various sorts. Mercedes García-Arenal is surely on firm ground when she argues that the key factor in the generation of doubt was not the mere *existence* of multiple religions—which has been a fact of life in many historical contexts—but, rather, the mass conversions.

These conversions entailed, among other things, a breakdown of the boundaries separating Iberia's religioethnic populations. The boundaries had been maintained by legal and institutional means, by polemical attacks, and by the exclusive bonds of intimacy within each distinct community. Scholars have discussed at length the trauma that the forced conversions entailed for the converts. Less obvious is the fact that there were also consequences for *Old* Christians, something that has just begun to be explored.[47] With the expansion of the activity of the inquisitions, Old Christians learned to recognize and reflect on a variety of "other" beliefs, as they listened to edicts of faith, auto-da-fé sermons, and rumor. What their converso neighbors were doing on Friday night suddenly became important and interesting. Griffiths may have a point that post-Tridentine indoctrination played a role in provoking

---

[47] Mercedes García-Arenal explores this in her article in this issue.

  Springer

skepticism about Church teaching; but the Church was also, despite itself, exposing Old Christians in this period to a variety of alternative teachings. Moreover, not every Old Christian found the spectacle of autos-da-fé inspiring, or saw burnings at the stake as a fulfillment of divine justice. For some Old Christians, the Inquisition's heavy-handed rhetoric of mercy, alongside its harshness and cruelty, sparked internal conflict and even articulated opposition.[48]

Surprisingly, in the discussion of the various ways in which heterodox thinking may have been provoked there has been only limited discussion of the impact of repression and persecution on those most directly affected. Yet there is ample evidence that inquisitorial punishment not only disturbed the thoughts of some untouched observers, but destabilized the beliefs of victims as well. Once arrested, suspects were kept for long periods in their cells, where they were forced in on their own thoughts. The stresses of imprisonment, interrogation, lack of information, and the expectation of punishment could lead to depression and hopelessness. The situation was made more acute by the prisoners' isolation from the social institutions and emotional bonds of fellowship that serve to validate and ground religion in everyday life. It should not be surprising that long-term imprisonment on charges of heresy sometimes bred new heresy. Let me enumerate some of my own findings that, given the focus of my research, involve conversos.

An anonymous rhymester in early seventeenth-century Amsterdam noted an occurrence among Iberian conversos who were wrongly accused of judaizing. He described the fate of these conforming Catholics in this way: "The upright soul becomes a criminal here, / Swearing to words and deeds that never were. / Here such tricks are played, and clever abuse, / That Christians are converted into Jews."[49] The author presumably expected his readers to take delight in his little verse because it reflected a recognizable reality: namely, that conversos who adhered to Catholic teaching, when imprisoned for judaizing, could actually be driven to judaize. While a single such source might seem less than compelling, the recurrence of the theme suggests a widely known phenomenon. Stuart Schwartz noted the case of a New Christian who condemned the inquisitors as unscrupulous men whose goal was the confiscation of property. He said that "he had entered in the Inquisition

---

[48] As mentioned, Stuart Schwartz has discussed several cases in which Old Christians criticized the cruelty of the Inquisition and expressed sympathy for New Christians. See Schwartz, *All Can Be Saved*, 106–7.

[49] Miriam Bodian, *Hebrews of the Portuguese Nation: Conversos and Community in Early Modern Amsterdam* (Bloomington, IN, 1997), 78–79. The original Portuguese: "Aqui se faz o justo criminozo, / Jurando o que não viu, nem foy soñado, / Aquy se fazem trassas e ardis seus, / Que os Christãos se convertem em Judeos." Herman Prins Salomon, *Portrait of a New Christian: Fernão Álvares Melo, 1569–1632* (Paris 1982), xiv.

as a good Christian, and now he was the biggest Jew in the world."[50] Similarly, an ex-converso who settled in Amsterdam in 1660 wrote of "the many imprisoned for observing the Law of Moses who had never done so"; such persons, imprisoned, tried and impoverished by the Inquisition, "confessed to things they had never done," an experience that caused some of them to change heart and become "perfect Jews."[51]

Inquisitorial persecution was a factor that led even a few disenchanted Old Christian Catholics to openly and defiantly adhere to the Law of Moses. In two cases of Old Christian judaizing—that of the Capuchin friar Diogo d'Assumpção and that of the Hebrew scholar Lope de Vera—such a mechanism seems to have been at play.[52] Iberian crypto-Judaism was present throughout the Peninsula and was the most readily accessible counter-theology to Catholicism. This may help explain the astonishing ease with which the fervent university-educated judaizer Francisco Maldonado de Silva, escaping from his cell by fashioning a rope from corn husks and proclaiming a fresh, energetic, Bible-centered, counter-Catholic creed, reportedly managed to persuade two prisoners whose cell he entered "to follow his Law."[53] Likewise, an Old Christian friar placed in the cell of the converso judaizer Luis Carvajal was persuaded by his charismatic cellmate to convert to the Law of Moses. (Two years later the friar was actually tried and punished as a judaizer.[54]) At least temporarily, ardent judaizers like Maldonado de Silva and Carvajal offered hope and purpose to dispirited prisoners. Still, it is testimony to the often unrecognized fluidity of belief in the Iberian Peninsula that these Old Christians were open to accepting an officially vilified religion.

Cases like these suggest that inquisitorial imprisonment could itself lead to conversion and, paradoxical as it might seem, could be a catalyst for a radical rethinking of habitual orthodox beliefs. It could lead to a shift in religious loyalties, as illustrated above, but it could also lead to despair, doubt, and skepticism. An interesting case in point is that of the New Christian merchant Diogo Lopes Pinhanços, who died at the stake in 1571. A century later, Pinhanços was hailed as a crypto-Jewish martyr in a Portuguese-Jewish apologetic work, presumably because he was known to have been a judaizer by his contemporaries and initially confessed to judaizing in his trial. However, after a wrenching set of audiences in which he became hopelessly entangled

---

[50] Schwartz, *All Can Be Saved*, 106.

[51] B. N. Teensma, "Fragmenten uit het amsterdamse convoluut van Abraham Idaña, alias Gaspar Méndez Arroyo (1623–1690)," *Studia Rosenthaliana* 11 (1977): 153.

[52] Miriam Bodian, *Dying in the Law of Moses: Crypto-Jewish Martyrdom in the Iberian World* (Bloomington, IN, 2007), 79–116, 153–77. Lope de Vera, it seems, also toyed mentally with Islam as an option.

[53] Bodian, *Dying in the Law*, 135–37.

[54] Bodian, *Dying in the Law*, 62–65.

as he sought to save members of his family against whom he had previously informed, he declared his conclusion that "there was no God in heaven." He persisted in this stance for eight months, apparently up to his death at the stake, saying that he regretted everything he had done to try to gain salvation and everything he had done in the name of God.[55]

I certainly do not mean to echo the "Black Legend" image of Spain as *the* land of persecution in early modern Europe. Religious persecution was a fact of life everywhere in Europe, and Iberian responses were not unique. Carsten Wilke has recently pointed to the similarity of skeptical ideation among both French libertines and Iberian New Christians, arguing that this coincidence was likely due not to direct connections, but rather to the "experience of marginality, persecution, and abrupt changes of allegiance" endured by both groups.[56] As the independent discovery of calculus by Newton and Leibniz famously illustrates, people living in different environments may produce similar sets of new ideas because they are living in the same broad intellectual climate. In any event, with the unearthing of further Iberian voices in the future, it may be possible to integrate Spain and Portugal more fully into the scholarly mapping of early modern European opposition to religious repression.

The fourth issue has to do with the relationship between expressions of doubt and the emergence of new forms of certainty. Competing religious truths, forced conversions, and religious repression were among the factors that fostered religious doubt. But as these doubts arose, they provoked a search for certainty on new, more secure foundations. Too great a scholarly focus on the phenomenon of doubt can obscure the important concomitant emergence of intense, fervent, "invincible" belief, sometimes fueled by persecution, seemingly immune to challenges, and maintained, in some cases, to the point of martyrdom.

Since doubt drives the search for certainty, anxious doubt and firm new belief cannot be easily disengaged. Both doubt and the search for secure truth entail a process of detachment from an unquestioning, tradition-rooted religious outlook. Both the doubters and the seekers in early modern Iberia had to one degree or another lost confidence in existing structures of religious authority. Both doubters and seekers at times looked across established religioethnic boundaries for spiritual support. We find, for example, that the passionate judaizer Luis Carvajal and the heterodox Old Christian hermit Gregorio López forged a spiritual friendship based on a literalist and historicist reading of the Hebrew Bible/Old Testament, a reading that among other

---

[55] Bodian, *Dying in the Law*, 42–45.

[56] Carsten Wilke, "'That Devilish Invention Called Faith': Seventeenth-Century Free-Thought and its Use in Sephardi Apologetics," in *Conversos, Marrani e Nuove Comunità ebraiche in età moderna*, ed. Myriam Silvera (Florence, 2015), 133–37.

things supported their shared apocalyptic expectations and rejection of image worship.[57]

If literal biblicism was an increasingly popular anchor of faith, so was the idea that all human beings were endowed with the capacity to apprehend a universal natural law—not the marginal, deficient natural law of Aquinas, but the emerging notion of a robust expression of God's will implanted in every human being. When the Old Christian Latin student Francisco de Marcilla came before the Inquisition in 1609 with nagging doubts about Church teaching, including the divinity of Christ, he expressed his opinion that the surest measure of truth was "natural law."[58]

The conviction that natural law provided a moral and theological north star was also firmly fixed in the mind of the Old Christian Hebraist Lope de Vera. This young man, who was burned at the stake for judaizing in 1644, asserted that Judaism and Islam were more "in conformity with natural reason" than the teachings of the Church.[59] In his case as in others, heterodox leanings brought him into conversation with others who lived in the shadows. He shared his rationalistic ideas with a fellow student at the University of Salamanca whom he described as "Portuguese" and a crypto-Jew, who may have persuaded him to take a more serious interest in Judaism.[60] The two agreed, among other things, that religions contrary to "*el precepto y bendición natural*" were pernicious. The case of Lope de Vera nicely illustrates the role of the Inquisition in precipitating a psychic shift toward certainty: this prisoner's trajectory from a state of vacillation and doubt to a posture of defiant judaizing martyrdom is clear even from the limited documentation of his trial.[61]

The proliferation of forms of interior spirituality was another reflection of the striving for religious certainty. For those who were conflicted about (or antagonistic toward) the institutions and rituals of the Church, turning inward could provide an alternative, or at least a viable compromise. The sixteenth century saw a burst of interest in a more intimate religiosity throughout Europe. In Iberia, echoes of this trend can be found in the thinking of certain

---

[57]Bodian, *Dying in the Law*, 57–58.

[58]Griffiths, "Popular Religious Skepticism," 110–12; see also García-Arenal, "Mi padre moro," 332–33; eadem, "What Faith to Believe?" García-Arenal mentions two other cases in which natural law was invoked, "Mi padre moro," 330–31.

[59]Bodian, *Dying in the Law*, 158.

[60]On Lope's discussions with this student as well as with a Portuguese physician, also surely a converso, see Bodian, *Dying in the Law*, 159–63.

[61]We have only annual trial summaries sent to the Suprema. On Lope de Vera, see Bodian, *Dying in the Law*, 153–77, and Kenneth Brown, ed., *De la cárcel inquisitorial a la sinagoga de Amsterdam* (*Edición y estudio del "Romance a Lope de Vera" de Antonio Enríquez Gómez*) (La Mancha, 2007).

judaizers and *luteranos*, but it is most conspicuous in the words and actions of the so-called *alumbrados*, sixteenth-century Catholics who were accused of overstepping the bounds of Catholic orthodoxy. It is abundantly clear that those accused of *alumbradismo* followed diverse and often incompatible trajectories. Yet the fact that the great majority of them suffered the stigma of Jewish ancestry suggests common psychic origins. Stefania Pastore has shown compellingly how anguish caused by the Spanish Church's suspicion and stigmatization of New Christians propelled many of them toward an anti-institutional, egalitarian conception of the Church and a radical Pauline quest for inner "perfection."[62]

The search for certainty, in its different manifestations, was of course not a phenomenon unique to the Iberian Peninsula. In Reformation Europe as a whole, religious doubt and alienation in the face of irresolvable religious dilemmas often led to a creative process of exploration and reintegration.[63] What I want to underscore is that the search for new certainties was as much a part of Iberia's entrance into a new European age as were expressions of doubt and skepticism. The cultivation of subjective religious consciousness, for example, was to have far-reaching and powerful consequences, not least for the debate on toleration. A balanced reevaluation of the intellectual and religious contours of early modern Spain and Portugal, eschewing the simplistic view that religious faith and "modernity" are somehow antithetical, should include a nuanced analysis of the full range of shifting religious perspectives.

Fifth, and finally, is the question of the dimensions of heterodoxy. What does the discovery of widespread popular expressions of doubt and dissent say about the faith and practice of the Iberian population as a whole? Inquisitorial records have shed unparalleled light on the religious lives of ordinary men and women in Iberian lands. Scholars continue to scour them for new material. But just as it is difficult to draw conclusions about the life of a city from its police records, it is problematic to try to wrest from Inquisition material an impression of the religious landscape of early modern Spain and Portugal. It seems reasonable to assume that most early modern Spaniards and Portuguese respected the authority and sanctity of the Church, the Inquisition, and the clergy. For some, the fear of punishment for deviation from orthodoxy only reinforced a reverence for authority; indeed, this was the effect that autos-da-fé were designed to produce. In any case it seems evident

---

[62] On the *alumbrados* there is a considerable literature. See, recently, Stefania Pastore, *Una herejía española: Conversos, alumbrados e Inquisición (1449–1559)* (Madrid, 2010) and bibliography there.

[63] On this topic see Susan Elizabeth Schreiner, *Are You Alone Wise? The Search for Certainty in the Early Modern Era* (Oxford, 2011).

that most people have little interest in complex issues of ideology and theology. Unless led firmly by a charismatic oppositional leader—an impossibility in lands under inquisitorial control—the inclination of most would have been to muddle through, avoiding significant risks and conforming until it became second nature.

Again, this is not to diminish the importance of identifying and analyzing instances of dissent and resistance. They offer a much-needed correction to deep-seated ideas about early modern Iberian religious life. To be sure, what lies behind the expressions of heterodox opinion recorded by notaries of the Inquisition is usually unknowable. Often enough we learn about a suspected person nothing more than a reported phrase or two, or a few reported behaviors. The difficulties presented by Inquisition testimony, the limited preservation of Inquisition documents, the uneven practices of tribunals over time and space, and the lack of more than a very small number of texts actually authored by persons with heterodox opinions, means that the actual extent of popular dissatisfaction with Church teaching is likely to remain a mystery.

A word by way of conclusion. Even if there is no good way to assess the dimensions of heterodox thought, we do now know that confining analysis to one or another of the categories of heresy established by the Holy Office—categories that have been defining for generations of scholars—serves to conceal the existence of intersecting pathways of heterodox discourse in Iberian lands. Research in recent years has begun to elucidate some of the connections. The evidence of the formation of these connections is testimony to the inventiveness of men and women living under a repressive regime, cautiously sharing ideas across apparent barriers, learning from each other's behaviors, and unwittingly creating a hidden ecosystem of dissent. Yet the picture is still only impressionistic. A more fine-grained picture will not be produced without further research in the vast archives of the inquisitions.

Publisher's Note Springer Nature remains neutral with regard to jurisdictional claims in published maps and institutional affiliations.

Jewish History (2021) 35: 351–377
https://doi.org/10.1007/s10835-021-09413-3

Rabbi Isaac of Rus' and His Esoteric Teachings

ALEXANDER KULIK

Department of Russian and Slavic Studies, Hebrew University of Jerusalem, Jerusalem, Israel
E-mail: kulik@mail.huji.ac.il

Accepted: 4 September 2020 / Published online: 10 September 2021

Abstract The paper focuses on the enigmatic thirteenth-century figure of R. Isaac of Rus'. A case study in the reconstruction of early East European Jewish history, it tests an integrative approach that brings together different types of evidence and disciplinary methods, while involving some new or neglected sources. Also examined are connections between Rabbi Isaac's esoteric teachings and those of Ḥasidei Ashkenaz and related themes in contemporary and subsequent rabbinic literature.

Keywords Eastern Europe · Kabbalah · Middle Ages · Mysticism · Isaac of Rus' · Ḥasidei Ashkenaz

לזכר מורי ורבי המקובל הגדול ר' מיכאל שניידר זצ"ל

Most of the evidence indicating the existence of a Jewish population in Eastern Europe prior to the mass migration from the German lands pertains specifically to territories inhabited by East Slavs. In particular, most of the known records are connected to the southwestern principalities of Rus'. Here a Jewish presence is attested as early as the tenth century and may go back to Jewish settlement in the cities of western Khazaria, i.e., in the territory of Kievan Rus' prior to its political formation. Evidence concerning the presence of Jews in Rus' after the Mongol invasions of the 1240s and up to the end of the fourteenth century becomes even more restricted geographically. The known sources from the time of the Mongol invasion on pertain almost exclusively to the territories of Halych-Volhynia, which suffered comparatively less from the invasion.

The historical evidence of a Jewish presence in Rus' during the Middle Ages has been preserved in extremely diverse sources mainly composed outside the region itself. Although modern scholarship often tends to neglect the cultural specificity of early East European Jews—regarding them as offspring of the Jews of Ashkenaz[1]—analyzing this disparate evidence sometimes permits us to identify a unique cultural reality unattested elsewhere. The specific

---

Chapter 6 was originally published as Kulik, A. Jewish History (2021) 35: 351–377. https://doi.org/10.1007/s10835-021-09413-3.

[1] See, for example, Bernard D. Weinryb, "The Beginnings of East-European Jewry in Legend and Historiography," in *Studies and Essays in Honor of Abraham A. Neumann*, ed. Meir

or peculiar cultural characteristics of this group still await a thorough investigation. In this microhistorical study I will focus on one case that, in addition to its historical value (accentuated by the poor state of documentation in this field), enables us to raise methodological questions regarding the reconstruction of early East European Jewish history. Since this reconstruction is based primarily on West European evidence, which has been preserved to a much greater extent, the results may also add new data for our understanding of the relations between Eastern and Western Europe in this period.

Our starting point is connected to the curious fact that upon review of the scant evidence regarding an early Jewish presence in early medieval Eastern Europe,[2] one cannot overlook the phenomenon of a disproportionate number of personae called *Isaac*, especially among Jews residing in or originating from Rus'. Among the forty-four named Jews (including fifteen patronyms) in the extant documents related to Rus' from the tenth to the fourteenth centuries, eight are named Isaac (Yitzhak).[3] Most of these belong to the late twelfth or thirteenth century, and in this narrower period the proportion is even more striking: of twelve persons known by name, six are called Isaac.

This name, of course, was also quite popular in Ashkenaz and elsewhere; but the extent of its popularity in Rus' during a single lifespan is remarkable. This circumstance prompts us to look for an alternative explanation and to raise the question of whether all or at least some of these Isaacs could be simply one and the same person.

Pinpointing each of these name-bearers chronologically and geographically may help to corroborate or eliminate this possibility. Criteria of time and place may not always be very reliable, however, taking into account the largely conjectural and relative dating of the majority of our evidence as well as the extraordinary mobility shown by medieval Jews—especially those hailing from Rus'. From the eleventh to the early fourteenth centuries Jews from Rus' are attested in the widest possible range of locations, including Byzantium, Germany, France, Spain, Italy, Sicily, Mallorca, and England.[4]

Ben-Horin, Bernard D. Weinryb, and Solomon Zeitlin (Leiden, 1962), 445–502; idem, "The Myth of Samuel of Russia, 12th Century Author of a Bible Commentary (A Study in Jewish Historiography)," *Jewish Quarterly Review* 57 (1967): 528–43; Israel M. Ta-Shma, "On the History of the Jews in Twelfth- and Thirteenth-Century Poland," trans. David Louvish, *Polin* 10 (1997): 287–317.

[2] For purposes of periodization of East European Jewish history, I would loosely define this period as commencing with the earliest known evidence of Jewish presence in the East Slavic areas in the tenth century and continuing up to the beginning of documented Jewish settlement in the Grand Duchy of Lithuania at the very end of the fourteenth century.

[3] For these numbers I rely on the corpus of all known evidence attesting to Jews in Old Rus', to be published in Alexander Kulik, *Jews in Old Rus': A Documentary History* (Cambridge, MA, forthcoming).

[4] On this, see Alexander Kulik, "Jews from Rus' in Medieval England," *Jewish Quarterly Review* 102 (2012): 371–403, esp. 375–76.

An additional consideration that may help to refine the result is that our sources mostly belong to rabbinic literature. This type of literature tends to mention by name those responsible for learned opinions or transmitted traditions, in accordance with the noble tannaitic principle encouraging correct reference: "One who cites his source, mentioning him by name, brings redemption to the world" (M. Abot 6:6). Frequently a person's name accompanies a saying attributed to him. In consequence, the content of the traditions or teachings ascribed to our Isaac(s) may also be of help, if we are able to extract material information about the author or connect it to other sources.

Below I attempt an integrative approach that brings together all of these methods and types of evidence while also involving some new or neglected sources referring to Isaac (or Isaacs) of Rus.[5] Our task, therefore, is threefold, including efforts to: (a) reconstruct R. Isaac's prosopography from all extant evidence; (b) analyze his/their teachings whenever available; and (c) on the basis of these data, seek to determine if or when we are dealing with the same or different persons. The structure of the following analysis is conditioned by these interconnected tasks. I begin by analyzing each of the sources without presupposing any common historical framework (but with historical comments where they seem plausible) and then proceed to suggest some more general conclusions.

"This and not any other organ"

The following commentary purporting to reveal the true reasons for circumcision and ascribed to R. Isaac of Chernigov has never previously been included in a discussion of Jews in Rus'. It appears in a kabbalistic essay on circumcision known in two manuscripts of Ashkenazi kabbalistic anthologies dating from the fifteenth century.[6]

Due to the uniqueness of the source and significant discrepancies in wording, we present both versions in full:

---

[5] Some of the primary sources collected below in support of the argument have been treated in Kulik, "Jews from Rus'," in connection with the presence of East European Jews in medieval England. That discussion is significantly updated here with crucial new evidence.

[6] BnF, Paris, MS hebr. 843 (Ashkenazi script, fifteenth century) and Vatican Apostolic Library, MS ebr. 236 (Ashkenazi script, fifteenth century). The fragment was published in Daniel Abrams, "Traces of the Lost Commentary to the Book of Creation by R. Jacob ben Jacob ha-Kohen: An Edition of a Commentary to the Book of Creation Based upon the Earliest Kabbalistic Manuscript" [in Hebrew], *Kabbalah* 2 (1997): 311–42 (see esp. pp. 335, 338–39). See also Amos Goldreich, *Sefer Me'irat Eynaim by R. Isaac of Acre: A Critical Edition* [in Hebrew] (Jerusalem, 1984), 395. I thank Michael Schneider z"l who brought this source to my attention.

Version A: Paris, MS hebr. 843

I heard a good and solid explanation in the name of R. Isaac of Chernigov[7] (of blessed memory) of why [the commandment of circumcision is performed] on this and not on any other organ of the body. He gave an explanation of why our forefather Abraham was given the commandment of circumcision. While he was uncircumcised, the Shekhinah (Divine Presence) would appear to him in most cases only when he was prostrated facedown or when he was asleep or drowsy. After his circumcision, it would appear to him when he was standing up, under any circumstance, so that you will not find any instance in which it did not appear. The reason is that an uncircumcised person cannot be pure and holy. For even if he immerses himself time and again [in water], the semen will not be washed away, because the water cannot reach it.[8] Consider [then] that he is condemned to being uncircumcised and impure, while [the sages] said that one who ejaculates is forbidden to study Torah or pray until he immerses himself—although today this immersion has been abolished.[9] All the more so [would Torah study and prayer be forbidden] in the case of one who is uncircumcised, for whom any [number of] immersions will not help—and all the water in the sea will not wash him clean. A circumcised person is different—if he experiences an ejaculation, he goes and immerses himself and then he becomes pure. He does not worry and fear that some of the semen remained there, because the crown [glans penis] is uncovered and it can be washed with water. This is why Abraham was called perfect (*tamim*)[10]—to say that he was pure and clean and the Shekhinah came to him in any state, whether prostrate or standing upright. At that time God added the letter *heh* [which has a numerical value of five] to his name [which was formerly Abram],[11] making [the numerical value of his new name] Abraham equal to the 248 [organs of the human body], which is the same as the number of positive commandments in the Torah. All of Israel have this potential to become perfect and pure and holy and to have the Shekhinah upon them like Moses our teacher. This is a correct and wonderful explanation.

וטעם למה באותו אבר יותר
משאר איברים שמעתי בשם הר"ר
יצחק מסרנגוב ז"ל דבר נכון וקיי'
נתן טעם למה נצטווה אברהם
אבינו על מילה. בהיותו ערל לא
שרתה עליו שכינה אלא בנפילה
על פניו או בשינ' בנמנום ברוב
המקומות. ואחר שמל שרתה אליו
בעמידה ובכל עניין ולא תמצא
מקום אחר אולי שלא תשרה.
והטעם מפני שאדם ערל אינו
טהור וקדוש אפי' יטבול כמה
פעמים לא יתרחץ אותו הזרע
מפני שלא יגיעו אליו המים. וראה
אם דינו להיות ערל וטמא שהרי
אמרו בעל קרי אסור בדברי תורה
ואסור להתפלל עד שיטבול אלא
בזמן הזה בטלוה לטבילותא. ועל
אחת כמה וכמה זה שהוא ערל
שלא יעלו לו כל טבילות ולא
יטהר בכל מימי הים. והמהול אינו
כן שאם ראה קרי הולך וטובל
ויהיה טהור ולא יפחד ולא יראה
שהוא הניח מן הקרי שם שהרי
העטרה מגולה היא ויכול להדיחה
במים. ועל כן נקרא אברהם תמים
כלומ'[ר] שיהא טהור ונקי ושרתה
עליו שכינה בכל עניין בין בנפילה
בין בעמידה. ובאותה שעה הוסיף
הקב"ה [הקדוש ברוך הוא] ה"א
בשמו להשלים בו מניין רמ"ח
ומניין רמ"ח כל מצות עשה
שבתורה כמניין אברהם. וכל
ישראל ראויין על זה להיותם
תמים וטהורים וקדושים ולשרות
שכינה עליהם כמשה רבינ' ע"ה.
וזה טעם נכון ומפואר.

---

[7] In Hebrew, *Sernegov* or *Sernigov*.

[8] According to Lev 15:16–18 and Deut. 23:10[11] emission of semen requires immersion in water.

[9] See BT Berakhot 21b–22b.

[10] See Gen 17:1. Cf. Jub. 23:10 (probably not known to Ḥasidei Ashkenaz).

[11] See Gen 17:5.

And the reason why circumcision takes precedence over the Sabbath is as follows. Circumcision is called a sign (*'ot*), and the Sabbath is also [called] a sign;[12] but the sign of circumcision is greater than the sign of the Sabbath, because it is an actual letter (*'ot*) [rather than a figurative sign]. And for the purposes of law, a greater sign takes precedence over a lesser one.[13]

וטעם מפני מה מילה דוחה שבת
מפני שהמילה נקראת אות ושבת
אות וגדול אות של מילה מאות
של שבת מפני שהוא אות ממש
לשון אותיות לענין דין הוא שיהא
האות קטן נדחה מפני גדול.

Version B: Vatican, MS ebr. 236

I heard in the name of R. Isaac Barbagov[14] that circumcision is commanded for this organ rather than for any other organ, because during sexual intercourse it is unavoidable that some drops of semen will remain within the foreskin of the [uncircumcised] penis, even if it is washed. The sages said that one who ejaculates is forbidden to study Torah or pray until he immerses himself. The immersions will not help in the case of an uncircumcised man. As long as Abraham was uncircumcised, the Shekhinah did not come to him except when he was prostrated on his face. After he was circumcised, it would come to him when he was standing upright. Therefore, Abraham was called perfect (*tamim*)—to say that he was pure and clean and the Shekhinah came to him in any state, either prostrate or standing upright. At that time God added the letter *heh* [which has a numerical value of five] to his name [which was formerly Abram], making [the numerical value of his new name] Abraham equal to the 248 organs [of the human body], which is the same as the number of positive commandments in the Torah. Therefore, he deserved to have the Shekhinah come to him as it did to Moses our teacher. This is why circumcision takes precedence over the Sabbath: for the Sabbath is a sign (*'ot*) and circumcision is also a sign, and the sign of circumcision is greater than the sign of the Sabbath, because it is an actual letter (*'ot*).[15]

ושמעתי בשם הר"ר יצחק ברבגוב
ז"ל שלכך נצטוה המילה באבר
יותר מבשאר איברים לפי דבשמש
אי אפשר שלא ישאר טיפי קרי
תוך הערלה ואפי' ירחץ לא יצא.
והרי אמ' רז"ל בעל קרי אסור
בדברי תורה ואסור להתפלל עד
שיטבול. וא"כ כ"ש בערל שלא
יעלו טבילות. וכל זמן שלא היה
אברהם נמול לא שרתה עליו
שכינה אלא בנפילת פנים. וכשמל
אז שרתה עליו בעמידה. ולכך
נקרא אברהם תמים כלומ'[ר]
שהיה טהור ונקי ושרתה עליו
שכינ' בכל ענין ובאותה שעה
הוסיף הקב"ה [הקדוש ברוך הוא]
ה"א לשמו להשלים רמ"ח איברים
וכן מנין מצות עשה שבתורה
כמנין אברהם ועל זה ראויה
שתשרה עליו שכינ' כמשה רבינו.
ומשום הכי מילה דוחה שבת לפי
ששבת אות ומילה נמי אותו וגדול
אות מילה מאות שבת לפי שהוא
אות ממש מלשון אותיות.

---

[12] See Gen 17:11; Exod 31:13, 31:17; Ezek 20:12, 20:20.

[13] Paris, MS hebr. 843, fol. 84a–85b, as published in Abrams, "Traces," 338–39. I thank Adina Luber for her collaboration in translating this and most other Hebrew texts in this paper.

[14] An obvious corruption of סרנגוב to ברבגוב.

[15] Vatican, MS ebr. 236, fols. 77b–80a, as published in Abrams, "Traces," 338–39.

Jewish tradition provides multiple alternative justifications for circumcision.[16] Some of them also relate to issues of purity, but not in the exact sense described in our text. Thus, Shaye Cohen shows how "Leviticus 12 implicitly equates circumcision with purification: the circumcision of the infant boy parallels the purification sacrifice of the mother," and that "many biblical and rabbinic passages see the foreskin as a source of impurity, and consequently the foreskinned as impure."[17] We will analyze the above text in conjunction with other related evidence below.

A Russian Word

In another source, a person also titled "Isaac of Chernigov" presents a scholarly opinion of a suspiciously similar character.[18] He was cited in *Sefer ha-Shoham* (The Onyx Book), a work on Hebrew grammar organized as an alphabetical listing and explanation of roots and authored by R. Moses ben Isaac (ben ha-Nesiah) of England,[19] a student of R. Moses ben Yom Tov ha-Nakdan of London (d. ca. 1268).[20] According to this text, R. Isaac of Chernigov[21] provided a sort of comparative linguistic information concerning East-Slavic language for insight into Hebrew grammar:[22]

---

[16] See, for example, Shaye J. D. Cohen's survey of "a canonical history of Jewish circumcision" in his *Why Aren't Jewish Women Circumcised? Gender and Covenant in Judaism* (Berkeley, 2005), 3–55. There are many other discussions of circumcision in thirteenth-century Kabbalah; see, for example, the *Bahir*, composed in southern France during the late twelfth and early thirteenth centuries (with apparent Ashkenazic influences) and additional sources discussed by Daniel Abrams in his *The Book Bahir: An Edition Based on the Earliest Manuscripts* [in Hebrew] (Los Angeles, 1994).

[17] Cohen, *Why Aren't Jewish Women Circumcised?*, 18-21, 52.

[18] See the discussion in Kulik, "Jews from Rus'," 380–82.

[19] Hebrew שהם is an anagram of his name משה.

[20] For more on R. Moses ben Isaac (ben ha-Nesiah), see Cecil Roth, "Moses ben Isaac Nessiah and His Work, the *Sefer ha-Shoham*" [in Hebrew], in *Sefer ha-Shoham (The Onyx Book)*, ed. Benjamin Klar (Jerusalem, 1947), 5–16.

[21] Note that the form "Yitse of Chernigov," often repeated in scholarly literature in connection with this text, is incorrect (see Kulik, "Jews from Rus'," 380–81). The two manuscripts that preserve this excerpt present a nearly identical text with the name in unabbreviated form.

[22] Oxford, Bodleian Library, MS Opp. 152 (Neubauer 1484; Ashkenazi script, thirteenth–fourteenth century), fol. 38a; National Library of Russia, St. Petersburg, MS EVR II. A 34, fol. 39v (Ashkenazi script, fourteenth century). Editions: Klar, *Sefer ha-Shoham*, 142 (partial); Franciszek (Efraim) Kupfer and Tadeusz Lewicki, eds., *Źródła hebrajskie do dziejów Słowian i niektórych innych ludów środkowej i wschodniej Europy: Wyjątki z pism religijnych i prawniczych XI–XIII w.* (Warsaw, 1956), 173 (partial excerpt). See also Kulik, "Jews from Rus'," 380; idem, "Jews and the Language of Eastern Slavs," *Jewish Quarterly Review* 104 (2014): 119.

Yabbam. Strong [verb]. [As it is written:] Come to your brother's wife and *yabbem* her.[23] R. Isaac of Chernigov told me that in the language of Tiras, which is Rus', they call sexual intercourse *yibbum*. [Thus], *yabbem* here means: have intercourse with her.[24]

יבם. חזק. בא אל אשת אחיך ויבם
אתה. אמ'[ר] לי ה"ר יצח'[ק]
מסרנגוב כי בל'[שון] תירס הוא
רושיאה קו'[ראים][25] ליבום
בעילה. ויבם אותה ובעול אתה.

Although "Tiras" (the youngest son of Japheth in Gen 10:2 and 1 Chr 1:5) had alternative and more popular attributions in Jewish tradition (such as Thracia or Persia; see Josephus, *Ant.* 1.6.1; BT Yoma, 9b-10a; YT Meg. 1.8 [71b]), here it is obviously identified with Rus'. This identification must follow the *Book of Josippon*.[26] Therefore, Hebrew "Sernegov" here can be nothing other than Chernigov, one of the most powerful cities and principalities of Kievan Rus'. For a time the princes of Chernigov also ruled the principality of Tmutorokan, located on the coast of the Taman Strait between the Black Sea and the Sea of Azov, where there may have been a considerable Jewish population.[27]

It is also noteworthy that R. Isaac ben Samuel of Acre, a thirteenth-century kabbalist, attributed *Sefer ha-Kuzari* (*The Book of the Khazars*, by R. Judah ha-Levi) to R. Isaac of "Sernegov." Although this would appear to be a confusion stemming from the fact that the defender of Judaism in that book is

---

[23] Gen 38:8.

[24] Oxford, MS Opp. 152, fol. 38a.

[25] St. Petersburg, MS EVR II. A 34, fol. 39v: קורין.

[26] Kupfer and Lewicki, *Źródła*, 175. For Tiras as Rus', see Alexander Kulik, "Locating Hebrew *Rusia*: A Problem of Medieval Hebrew Nomenclature for Old Rus'," *Jewish Quarterly Review* 110 (2020): 702–32.

[27] See Авраам Я. Гаркави [Avraham Harkavi], "Еврейские надгробные памятники, найденные на Таманском полуострове" [Jewish Tombstones Found on the Taman Peninsula], *Еврейские Записки* 5 (1881): 313–18. Cf. Daniel Chwolson, *Corpus Inscriptionum Hebraicarum* (St. Petersburg, 1882). The Jews of the region are mentioned by Theophanes in his *Chronography* under the year 678/9 (6170), who speaks of "Phanagoria and the Jews who live there" (Carl de Boor, *Theophanes Chronographia*, 2 vols. [Leipzig, 1883–1885], 1:357), and by Ibn al-Faqih in *Kitâb al-Buldān*, who calls one of the towns there "Jewish Samkersh" (Michael Jan de Goeje, *Ibn al-Fakīh al-Hamadhānī: Compendium libri Kitāb al-Boldān* [Leiden, 1885], 271). Cf. סמכרץ in the letter of King Joseph from the "Jewish-Khazar Correspondence" in P. K. Kokovtsov, *Evreisko-khazarskaia perepiska v X veke* [Jewish-Khazar Correspondence in the Tenth Century] (Leningrad, 1932), 31, and סמכריו/סמכריי in the "Schechter Text," Solomon Schechter, "An Unknown Khazar Document," *Jewish Quarterly Review* 3 (1912): 207–8, line 65; Norman Golb and Omeljan Pritsak, *Khazarian Hebrew Documents of the Tenth Century* (Ithaca, NY, 1982), 106–20. See also the most recent survey by Jonathan Shepard, "Closer Encounters with the Byzantine World: The Rus at the Straits of Kerch," in *Pre-Modern Russia and its World: Essays in Honor of Thomas S. Noonan*, ed. Katherine Louise Reyerson et al. (Wiesbaden, 2006), 15–78.

sometimes called Isaac ha-Sangari,[28] this mistake still confirms that the name could have been known more broadly than is demonstrated by the extant sources.

For the purposes of our analysis, it is noteworthy that the gloss introduced by R. Isaac represents the earliest known attestation of the most fundamental obscene item in the Slavic vocabulary.[29] In some forms it happens to be a homophone of the Hebrew יבם. The term belongs to a group of taboo words associated with pagan practices, witchcraft, and non-Christian identities during the Middle Ages.[30] Moreover, obscene speech could be referred to as "Hebrew" or "Jewish." Uspenskij adduces examples including "Jewish speech" (*жидовское слово*; *zhidovskoe slovo*) and "Do not speak Jewish; do not swear in foul language" (*по жидовскыя не говорите, матерны не бранитеся*; *po zhidovskyia ne govorite, materny ne branitesia*). The term "Jewish" was also very likely used as a synonym for "pagan" (though never "Hellenic," itself a far more common designation for "pagan" in Church Slavonic literature, following a similar turn of phrase in the New Testament).[31]

The Paris manuscript that cited Isaac of Chernigov only provided a place of residence (or rather origin) and a general dating (prior to the fifteenth century). However, if that Isaac and the Isaac of Chernigov in *Sefer ha-Shoham* are one and the same person, then the dating can be narrowed, as we know that R. Moses ben ha-Nesiah's teacher, R. Moses ben Yom Tov ha-Nakdan of London, died around 1268. The next source also provides us with information on R. Isaac's English contacts.

English Taxes

Regarding the English connection, a certain "Ysaac de Russie" is one of a group of three Jews mentioned twice in the *Pipe Rolls*, financial records maintained in Latin by the English Royal Exchequer. Entries were made under the "27[th year of the reign of] Hen.[ry] II [= 1180–1181]" and the "28[th

---

[28] See Goldreich, *Sefer Me'irat Eynaim*, 395. On Isaac ha-Sangari, see Dan Shapira, "Yitshaq Sangari, Sangarit, Bezalel Stern, and Avraham Firkowicz: Notes on Two Forged Inscriptions." *Archivum Eurasiae Medii Aevi* 12 (2002–2003): 223–60. Russian edition in *Материалы по археологии, истории и этнографии Таврии* [Materials on the Archeology, History, and Ethnography of Taurida] 10 (2003): 535–55.

[29] See Трубачев [O. N. Trubachev], ed., *Этимологический словарь славянских языков: Праславянский лексический фонд* [Etymological Dictionary of Slavic Languages: The Lexical Store of Proto-Slavic], vol. 8 (Moscow, 1981), 188 (s.v. *jěbati*).

[30] See Борис А. Успенский [Boris Uspenskii], "Мифологический аспект русской экспрессивной фразеологии" [The Mythological Aspect of Russian Expressive Phraseology], in idem, *Избранные труды* [Selected Works], 2 vols. (Moscow, 1994), 2:53–128, esp. 60.

[31] Ibid., 61.

year of the reign of] Hen.[ry] II [1181–1182]" in "Svdhantescr'," i.e., Syd-hantescire, South Hampshire:[32]

Ysaac Ruffus,[33] Ysaac of Rus', and Ysaac of Beverly, Jews, render account of ten marks to be cleared of a charge, because they were said to have exchanged [money]. [They paid] to the Treasury 55 shillings and 7 pence and [still] owe 77 shillings and 9 pence.[34]

Ysaac Ruffus et Ysaac de Russie et Ysaac de Beuerl' Judei reddt. [irunt] comp.[otum] de .x. m. ut sint quieti de calumpnia quod dicebantur cambuisse. In thesauro lv. s. et .vij. d. et debent lxxvij. s. et ix. d.

Ysaac Ruffus, Ysaac of Rus', and Ysaac of Beverly, Jews, render account of 77 shillings and 9 pence to be cleared of a charge, because they were said to have exchanged [money]. They paid into the Treasury and were cleared.[35]

Ysaac Ruffus et Ysaac de Russia et Ysaac dc Beuerl' Judei redd [irunt]t. comp.[otum] de lxxvij. s. et ix. d. ut sint quieti de calumpnia quod dicebantur cambuisse. In thesauro liberaverunt. Et quieti sunt.

The relatively late date of death of R. Moses ben ha-Nesiah's teacher in the third quarter of the thirteenth century, when compared to this documentation of 1180–1182 about "Ysaac de Russie" of South Hampshire, prompted Roth to assert, "We can definitely discard Joseph Jacobs' hypothesis that this Isaac [of Chernigov] is identical with the Isaac of 'Russia' [sic] who figures in some twelfth-century English records."[36] However, it is actually not beyond the realm of possibility that Ysaac of South Hampshire (though apparently already an adult in 1180) may have lived well into the thirteenth century and met R. Moses ben Isaac, whose teacher died ca. 1268.[37]

---

[32] Pipe Rolls (1180–1182): The National Archives, Kew, MSS E372/27 and E372/28. Editions: *The Great Roll of the Pipe for the Twenty-Seventh Year of the Reign of King Henry the Second, A.D. 1180–1181* (London, 1909), 134 (first excerpt); *The Great Roll of the Pipe for the Twenty-Eighth Year of the Reign of King Henry the Second, A.D. 1181–1182* (London, 1910), 143 (second excerpt). See also Joseph Jacobs, *The Jews of Angevin England: Documents and Records from the Latin and Hebrew Sources* (London, 1893); В. И. Матузова [V. I. Matu-zova], *Английские средневековые источники, IX–XIII вв.: Тексты, перевод, комментарий* [English Medieval Sources, Ninth to Thirteenth Centuries: Texts, Translation, Commentary] (Moscow, 1979), 49–50; Kulik, "Jews from Rus'," 376–80.

[33] The cognomen *Ruffus* would appear to signify "the Red," or possibly "of Rochester."

[34] The National Archives, Kew, MSS E372/27, Rot. 9, membr. 2; *Great Roll of the Pipe for the Twenty-Seventh Year*, 134.

[35] The National Archives, Kew, MSS E372/28, Rot. 11, membr. 2; *Great Roll of the Pipe for the Twenty-Eighth Year*, 143.

[36] Roth, "Moses ben Isaac," 11; Cecil Roth, *A History of the Jews in England*, 3rd ed. (Oxford, 1964), 93 n. 4.

[37] See Kulik, "Jews from Rus'," 381–82.

This R. Isaac of Rus' / "Ysaac de Russie" could have reached England via Germany or France (and we will examine these possibilities below); but could he (or they) have come directly from Rus'? The Baltic trade route from Rus' to the North Sea is very well documented, so that Isaac could hardly have been "the first Russian ... on English soil," as Jacobs suggests.[38] The East-Slavic Jewish presence in England may also be attested by a Cyrillic-Hebrew abecedarium composed in England in the same thirteenth century.[39]

An Italian Precaution: "... revealing it to myself, but not to my organs"

Another (or the same) Isaac, cited this time with his patronym and a more general toponym—"R. Isaac ben Ezekiel of Rus'"—appears in *Sefer Minhag Tov* (*The Book of Good Custom*), a work of rabbinic ritual law by an anonymous author. The publisher called this text *The Book of Good Custom* since it opens each paragraph with the words, "And it is a goodly custom [to do such and such]." However, the manuscript is corrupt at the beginning, and the work lacks any original title. Though discovered in Hungary, the manuscript has Italian glosses and refers to Italian realia probably connected to seaside cities.[40] The work has been dated based on the author's statement that he met R. Moses ben Meir in the year "33," i.e., 5033 (1273).

In this book, the author records that he learned the reason for one of the "goodly customs" from R. Isaac from Rus':[41]

It is a good and proper custom for every man in whom the Divine Spirit rests to rise and shake himself a bit when he pronounces the Revered and Awesome Name, the Four-Letter Name. One has to pronounce it in purity and holiness and with concentration, not in a distracted, absentminded manner. For—making a thousand thousands upon thousands and myriads upon myriads of distinctions—when one mentions a human king of flesh and blood by name and in his presence, one removes his hat if he is wearing one and speaks with attentiveness and thought, in order not to err in the king's name or in his praise.	ומנהג טוב וכשר לכל איש אשר רוח שמעים [sic] בו לקום ולנענע עצמו קצת בשעה שהוא מוציא מפיו ומזכיר את השם הנכבד והנורא הוא השם של ד' אותיות ולהזכירו בטהרה וקדושה ובכוון. ולא יזכירינו דרך עראי ובהסח הדעת כי להבדיל אלף אלפי אלפים ורבי רבאות כשאדם מזכיר מלך בשר ודם בשמו ובפניו אם יש לו כובע בראשו מסירו

---

[38] Jacobs, *Jews of Angevin England*, 73. On early connections between Rus' and England see Kulik, "Jews from Rus'," 388.

[39] See Kulik, "Jews from Rus'," esp. 389–402.

[40] Meir Tzvi Weiss, "*Sefer Minhag Tov*," *Ha-Zofeh le-Hokhmat Yisrael* 13 (1929): 217–44, 224–25; in Hungarian, idem, *Minhag Tob* (Budapest, 1911); see no. 22 there.

[41] Hungarian Academy of Sciences, Budapest, MS Kaufmann A 89 ((Italian script, fourteenth century). Edition: Meir Tzvi Weiss, ed., *Sefer Minhag Tov, the First Edition apud ms. Kaufmann in Budapest* [in Hebrew] (Budapest, 1929; repr., Jerusalem, 1986). See also Ta-Shma, "History," 312; Kulik, "Jews from Rus'," 384–86.

[How much more care, then, should one exercise when addressing God.] I heard an additional explanation from R. Isaac ben Ezekiel of Rus', who spoke in the name of the author of *Sefer Yeẓirah*.[42] And I set [his explanation] deep within my heart, revealing it to myself, but not [relating it even] to my own organs. Additionally, it is written: And the posts of the door were moved from the voice of him who called [Isa 6:4]. If mere stones, devoid of wisdom and the ability to speak and hear, moved at the sound of God's Name, how much more so should a human being who possesses wisdom, speaks, and hears! An additional source [records]: King Eglon of Moab rose from his seat when Ehud ben Gera announced that he had a message from God [Judg 3:20]. [Concerning this incident] our rabbis said in tractate Sanhedrin [BT Sanh. 60a] that one must rise when God's Name is mentioned.[43]

גם מזכירו בדעת ובתבונה שלא
יטעה בשמו ובשבחו. וטעם אחר
שמעתי מר' יצחק בר' יחזקאל
מרוסייא שאמ'[ר] בשם בעל ספר
יצירה. ובתוך חדרי לבי קבעתי
ולי גליתי ולאיברי לא הודעתי.
ועוד דכת'[יב] וינועו אמות
הסיפים מקול הקורא. והלא
דברים קל וחומר ומה אבנים שאין
בהן חוכמה ולא מדברים ולא
שומעים כך אדם שיש בו חוכמה
ושומע ומדבר עאכ'ו [על אחת
כמה וכמה]. ועוד שמצינו בעגלון
מלך מואב כשאמ'[ר] לו אהוד בן
גרא דבר שמוים [sic] לי אליך
ויקם מעל הכסא. וכן אמ'[רו]
רבותי'[נו] במסכת סנהדרין שחייב
אדם לקום מפני מזכירי השם.

Among various reasons for swaying while mentioning the name of God, the author of *Sefer Minhag Tov* mentions one he heard from R. Isaac ben Ezekiel of Rus', who spoke in the name of the author of *Sefer Yeẓirah*. Rabbi Isaac's reason is so secret that the author keeps it to himself. The question is whether we can reconstruct an explanation that has not actually been given.

One possible hint is provided by the reference to the *Sefer Yeẓirah*. R. Isaac may well have meant verses 1:12-13 (§ 15), which deals with the sealing of the world with the letters of the Divine Name. Early mystics had already connected this passage to the swinging of the body or of the *lulav*[44] at the moment of enunciating the Divine Name.[45] But why would this explanation be described so dramatically as a secret to be kept "deep in one's heart" and that the author of *Sefer Minhag Tov* could not disclose even to his "own organs"?

This very wording, together with what we know about R. Isaac's interests from other sources, provides us with another lead. We can hazard a guess as to which organs are referred to and why the esoteric teaching was deemed

---

[42] *Sefer Yeẓirah* (*The Book of Creation* or *The Book of Formation*) is an influential esoteric work dated variously between the first and ninth centuries CE. In the period under discussion its mystical, and especially kabbalistic, interpretation becomes predominant; see Tzahi Weiss, *Sefer Yeṣirah and Its Contexts: Other Jewish Voices* (Philadelphia, 2019).

[43] Budapest, MS Kaufmann A 89, fol. 6b; Weiss, *Sefer Minhag Tov*, 224.

[44] A frond of the palm tree used in the prayer services during the holiday of Tabernacles.

[45] See, for example, Shalom Albeck and Chanoch Albeck, eds., *Sefer ha-Eshkol by R. Abraham ben Isaac of Narbonne*, 2nd ed., 2 vols. (Jerusalem, 1984), 1:14, or R. Avraham of Rimon, *Berit Menuḥah* (Amsterdam, 1648), 16b–25a. For more sources, see Yitzhak Zimmer, "Poses and Body Movements during Reading of Shema'" [in Hebrew], *Asufot* 8 (1994): 359–62.

unfit for them. The word אבר "organ" has sexual connotations in certain contexts but could also be used in its primary meaning. The very turn of phrase here is borrowed from BT Sanhedrin 99a, where in the context of calculations of "the days of the Messiah," R. Yohanan interprets כִּי יוֹם נָקָם בְּלִבִּי ("For the day of vengeance is in mine [God's] heart," Isa 63:4) free of any sexual connotations as: "I [God] revealed it to my heart but not to my organs" (ללבי גליתי לאברי לא גליתי). The phrase is also reminiscent of Eccl 5:5[6], "Let not your mouth cause your flesh to sin," which the Zohar interprets as referring either to sins of a sexual nature and/or to the sin of disclosing esoteric truths.[46] *Sefer Yezirah* also connects "the covenant of the tongue and the circumcision of the flesh" (ברית לשון ובמילת המעור).[47]

However, if we explore a possibility of well-attested sexual semantics of אבר here[48] or more simply suggest an interpretation consistent with other teachings ascribed to R. Isaac of Rus', we can connect apparently distinct practices that he analyzes in our two different sources: circumcision and swaying during prayer. R. Isaac's teaching about swaying may complement his theory of circumcision by explaining the nature of the relations between a circumcised person and the Shekhinah (which may be referenced only implicitly in his discussion of circumcision). With or without specific sexual connotations, midrashic and kabbalistic roots of the conceptual affinities between circumcision and revelation may clarify R. Isaac's teaching. By its very nature, this reconstruction can be only speculative.

I propose tracing the connection between circumcision and swaying during prayer to the rabbinic doctrine that *unio mystica* can be achieved only through circumcision. Elliot Wolfson has explored the correlation between two apparently unrelated phenomena—circumcision and the ability to see the Shekhinah. Characterizing this as "the phenomenological reciprocity between the opening of circumcision and visionary experience of God," he points out that Zoharic discussions depict the mystical experience as a sexual union between the mystic and the Divine.[49] Wolfson demonstrates a complex and deep connection between the two phenomena in the history of Jewish

[46]Zohar I, 8a; II, 87a; etc.; see Elliot R. Wolfson, "Circumcision, Vision of God, and Textual Interpretation: From Midrashic Trope to Mystical Symbol," *History of Religions* 27 (1987): 189–215, 207. See also his "Circumcision and the Divine Name: A Study in the Transmission of Esoteric Doctrine." *Jewish Quarterly Review* 78 (1987): 77–112; and Cohen, *Why Aren't Jewish Women Circumcised*, 43–45.

[47]A. Peter Hayman, ed., *Sefer Yesira: Edition, Translation and Text-Critical Commentary* (Tübingen, 2004), 67, 182 (§§ 3, 61).

[48]As in, for example, YT Ketubbot 5, 8b, etc.; see E. E. Ben Yehuda, *A Complete Dictionary of Ancient and Modern Hebrew by Eliezer Ben Yehuda of Jerusalem* [in Hebrew] (Jerusalem, 1908–1959, 1960).

[49]See Wolfson, "Circumcision, Vision of God," 189–90.

thought, from Philo and early rabbinic texts to the medieval mystical tradition that reached its climax in the kabbalistic works of the thirteenth century (which is also the date of our sources). At this time the correlation was given elaborate treatment in the theosophic system of the Zohar.[50]

Thus, already Genesis Rabbah (fifth century) connects circumcision with revelation:

Gen. Rab. 48, 1:	R. Isaac of Rus', Paris, MS hebr. 843:
"But I would behold God from my flesh," [Job 19:26]—for had I not done this [i.e., performed the act of circumcision], on what account would God have appeared to me? [As it is written] "The Lord appeared to him, etc." [Gen. 18:1 *et passim*].	While he was uncircumcised, the Shekhinah would appear to him in most cases only when he was prostrated facedown or when he was asleep or drowsy. After his circumcision, it would appear to him when he was standing up.

Wolfson notes that Genesis Rabbah makes its statement on the impossibility of a Divine manifestation to the uncircumcised "in disregard of other biblical contexts to the contrary (e.g., Gen 17:1)," where God appears to Abraham before his circumcision.[51] While Wolfson explains this contradiction by the "verse-centerednesss" of midrash, in James Kugel's terminology,[52] our R. Isaac (or rather his sources, as we will see below) solves the problem philologically: he harmonizes the early rabbinic interpretation with Scripture by remarking that although Abraham had a revelatory experience before his circumcision, in the earlier period he had to prostrate himself facedown (as in Gen 17:3, 17) to hide the impure organs.

This idea, though not completely innovative, was unknown to Genesis Rabbah, which in another passage establishes quite a different connection between the two phenomena: "'And Abraham fell on his face,' etc. [17:3]. R. Pinchas said in R. Levi's name: 'Abraham fell on his face on two occasions. In consequence, his children were deprived of circumcision once in the wilderness and once in Egypt'" (Gen. Rab. 46:6). Here prostration is understood as either an indication of disobedience to God's command or a prayer for one's descendants.16

However, other early rabbinic sources must already imply a different kind of connection between facedown prostration and revelation—one close, if not identical, to the one explicitly articulated by R. Isaac. Thus, the Targum Pseudo-Jonathan (eighth century) states for Gen 17:3: "And because Abram

---

[50] Ibid.

[51] Ibid., 193.

[52] James Kugel, "Two Interpretations of Midrash," in *Midrash and Literature*, ed. Geoffrey H. Hartman and Sanford Budick (New Haven, CT, 1986), 94–95.

was not circumcised, he was not able to stand, but he bowed himself upon his face." Similarly, in Midrash Tanhuma (seventh–ninth centuries): "'And Abraham fell on his face,' [17:3]. Before he [Abraham] circumcised himself, every time when the Shekhinah was speaking to him, he would fall [face-down]. And since he circumcised himself, whenever He [God] was speaking to him, he [Abraham] would stand: 'And Abraham was still standing before the Lord' [Gen 18:22]" (Tanhumah, Lech Lecha 20). Similarly, in Pirqe Rabbi Eliezer (eighth century), we read: "Before Abraham was circumcised he fell on his face, and afterwards I spoke with him, as it is said, 'And Abraham fell on his face' [17:3]. Now that he is circumcised he sits and I stand! Whence do we know that God was standing? Because it is said, 'And he looked up and saw three men standing over him' [Gen 18:2]" (Pirqe R. El. 29). Similarly with the gentile prophet Balaam, "'who falls down with eyes wide open' [Num 24:4]. When God wanted to speak to him [Balaam], he would prostrate himself on the ground and throw himself to the ground,[53] and God would immediately show him all that he asked. And why could he not see the Shekhinah without falling [facedown]? Because he was uncircumcised and could not stand on his feet [during revelation]" (Midrash Aggadah, Num 24:4; cf. also Num. Rab. 12, 10, quoted below).

Another early rabbinic tradition connects this issue to impure ejaculation, exactly as in R. Isaac's teaching: "'And God met Balaam' [וַיִּקָּר אֱלֹהִים אֶל בִּלְעָם; Num 23:4]. R. Issachar of Kefar Mandi said: 'The term וַיִּקָּר signifies uncleanness, as in the verse, "If there be among you any man that is not clean by reason of that which chanceth him by night" [כִּי-יִהְיֶה בְךָ אִישׁ, אֲשֶׁר לֹא-יִהְיֶה טָהוֹר מִקְּרֵה-לָיְלָה; Deut 23:10[11])'" (Gen. Rab. 52, 5; cited also by Rashi on Num 23:4). As we have seen, R. Isaac claims that "a circumcised person is different—if he experiences an ejaculation, he goes and immerses himself and then he becomes pure." This practice, known as "an enactment of Ezra" (תקנת עזרא), was largely abandoned after the destruction of the Temple (see BT Baba Qamma 82a). It was preserved or revived mainly in mystical circles, being especially popular among Ḥasidei Ashkenaz.[54] This detail, therefore, may favor the possibility that R. Isaac belonged to their circle (see below).[55]

---

[53] Aramaic ומפיל עצמו לתרעא, lit. "and throws himself to the gate" (כשהיה רוצה לדבר עמו הקב״ה היה משתטח לארץ ומפיל עצמו לתרעא). Here the reference is either to the "gates of prayer," a notion well attested in rabbinic literature (cf. YT Berakhot 4.7c; BT Berakhot 32b; Pesiqta de Rab Kahanah 24.2; Pirqe Rabbi Eliezer 35; etc.), or else a textual corruption of Aramaic ארעה "ground," as translated above, despite a certain tautology.

[54] See Yedidyah Dinari, "The Profanation of the Holy by the Menstruant Woman and Taqqanot Ezra" [in Hebrew], Te'udah 3 (1982): 17–37.

[55] It may additionally be noted that, taken separately, R. Isaac's technical explanation—according to which impurity stems from the lack of ability to clean the folds of the foreskin—shows that this was not an immanent kabbalistic secret as in his teaching from Sefer Minhag

None of these sources provides any explicit explanation of the nature of the connection between circumcision and revelation. R. Isaac's commentary is close to Numbers Rabbah (seventh–twelfth centuries), which does offer an explanation for the connection between the two phenomena.

> If they were uncircumcised, they would not have been able to look upon the Shekhinah. Rather, they would have fallen as Abraham fell, as it is said, "Abram fell on his face, and God spoke to him" (Gen 17:3). ... This may be compared to a shopkeeper who has a friend who is a priest. He had some unclean thing in his house, and he wanted to bring him [the priest] into the house. The priest said to him: If you want me to go into your house, listen to me and remove that unclean thing from your house. When the shopkeeper knew that there was no unclean thing there, he went and brought the priest into his house. Similarly [with respect to] the Holy One, blessed be He, when He wanted to appear to Abraham, His beloved, the foreskin was hanging from him. When he circumcised himself, immediately [God] was revealed, as it says, "On that very day Abraham was circumcised" [Gen 17:26], and afterward "The Lord appeared to him" [Gen 18:1] (Num. Rab. 12, 10).

Numbers Rabbah provides two justifications for the conjunction of circumcision and revelation. One justification is textual, based on the conjunction of the passages about Abraham's circumcision in Gen 17:10–23 and about the theophany at the Oaks of Mamre in Gen 18:1–15. The other justification is ontological: an association of the foreskin with impurity.

The section of Numbers Rabbah quoted here is from parashat Naso and must belong to or be based on the teaching of R. Moses ha-Darshan of Narbonne, who was active in the eleventh century, close in time to R. Isaac.[56] It is difficult to determine if we are dealing here with influence from one scholar on another or two scholars who reached similar conclusions independently.

Tov. While the rabbinic tradition (going back to Ezra 44:9) saw the foreskin as an impurity in itself that prevented a man from entering the temple, R. Isaac argues here that the foreskin only creates a technical difficulty in the act of purification. This may show that R. Isaac did not ascribe a fundamental significance to the foreskin.

[56]Leopold Zunz and Chanoch Albeck, *Jewish Synagogue Expositions* [in Hebrew] (Jerusalem, 1947), 125–27, 397–400. R. Moses ha-Darshan (eleventh century) was head of the yeshivah in Narbonne and often considered the founder of Jewish exegetic studies in France. See also the work of Hananel Mack, who demonstrated the ties between Numbers Rabbah and early kabbalistic writings; see, for example, his "Midrash Bamidbar Rabbah and the Beginning of the Kabbalah in Provence" [in Hebrew], in *Myth in Judaism*, ed. Haviva Pedaya (Jerusalem, 1996), 78–96, and idem, *The Mystery of Rabbi Moshe Hadarshan* [in Hebrew] (Jerusalem, 2010).

To the spiritual dimensions of circumcision as formulated in the cited traditions, R. Isaac adds rationalistic arguments that provide a physiological basis for the physical impurity of an uncircumcised organ. He may also allude to the theory of circumcision as "the holy sign" (the Zoharic *reshima qadisha*; cf. R. Isaac's "actual letter" or "real sign," *'ot mamash*, above) and/or to the identification of circumcision with one of the letters of the Divine Name, in this case possibly *heh* (because, as our source says, "God added the letter *heh* to his [Abraham's] name")[57] instead of the better-attested identification with the letter *yod*.[58] If both his sayings may be regarded as constituents of a single teaching, then R. Isaac additionally provides a way to connect circumcision with the Divine Name. Both these topics were extensively developed in the thirteenth-century Zohar,[59] which supplies the missing "secret"[60] element absent or not explicit in the early rabbinic sources: that is, the idea of sexual union between the circumcised mystic and the Divine.[61]

The Zohar, of course, was not the only source that dealt with this topic. As mentioned by Moshe Idel, "Some forms of Judaism may be described as a culture of eros. Indeed, at least since the medieval masters discussed above, main religious topics have been understood as fraught with erotic overtones."[62] Compare, for example, the overtly sexual language of R. David ben Judah he-Ḥasid in his description of the nature of prophecy in *The Books of Mirrors*,[63] or how Abraham Abulafia (influenced by Eleazar of Worms)[64] explains the nature of the Divine Name as "composed from two parts, since there are two parts of love [divided between] two lovers. ... This is the [great] power of man: he can link the lower part with the higher one, and the lower

---

[57] See Eliot Wolfson's analysis of *Tiqqune ha-Zohar* ("Circumcision and the Divine Name," 109), where "the first and last *heh* are the place of the foreskin and the act of *peri'ah*" (ה"ה דא אתר דערלה ופריעה; *Tiqqune ha-Zohar* 61, 94a). Cf. Moshe Idel's criticism of Wolfson's "phallocentric" interpretations in *Kabbalah and Eros* (New Haven, CT, 2005), 22 n. 16, 54 n. 2, passim.

[58] As, for example, in Tanhumah, Tsav, 14 and Shemini, 8; see Yitzhak Raphael, ed., *Sefer ha-Manhig of R. Abraham b. Nathan ha-Yarḥi*, 2 vols. (Jerusalem, 1978), 2:579. See Wolfson, "Circumcision and the Divine Name," 78, 86.

[59] For the former, see, for example, Zohar I, 245b; Wolfson, "Circumcision, Vision of God," 210–13; for the latter, see Zohar I, 95a, 96b; II, 3b, 32a, 87b; III, 91a; *Tiqqunei Zohar* 24 (70a), 22 (65b), 61 (94b); Wolfson, "Circumcision, Vision of God," 202.

[60] Cf. also the term "the secret of circumcision/covenant" (*raza de-berit*) connected to the level of visionary experience (Zohar I, 91a–b; Wolfson, "Circumcision, Vision of God," 200ff.).

[61] See Wolfson, "Circumcision, Vision of God," 198ff.

[62] Idel, *Kabbalah and Eros*, 240.

[63] *Books of Mirrors*, 214, *apud* Idel, *Kabbalah and Eros*, 117.

[64] Eleazar ben Judah ben Kalonymous of Worms (ca. 1176–1238), known as Rokeach, was one of the last major members of Ḥasidei Ashkenaz. Abraham ben Samuel Abulafia (Spain, 1240–after 1291) was the founder of the school of "prophetic kabbalah."

[part] will ascend and cleave to the higher, and the higher [part] will descend and will kiss the entity ascending toward it, as a bridegroom actually kisses his bride out of his great and real desire, characteristic of the delight of both." (*Sefer Or ha-Sekhel*)[65]

A Ḥasidic Digression

While reservations regarding attempts to read earlier texts in light of much later ones are justified, it is inadvisable to dismiss late evidence completely. Such parallels may demonstrate ways of developing the same ideas, uncover tendencies immanent but implicit in earlier sources and, at the very least, may be interesting from a typological perspective.

In none of the Zoharic or other medieval mystical texts do we find the explicitly erotic language used by later East European Ḥasidic teachers.[66] For example, here is how the anonymous *Zava'at ha-Ribash*, attributed to the Besht,[67] explains the custom of swaying during prayer:

> Prayer is a form of intercourse with the Shekhinah, and just as at the beginning of intercourse one moves one's body, so is it necessary to move one's body at first in prayer, but afterwards one can stand still, without any movement, when there is a great union with the Shekhinah. The power of this movement causes a great arousal, for it causes one to think, "Why am I moving myself?" [And he answers himself,] "Because perhaps the Shekhinah is actually standing in front of me." And from this great power, he comes to a great passion. (*Testament of the Besht*, par. 68)

It is notable that some of the contemporary Mitnaggedim critics of Ḥasidism presented such practices as a Ḥasidic innovation. R. David Makov, in his anti-Ḥasidic *Breaking of Sinners* states: "And they say that in their prayer they have to give birth, and therefore the sex organ must bring about the unifications; and he must sway like a man and a woman coupling when they are united."[68]

---

[65] Vatican MS ebr. 233, fol. 115a, as cited in Idel, *Kabbalah and Eros*, 79.

[66] Which does not necessarily imply a historic connection between these two homonymic groups; see Joseph Dan, *R. Judah he-Ḥasid* [in Hebrew] (Jerusalem, 2006), 9–10.

[67] Israel Baal Shem Tov (1698–1760), the founder of East European Ḥasidism.

[68] Mordecai Wilensky, *Ḥasidim and Mitnaggedim: A Study of the Controversy Between Them in the Years 1772–1815* [in Hebrew], 2 vols. (Jerusalem, 1970), 2:159; Mor Altshuler, *The Messianic Secret of Hasidism* (Leiden, 2006), 375.

Even the Ḥasidim themselves ascribed introduction of excessive bodily movements in prayer to the innovations of the Maggid of Zlotchov.[69] However, these ideas are so well developed and widespread in East European Ḥasidism,[70] that it is reasonable to suppose that they may have had earlier sources.

Of course, sexual imagery in relations between the human and divine, as known from Kabbalah and other mystical teachings,[71] crosses sectarian and confessional borders. Nor was it alien to Christian usage. This type of imagery was present already in the biblical texts, which often presented Israel as God's bride or spouse; it received further development in common ancient apocalyptic and mystical traditions, with motifs and symbolic language attested in early Judaism, Gnosticism, and Neo-Platonism. (Compare, for example, the rich tradition of Jesus as a true bridegroom in, inter alia, Matt. 25:10; Luke 12:36; and Acts of Thomas 124.) No less expressive is the language of, for instance, the Beguine mystics who flourished in the same thirteenth century. In her *Das fliessende Licht von Gottheit*, Mechthild of Magdeburg (ca. 1207–ca. 1282/94), a contemporary of our Isaac, describes a "naked soul" in the celestial bed of love with Jesus.[72] Distinct, however, in the teachings of R. Isaac and the *Testament of the Besht* is that here these spiritual concepts and metaphors of erotic *unio mystica* are connected to concrete physical practices—namely bodily movement in prayer and circumcision.

The Third Man – German Traces

Could the author of *Sefer Minhag Tov* have met his Rusian informant in Italy? Precedents to consider include a visit to Sicily in the early fourteenth century by a disciple of the Rosh, R. Asher ben Sinai of Rus', on his way home from

---

[69] See Rivka Schatz Uffenheimer, *Hasidism as Mysticism: Quietistic Elements in Eighteenth-Century Hasidic Thought*, trans. Jonathan Chipman (Princeton, 1993), 140; Altshuler, *Messianic Secret*, 53, 377. R. Yekhiel Michel Rabinowitz, known as the Maggid of Zlotchow (1721–1786), was the Besht's younger disciple.

[70] See David Biale, "The Lust for Asceticism in the Hasidic Movement," in *Jewish Explorations of Sexuality*, ed. Jonathan Magonet (Providence, RI, 1995), 51–67, 62; Altshuler, *Messianic Secret*, 374–75; cf. Hebrew edition (Haifa, 2002), 297–99.

[71] See, for example, Moshe Idel, "Sexual Images and Actions in Kabbalah," *Zemanim* 42, no. 2 (1992): 30–39; Idel, *Kabbalah and Eros*.

[72] 1:44; see Gallus Morel, ed., *Offenbarungen der Schwester Mechthild von Magdeburg, oder Das fliessende licht der Gottheit, aus der einzigen handschrift des Stiftes Einsiedeln* (Darmstadt, 1963)); for English, see *Mechthild of Magdeburg: The Flowing Light of the Godhead*, trans. and introd. Frank J. Tobin (New York, 1998), 61ff.

Toledo (*'Even ha-'ezer* 118);[73] and the *Sefer Russiano* of 1124, ascribed to R. Samuel of Rus', which has been preserved exclusively in Italian copies.[74] But this suggested encounter is not really necessary. The same *Sefer Minhag Tov* cites a wide range of authorities from France, the German lands, Languedoc, and Italy; moreover, it was heavily influenced by Ḥasidei Ashkenaz. This is also evident in the case of R. Isaac, with his attested interest—characteristic of Ḥasidei Ashkenaz—in the Tetragrammaton and the practice of ritual immersion after ejaculation. The inclusion of R. Isaac ben Ezekiel of Rus' in *Sefer Minhag Tov* constitutes only one of several pieces of evidence that demonstrate close connections between Ḥasidei Ashkenaz and Jewish scholars in Eastern Europe.[75]

This possible "German trace" merits exploration. In his later years R. Judah he-Ḥasid (ca. 1150–1217)[76] lived in Regensburg (an important center of the East European trade in this period) and communicated with scholars in Eastern Europe.[77] Several sources connect R. Judah he-Ḥasid with R. Jacob ha-Kohen of Kraków or Poland, R. Mordekhai of Poland, and R. Isaac of Poland.[78] An anonymous compiler of Torah commentaries mostly by R. Judah he-Ḥasid ascribes the main part of one interpretation to R. Israel of Poland.[79]

A certain "R. Isaac of Rus'" (ר' יצחק מרוסיא) appears to have been another of R. Judah's East European correspondents or, more likely, his disciple. He is assigned responsibility for transmitting a substantial number of R. Judah's teachings (thirty-five texts) in R. Judah's commentary on the Pentateuch and

---

[73] Avraham Yaakov Bombach et al., eds., טור: עם כל המפרשים אשר נדפסו מקדם ומפרשים חדשים מכתבי יד... מוגה ומתוקן, 2 vols. (Jerusalem: 1993–1997), 1:384–85. R. Asher ben Yechiel (Rosh; d. 1327) was a leading disciple of R. Meir of Rothenburg (Maharam). In 1304 he established an academy in Toledo.

[74] Moshe Weiss, ed., *Sefer Russiano . . . by R. Samuel of Rus'* [in Hebrew], 4 vols. (Jerusalem, 1976–96). Although this book is generally regarded as composed in southern Italy and not in Rus' (thus Weinryb, "Myth"); cf. Israel Ta-Shma, *Studies in Medieval Rabbinic Literature*, vol. 3, *Italy and Byzantium* (Jerusalem, 2010), 295–316, it may possibly have Russian provenance; see Kulik, "Locating Hebrew *Rusia*."

[75] On this, see Dan, *Judah he-Ḥasid*, 11–13; Ta-Shma, "History," 316–17. For more on *Sefer Minhag Tov*, see Weiss, *Book of Minhag Tov*, 217–45.

[76] R. Judah ben Samuel he-Ḥasid, the primary leader of Ḥasidei Ashkenaz, was born in Speyer and moved at some point in his life to Regensburg or possibly lived there his entire life. See Ephraim Shoham-Steiner, "Reexamining the Migration of the Pietistic Kalonymides from the Rhineland to the Danube" [in Hebrew], *Zion* 81 (2016): 149–76; for more details see Dan, *Judah he-Ḥasid*.

[77] See Dan, *Judah he-Ḥasid*, 11–13; Ta-Shma, "History," 316–17.

[78] See Ta-Shma, *Knesset Meḥqarim: Studies in Medieval Rabbinic Literature* [in Hebrew], 4 vols. (Jerusalem, 2004–2010), 1:261.

[79] See Ta-Shma, "History," 312–13.

haftarot[80] known as *Perushe ha-Torah* (Interpretations of the Torah) and assembled by Judah's son, R. Moses ben Judah Zaltman.[81] However, some of the commentaries attributed to the transmission of R. Isaac do not mention R. Judah explicitly, and one cites R. Eleazar of Worms instead.[82] Moreover, the form of attribution to R. Isaac of Rus' varies. Fourteen texts clearly spell out "R. Isaac of Rus'," although one of these abbreviates the first name as "R. Y[itzhak]" (ר״י) and the typical *Rusi'a* (רוסיא) to *Rus* (רוס). Another one of the fourteen has both the full name and the acronym רי״מ, which presumably stands for "R. Y[itzhak] of [Rus']." The same (somewhat ambiguous) acronym appears alone in fourteen other texts. Six additional texts simply cite "R. Isaac" (ר׳ יצחק); two of these use the abbreviation "R. Y[itzhak]" (ר״י).

Could R. Isaac ben Ezekiel of Rus' of the *Sefer Minhag Tov* be identical to the Isaac of Rus' who belonged to the circles of Ḥasidei Ashkenaz? Chronologically, this is at least possible: the Italian text was composed sometime close to 1273, and the "German" R. Isaac of Rus' certainly outlived R. Judah he-Ḥasid, who died in 1217.

This "German" identification does not necessarily preclude the English one. During the long and relatively prosperous reign of Henry II, many Jews had good reasons to resettle or visit England, where they enjoyed a favorable position.[83] "Ysaac de Russie" or "Ysaac de Russia" and Isaac of Chernigov may well have been among such migrants. And they may not necessarily have come to England directly from Rus'. They could have come to England from Germany—for instance, as one/some of the Jewish emigrés to England against whom Emperor Frederick Barbarossa protested in 1168 (thirteen years before our Pipe Rolls entry).[84] However, this particular wave of migra-

---

[80] Selections from the Prophets, read as part of the service on Saturdays and other special occasions in addition to the readings from the Pentateuch.

[81] Caught up in controversy due to its bold critical approach to the biblical text and first published only in 1975; see Isaac S. Lange, ed., *Perushe ha-Torah* (Jerusalem, 1975). See also Efraim F. Kupfer, *Responsa et Decisiones: Ad fidem Codicis Bodleianensis 692* [in Hebrew] (Jerusalem, 1973), 162 n. 14; Ta-Shma, "History," 309–12; Kulik, "Jews from Rus'," 382–83.

[82] R. Eleazer ben Judah of Worms (Eleazar Rokeach, ca. 1165–1230), a relative of R. Judah he-Ḥasid, was born in Mainz to the same influential Kalonymous family and was deeply influenced by Judah he-Ḥasid. R. Eleazar also cited a *kashrut* ruling by R. Moses Poler (of Poland); see Urbach, *Tosafists*, 388–411. Cf. Simcha Emanuel, ed., *Oratio ad Pascam: Rabbi Elazar Vormensis* [in Hebrew] (Jerusalem, 2006); Joseph Dan, *History of Jewish Mysticism and Esotericism* [in Hebrew], 10 vols. (Jerusalem, 2008–2014), 6:493–669. For his evidence connected to Jews in Poland, see Paris, L'Ecole rabbinique de France, MS 147 (Ashkenazi script, 1465), fol. 51a; Simcha Emanuel, *Shivrei Luḥot: Lost Books of the Tosaphists* [in Hebrew] (Jerusalem, 2006), 241–43, n. 91.

[83] Roth, *History*, 10.

[84] William Stubbs, *The Historical Works of Gervase of Canterbury*. 2 vols. (London, 1879–1880), 1:205; Roth, *History*, 12.

tion is not a possibility for someone who was a disciple of R. Judah he-Ḥasid, who himself turned eighteen only during that year.

The French Connection

Kupfer noticed that the commentary on Ex 18:3 in R. Judah's *Perushe ha-Torah* also appears, albeit worded differently, in the commentarial work *Pe'aneah Raza'*, composed by R. Isaac ben Judah ha-Levi not earlier than 1300.[85] The oldest manuscripts of this latter text—Oxford (Bodleian Library; Italian script, fifteenth century), MS Opp. Add. Qu. 103 (Neubauer no. OX 2344), fol. 59a, and Munich (Bayerische Staatsbibliothek; Ashkenazi script, 1552), Cod. Hebr. 50, fol. 125b—ascribe the commentarial passage to "R. Y(ehudah he-Ḥasid) in the name of R. Y(itzhak) from Rus'" (רי״ח בשם ר׳י מרוסיאה), while multiple printed editions have instead "R. Judah he-Ḥasid in the name of Rabbenu from Moret [or Moriat]" (רי״ח בשם רבינו ממוראט). Ta-Shma suggested that these discrepancies provide the basis for identifying R. Isaac from Rus' and R. Isaac from Moret as one and the same person.[86] French residency of Rusian migrants is not entirely unprecedented: another scholar from Rus', R. Moses of Kiev—a disciple of the most prominent Tosafist, Rabbenu Tam—might have lived in Champagne in the late twelfth century.[87] However, no extant manuscript of *Pe'aneah Raza'* contains this alternative attribution, which makes this identification much less likely.

But even if our "German" Isaac is indeed identical to the "French" one, his further identification with our "English" Isaac is still not beyond the realm of

---

[85] Kupfer, *Responsa et Decisiones*, 162 n. 14. On *Pe'aneah Raza*, see Joy Rochwarger, "Sefer Pa'aneah Raza and Biblical Exegesis in Medieval Ashkenaz" (master's thesis, The Hebrew University of Jerusalem, 2000).

[86] See Ta-Shma, "History," 309, 312; idem, *Studies in Medieval Rabbinic Literature*, 1:245–48. See also Heinrich Gross, *Gallia Judaica: Dictionnaire géographique de la France d'après les sources rabbiniques* (Paris, 1897), 338–39. On R. Isaac from Moret, see Ephraim Kanarfogel, "Between the Tosafist Academies and other Battei Midrash in Ashkenaz in the Middle Ages" [in Hebrew], in *Yeshivot and Battei Midrash: Mordechai Breuer Jubilee Volume*, ed. Immanuel Etkes (Jerusalem, 2006), 85–108, 106 n. 86; Ephraim Kanarfogel, *The Intellectual History and Rabbinic Culture of Medieval Ashkenaz* (Detroit, 2013), 205 n. 1. Kupfer, *Responsa et Decisiones*, 162 n. 14, appears to reject the identification.

[87] See Simcha Emanuel, "A Responsum of Samuel ben Ali Gaon of Baghdad to the Talmudic Scholars of France" [in Hebrew], *Tarbiz* 66 (1996): 96–97; Avraham (Rami) Reiner, "Rabbenu Tam: His (French) Teachers and His Student From Ashenaz" [in Hebrew] (master's thesis, The Hebrew University of Jerusalem, 1997), 130–33; Israel M. Ta-Shma, *Creativity and Tradition: Studies in Medieval Rabbinic Scholarship, Literature and Thought* (Cambridge, MA, 2006), 42. R. Yaakov ben Meir of Ramerupt (commonly known as Rabbenu Tam), a grandson of Rashi, was often considered the most outstanding of the Tosafists.

probability. Jewish migration from France to England is well attested for this period. His departure from France could have followed naturally from the series of tragic events associated with the Blois blood libel of 1171 (and the subsequent accusations elsewhere in France).[88] Similarly, the scholar R. Yom Tov of Joigny removed from Troyes to York in 1180.[89] Other anti-Jewish outbreaks took place in Central France in the same years as well—from the imprisonment of the Jewish notables of Paris in 1180 to the general expulsion of the Jews from the royal estates by Philip II Augustus (1180–1223) in 1182.[90] Moret, not far from Paris, was part of the royal domain and therefore also subject to the edict of expulsion.[91]

To the French connection may also be added the proximity of R. Isaac's ideas with those of the school of R. Moses ha-Darshan of Narbonne discussed above.

A Polish Direction

Finally, one of the commentaries in R. Judah's *Perushe ha-Torah* cites "R. Isaac Poler," that is, "R. Isaac of Poland" (ר' יצחק פולער). A certain R. Isaac of Poland is also known from an unidentified Torah commentary extant in a fourteenth-century Ashkenazi manuscript (London, British Library, MS Or. 9931, fols. 121a–121b, 123b). Ta-Shma believed this to be R. Isaac of Rus' and a senior member of the circle of R. Judah he-Ḥasid in Regensburg.[92]

Ta-Shma[93] also proposed that R. Isaac ben Ezekiel was the son of the R. Ezekiel who called for the excommunication of R. Jacob Svara of Kraków, as

---

[88] This is the earliest ritual murder accusation made in France; it was followed by the burning of thirty-three members of the community.

[89] Roth, *Intellectual*, 21–22.

[90] Robert Chazan, *Medieval Jewry in Northern France: A Political and Social History* (Baltimore, 1973), 64–70, 74–75; idem, *The Jews of Medieval Western Christendom, 1000–1500* (Cambridge, UK, 2006), 137–41.

[91] The French form *Russie* in the first Pipe Rolls records above, rather than the Latin *Russia* (as in the second record), does not do much to help us make the choice between the German and the French options, considering that throughout this period Norman French was widely spoken in England; it influenced Middle English idiom and was probably also the language used by most Jews. This is especially noticeable in the French names common among English Jews; see Roth, *History*, 93–95; Robin R. Mundill, *England's Jewish Solution: Experiment and Expulsion, 1262–1290* (Cambridge, UK, 1998), 28. The same French form for "Rus'" is to be found, for example, in Layamon's *Brut* [The Chronicle of England] of about 1205, otherwise written in Middle English: *king of Rusie ræhzest alre cnihten*, "king of Rus', sternest of all knights"; see Frederic Madden, ed., *Layamons Brut, or Chronicle of Britain: A Poetical Semi-Saxon Paraphrase of the Brut of Wace*, 3 vols. (London, 1847), 2:132, verses 13322–23.

[92] Ta-Shma "History," 309–10.

[93] Ibid., 312.

cited in R. Isaac ben Moses of Vienna's *Or Zarua'* (first half of the thirteenth century).[94] The case of R. Jacob Svara mentions a scholar by the name of R. Aaron. As *Sefer Minhag Tov* also mentions a scholar by the name of R. Aaron, the two references might be to the same individual. Were this demonstrated, it would help establish the connection between R. Isaac ben Ezekiel and the case of R. Jacob Svara.

Suppositions regarding persons identified variably in different sources as both "of Rus'" and "of Poland" are possible, but for a different reason than Ta-Shma adduces. Based on the fact that R. Benjamin ben Jonah of Tudela in his *Book of Travels* (*Sefer Masa'oth*; year 1173) ignores the existence of Poland between Bohemia and Rus',[95] Ta-Shma assumed that medieval rabbinic texts did not distinguish between Poland and Rus'.[96] Generally speaking, however, this was not so, and many contemporary Jewish sources clearly distinguish between the two. But many border territories—including such important regions as Red Ruthenia—changed hands frequently between Poland and the principalities of Rus', while their politically divided Jewish population likely preserved a cultural continuity that could easily create such "ambiguous identities" (through continued utilization of the political conception of a previous era). Among the contemporary Polish scholars named Isaac we also find a R. Isaac of Wrocław, who R. Abraham ben Azriel of Bohemia cites in his *'Arugat ha-Bosem* dated to 1234.[97]

A Lithuanian Seal

Finally, we consider a recently-added piece of evidence from the then-Lithuanian Novogrudok region. In 2015 excavations at the Lavrishev Monastery on the banks of the Neman, some 30 km from Novogrudok (also known as "Little" or "Lithuanian Novgorod" and now part of Grodno

---

[94] See Ya'aḳov Farbshṭain, ed., *Sefer Or Zarua' of R. Isaac b. Moses*, 3 vols. (Jerusalem, 2010), 1:661–62 (§ 740). R. Jacob of Kraków (fl. first half of the thirteenth century) was a contemporary of R. Judah he-Ḥasid. He is known from several sources to have become embroiled in a controversy surrounding his own marriage and to have transmitted various commentaries and rulings. It is assumed that R. Jacob of Kraków was a single individual identified in the sources by various names, including, R. Jacob Svara (Savar, Savur), R. Jacob ben Shalom ha-Kohen, and R. Jacob of Poland. See Ephraim E. Urbach, *The Tosafists: Their History, Writings and Methods* [in Hebrew] (Jerusalem, 1980) 490–91; Ta-Shma, *Creativity and Tradition*, 44–51.

[95] Marcus N. Adler, ed., *The Itinerary of Benjamin of Tudela: Critical Text, Translation and Commentary* (London, 1907), 72.

[96] Ta-Shma, "History," 309–10.

[97] Ephraim E. Urbach, *Sefer Arugat ha-Bosem Auctore R. Abraham b. R. 'Azriel* [in Hebrew], 4 vols. (Jerusalem, 1939–1963).

---

province of Belarus), unearthed a presumed thirteenth-century seal matrix made of shale.[98] Its inscription consists of Hebrew letters and reads "יצחק [ק]איזי," i.e., "Isaac Ayyzi[k]," with the final letter missing due to damage.[99] Alternatively, the last letter could possibly have been ל, which would make the reading "Isaac Ayyzi[l]." Alternative vocalizations of the second name are possible, especially *Ayyzek/Ayyzel*. Beider's onomastic dictionary lists similar attested derivatives of the name *Yitzhak/Isaac*, including such pronunciations as *Ayyzik*, *Ayyzek*, and *Ayzel*.[100] The closest variants in form, date, and provenance to the Lavrischev seal inscription include Hebrew איזק ('*Ayyzeq*; Lviv/Lwów, 1599) and אייזיק ('*Ayyziq*; Lithuania, 1632); Cyrillic Айзик (*Aizik*; Brest, 1579) and Ейзик (*Eizik*; Volhynia, 1607); and Latin *Ayzel/Eyzel* (Hungary, 1400). The Lavrishev signet thus constitutes further evidence of the presence of Jewish traders and/or residents in the territory of western Rus' in the thirteenth century. In particular, this artifact attests to the existence of someone called Isaac who also utilized a localized form of his Hebrew name. The Black Ruthenian principality of Novogrudok was incorporated into the Grand Duchy of Lithuania in the mid-thirteenth century and became one of its most important centers—possibly even the first capital and later the see of the Orthodox Metropolitanate of Lithuania—with Jewish presence attested here as early as 1388.[101]

Conclusion

In summary, we have six references to R. Isaac, a resident of or migrant from Rus', and two more of persons from other places identified with "Isaac of Rus'" in sources dating from 1180 to circa 1273 and originating from England, Germany, France, Italy, Poland, and Lithuania:

---

[98] See Сяргей Галоўка [Siarhei Haloŭka], "Тайны Лаўрышаўскага манастыра: Шлях да разгадак" [Secrets of the Lauryshava Monastery: A Path to Decoding], *Беларуская думка* 11 (2015): 50–57; Сяргей Шупа [Siarhei Shupa], "Які Ііхак-Айзік згубіў пячатку XIII ста-годзьдзя ў Лаўрышаўскім манастыры?" [Which Yitzhak/Isaac Lost a Seal of the Thirteenth Century in the Lauryshava Monastery?], *Радыё Свабода* (Oct. 22, 2015), http://www.svaboda.org/content/article/27321253.html; "Надпіс на старажытнай пячатцы: іўрыт ёсьць, а габр-эяў не было?" [The Inscription on an Ancient Seal: Hebrew Where There Were No Jews?], Радыё Свабода (Oct. 28, 2015), http://www.svaboda.org/content/article/27331749.html.

[99] Some controversy arose in Belarus due to an earlier deciphering of the inscription as "Α[γιος]ΠΥ[C]TIN," i.e., "Holy hermitage" in a combination of Greek and Slavic. However, the *interpretatio hebraica* is both obvious and unambiguous.

[100] Alexander Beider, *A Dictionary of Ashkenazic Given Names: Their Origins, Structure, Pronunciation, and Migrations* (Bergenfield, NJ, 2001), 340–42.

[101] Stanislovas Lazutka and Edwardas Gudavichius, *Privilege to Jews Granted by Vytautas the Great in 1388* (Moscow, 1993).

1. R. Isaac of Chernigov (kabbalistic anthologies, prior to the fifteenth century), Ashkenaz
2. R. Isaac of Chernigov (*Sefer ha-Shoham*, mid–late thirteenth century), England
3. Ysaac de Russie (*Pipe Rolls*, 1180–1182), South Hampshire, England
4. R. Isaac ben Ezekiel of Rus' (*Sefer Minhag Tov*, ca. 1273), Italy
5. R. Isaac of Rus' (*Perushe ha-Torah*, after 1217), Regensburg, Germany
6. R. Isaac of Moret/Moriat (*Perushe ha-Torah*, after 1217), Moret or Moriat, France
7. R. Isaac of Poland (*Perushe ha-Torah*, after 1217), Poland
8. Isaac Ayzi[k] (seal matrix, thirteenth century), Novogrudok, Lithuania

Could all these Isaacs be one and the same person? The geographical range of the evidence should not pose a real challenge for such an identification, for the following two reasons.

In most cases the geographic attribution refers to the informants, that is, the authors of our sources, rather than to R. Isaac himself. Only references nos. 3 and 8 necessarily suggest Isaac's physical presence in South Hampshire and Novogrudok. respectively. The rest of the reported contacts might have taken place elsewhere, due to the mobility of the informant or intermediary informants, or even via correspondence. So, for example, the Italian *Sefer Minhag Tov* (no. 4) often refers to foreign informants, both German and French; and R. Judah he-Ḥasid (no. 5) was known for his contacts with East European correspondents (although the volume of traditions transmitted in his name by R. Isaac suggests rather intramural, teacher-pupil relations).

Additionally, even suggesting R. Isaac's physical presence in all or some of these locations would not be unprecedented, especially in the case of a Jew who settled in England with its relatively young community of migrants, mainly from France as well as from Germany and other places.[102] There are documented precedents of persons connected to all three of these countries. For the same period there is the example of Elhanan ben Yakar of London, who was also associated with Ḥasidei Ashkenaz and had studied in France.[103]

The chronology of such an identification of the different multiple Isaacs with each other is somewhat more difficult but still within the realm of the possible. In 1180 the "composite" Isaac should have been an adult paying his taxes or fines. He outlived R. Judah he-Ḥasid and communicated with

---

[102]On possible migrants to England from Rus', see Kulik, "Jews from Rus'," 374–76, 382, 386, 388–89, 402–3, passim.

[103]Cecil Roth, *The Intellectual Activities of Medieval English Jewry* (London, 1949), 62; Na'ama Ben Shachar, *Commentary to Sefer Yezira Attributed to R. Saadia Gaon* [in Hebrew] (Los Angeles, 2015), 31–38.

Moses Zaltman after that date. He made the acquaintance of two people: (a) R. Moses ben ha-Nessiah, whose birth and death dates are not known, but we do know that his teacher, R. Moses ben Yom Tov ha-Nakdan, died in 1268 (if he passed away at a ripe old age and his student was his junior by some twenty years, then R. Moses ben ha-Nessiah could have been born as early as 1220, if not earlier); and (b) the author of the *Sefer Minhag Tov*, sometime before 1273 (but after the book was composed).

A person living a fruitful life from approximately 1160 to 1240 could manage to proverbially dance at all these weddings, but it is rather more probable that we are dealing with more than one person. If so, for the sake of more cautious identifications we need to regroup the evidence, considering not only geographical and chronological technicalities, but also the content of the teachings ascribed to the manifold Isaacs. R. Isaac of Chernigov (nos. 1 and 2) may well be the same person, not only due to his place of origin, which is unique in rabbinic literature, but also because of an affinity between the scholarly interests (including erotic overtones) manifest in both sources. It seems that this scholar was famous enough that such an authoritative work as *Sefer ha-Kuzari* by R. Judah ha-Levi could be ascribed to him, even if erroneously.

It is also plausible that R. Isaac ben Ezekiel of Rus' (no. 4) is identical to R. Isaac of Chernigov (nos. 1 and 2). The esoteric teaching of the former, direct parallels to which we found a "mere" five centuries later (curiously enough, also in East European Ḥasidic tradition), not only shows similarity but may complement and explain what exactly was meant in the doctrine concerning circumcision attributed to R. Isaac of Chernigov (no. 1).

Due to the manifest dependence of the *Sefer Minhag Tov* on Ḥasidei Ashkenaz, it is tempting to extend this identification also to the disciple of R. Judah he-Ḥasid, the R. Isaac of Rus' of *Perushe ha-Torah* (no. 5). His literary heritage is the richest of all our Isaacs—approximately thirty commentaries transmitted in his name comprise more than a dozen pages. But, alas, none of these texts feature any resemblance to the teachings of R. Isaac of Chernigov / Isaac ben Ezekiel of Rus' (although it bears noting that these traditions are supposed to represent the interpretations of R. Judah, having only been communicated by R. Isaac).

Any further identification of the R. Isaac of Rus' who belonged to the circles of Ḥasidei Ashkenaz with R. Isaac of Moret (no. 6) or R. Isaac of Poland (no. 7) can hardly withstand examination. The former conjecture is based only on printed editions, while the manuscript evidence shows no trace of confusion between the two. Behind the latter identification lies Ta-Shma's approach—based on Weinryb's earlier skepticism as to the very existence of early Rus' Jewry—that seeks to eliminate all Rus' evidence and, whenever possible, explain it as Polish.[104] Since this approach fails the tests of source criticism and more balanced historical contextualization, I see no need to identify these two namesakes with R. Isaac of Rus' based solely on their common East European provenance.

Moreover, Ysaac de Russie, who paid his taxes in South Hampshire (no. 3) and Isaac Ayzi[k], who lost his seal matrix in Lithuanian Novogrudok (no. 8), provide us with no further data sufficient even for the most audacious speculations as to their identity. The very fact of the former's residency in England would have been a stronger argument for his identification with Isaac of Chernigov, who had English contacts, if one were to presume that the very appearance of a migrant from Rus' in that place represented a unique phenomenon. However, since this was not the case, we may just as well assume the simultaneous appearance in England of more than one migrant from Rus' bearing this popular name Isaac.

Acknowledgments The research leading to these results has received funding from the European Research Council under the European Union's Seventh Framework Programme (*FP7*/2007–2013) / ERC grant agreement no. 263293 and the Israel Science Foundation (grant no. 314/20). I am grateful to my dearly departed friend and teacher Dr. Michael Schneider z"l for his most valuable advice during the preparation of this article.

Publisher's Note Springer Nature remains neutral with regard to jurisdictional claims in published maps and institutional affiliations.

---

[104] See Ta-Shma, "History"; Weinryb, "Beginnings"; idem, "Myth."

Jewish History (2021) 35: 379–403
https://doi.org/10.1007/s10835-021-09425-z

A Sage of the Golden Age of Safed: Rabbi Moses Najara

YOEL MARCIANO

Ariel University, Ariel, Israel
E-mail: yoelma@ariel.ac.il

Accepted: 20 January 2021 / Published online: 2 December 2021

Abstract Many studies have been devoted to the prominent scholars who lived in Safed, such as R. Joseph Karo and R. Isaac Luria, but these figures were exceptional and do not accurately reflect the reality of the more typical Safed sage. This study deals with R. Moses Najara (R. Israel Najara's father), one of the sages during Safed's Golden Age. The author of *Leqaḥ Ṭov*, he was also a member of the rabbinical court of Safed, to which questions were sent from Jewish communities around the world. The article describes what is known about R. Moses, his literary work, and his role as a rabbi and member of the rabbinical court. Special attention is devoted to his attitude toward Kabbalah, which provides insight that tempers conventional wisdom about the dominance of Kabbalah among Safed sages in the mid-sixteenth century. There is no doubt that if figures like R. Moses had not lived in the shadow of figures who were extraordinary by any measure, they and their works would have received greater attention. This study of R. Moses, who was overshadowed in the eyes of historians by his exceptional peers, aims to provide a more balanced description of the rabbinic stratum of Safed in the period when the city was in its glory.

Keywords Safed sages · Safed kabbalists · Joseph Caro · Isaac Luria · Israel Najara · Jews of Spain · Biblical interpretation

The Jewish population of Safed blossomed dramatically during the sixteenth century, from a small community of 200 to 250 households at the beginning of the century to about 1,700 households in the second half. Safed went from a small Palestinian town in the Ottoman periphery to a city with a Jewish majority and was transformed into one of the most central and influential communities of the Jewish world.[1] Notable among the influx of immigrants from Jewish centers of the west and east were the large number of rabbinic scholars from the Iberian Peninsula. Some of these sages had initially immigrated to other urban centers of the Ottoman Empire—Istanbul, Solonika, Adrianople,

---

Chapter 7 was originally published as Marciano, Y. Jewish History (2021) 35: 379–403. https://doi.org/10.1007/s10835-021-09425-z.

[1] Safed's diverse population was divided into dozens of congregations (likely more than thirty), based on the places of origin of the members. See Bernard Lewis and Amnon Cohen, *Population and Revenue in the Towns of Palestine in the Sixteenth Century* (Princeton, NJ, 1978), 159–61; Joseph Hacker, "Romaniote Jews in Sixteenth-Century Safed: A Chapter in the History of Support for the Jews of Eretz Israel by Communities in the Ottoman Empire" [in Hebrew], *Shalem* 7 (2002): 133–35; idem, "The Payment of Djizya by Scholars in Palestine in the Sixteenth Century" [in Hebrew], *Shalem* 4 (1984): 92–98.

⚫ Springer

Cairo, Damascus, Jerusalem, and others—and from there moved to Safed between 1525 and 1550. Others were born in Safed between 1525 and 1575 to parents who had arrived earlier. Safed became a major center of prominent Torah scholars. Many yeshivas and Torah institutions were established there, and the city rapidly became a spiritual center that drew the attention of individuals and communities in the diaspora. In parallel, Safed developed into a fertile and innovative center of Kabbalah, giving rise to fresh and innovative lifestyles and practices that centered life around religious experience and spirituality. As a result of these developments, many diaspora Jews began to regard Safed as a model community. Communities, institutions, and individuals turned to its sages to adjudicate disagreements in religious and civil matters. Some accepted their rulings unreservedly, provided generous financial support, or even took oaths in their name.

The history of the Jews of Safed and its circle of sages in this golden age has merited considerable scholarly attention, but there has been no comprehensive monograph on the community of Safed in its golden age.[2] R. Joseph Karo and R. Isaac Luria, pathbreaking scholars of the highest rank of sixteenth-century Safed, are two prominent figures who have merited thorough and detailed investigation. However, these two examples are exceptional in many senses. The historian who seeks to describe the typical sage of Safed, whether a teacher in a congregation or another of the city's learned men, cannot rely on the sketches drawn of the personalities, creativity, and activities of the most prominent and truly outstanding individuals. In many respects, scholars of the first rank are not illustrations of the rule, but rather exceptions. If our goal is to understand and characterize the cultural and intellectual reality of Safed in the second half of the sixteenth century, we must first look at the personalities and production of the members of the religious establishment of the city. That is, not the trailblazers who changed future reality, but the vast majority of sages, who served as teachers of Torah, judges, and preachers in the city. R. Moses Najara was one of these figures. Research on R. Moses and other figures like him will give us a more credible depiction of the typical scholarly figure of Safed of that time. R. Moses's extant creative output consists of a single book, entitled *Leqaḥ Ṭov*. Other than that work, not much is known about him. Taking account of all that is

---

[2]There is a broad literature on Safed and the individuals who lived there. For a (nonupdated) bibliography on Safed, see Naftali Ben-Menachem, "Publications on Safed: Bibliography" [in Hebrew], *Sefunot* 6 (1962): 475–503. Even after more than a century, Schechter's article is still important: Solomon Schechter, "Safed in the Sixteenth Century: A City of Legists and Mystics," in *Studies in Judaism, Second Series*, ed. Solomon Schechter (1908), 202–306, 317–328. Recently, see the broad and comprehensive scholarship concentrated in Eyal Davidson, "Safed's Sages Between 1540–1615, their Religious and Social Status" [in Hebrew] (PhD diss., Hebrew University of Jerusalem, 2009).

known about him and his character from the available sources, in particular from his book, I will endeavor to sketch a portrait of R. Moses Najara as a sixteenth-century scholar of Safed.

Life of R. Moses Najara

Moses son of Levi Najara was a second-generation exile from Spain. His name indicates that the family originated from Nájera, in the province of La Rioja in northern Spain. After the expulsion of the Jews from Spain in 1492, his father Levi entered the Ottoman Empire and apparently settled in Constantinople.[3] His son Moses was born ca. 1510, and around 1530 Moses Najara immigrated with his father to Safed, like many other local scholars who had come from various Jewish communities across the empire.[4] R. Moses married into the family of R. Israel di Curiel, one of the four scholars ordained by R. Jacob Berab in the attempted revival of *semikhah* (the ancient chain of ordination that traditionally originated with the biblical Moses).[5] Around 1555,[6] R. Moses's son, the poet R. Israel Najara was born.[7] During the years of R. Moses's youthful studies, several of the greatest Torah scholars of the sixteenth century lived in Safed,. He himself became one of the sages of the city, and his son considered him to be one of his teachers. R. Israel Najara, in a eulogy for R. Moses Alsheikh, wrote of his father's membership in a rabbinical court alongside R. Alsheikh:

> How great is the punishment of one who is lax in eulogizing a sage, particularly a man outstanding in his generation as this. Furthermore, this obligation applies somewhat specifically to me, because he was a member of a rabbinical court in Safed with the

---

[3] See Israel ben Moses Najara, *Miqveh Israel*, ed. Shual Regev (Ramat Gan, 2004), 394.

[4] Many of them came to Safed from Salonica. See Joseph Hacker, "Links Between Salonican Jews and the Community of Safed in the Sixteenth and Seventeenth Centuries" [in Hebrew], *Shalem* 8 (2009): 249–326.

[5] Regarding the identity of those who were ordained by Rabbi Berab, see Meir Benayahu, "The Revival or Ordination in Safed" [in Hebrew], in *Yitzhak Baer: Jubilee Volume on the Occasion of His Seventieth Birthday*, ed. Salo W. Baron et al. (Jerusalem, 1960), 248–69. On R. Moses's marriage to the daughter of R. Israel di Curiel, R. Israel Najara wrote, "Saintly and righteous giants, members of our family like my father and teacher, bridegroom of the King [Israel Meir di Curiel]"; Israel Najara, *Miqveh Israel*, 125.

[6] According to Shaul Regev, the publisher of R. Israel Najara's *Miqveh Israel*, he was born around 1550. See Regev, introduction to *Miqveh Israel*, 14.

[7] See, for example, Najara, *Miqveh Israel*, 123.

great Rabbi, my father and teacher—brothers who shall not be parted.[8]

At the end of the 1570s, R. Moses and his family moved from Safed to Damascus. The events that precipitated the move are not completely clear, but we know of many troubles and difficulties, in particular an economic crisis in Safed during those years. A central cause of the crisis was an increase in the tax burden. The burden was increased by periodic censuses, following which the sums imposed on the community were reassessed. For example, between the years 1555/6 and 1567/8, the poll tax increased from approximately 1,175 to 1,785 gold coins.[9] The situation deteriorated further in 1574, the beginning of the reign of Murad III.[10] The difficulties led many Jews to leave Safed, including many of its sages.[11] The distress that provoked their departure can be seen in a letter R. Israel Najara sent to R. Abraham Hamon of Safed, in which he describes how his family was forced to leave.[12] In Damascus, R. Moses obtained a position as a judge, legal advisor, and preacher in the community, and also was a teacher of local yeshiva students.[13] He died in 1581, a few years after his arrival in Damascus.[14]

We do not know the name of R. Moses's wife, nor do we have many substantial details about her. Her son R. Israel Najara eulogized her,[15] ascribing to her the virtues of the wife of a Torah scholar in the terminology of the time,

---

[8] Ibid., 406. The legal rulings which R. Moses cosigned with R. Moses Alsheikh are discussed below.

[9] On the taxation crisis and its consequences for the community in general and for the scholars in particular, see Hacker, "Payment of Djizya," 64–104; tax data at 94.

[10] During his reign, the economic crisis in the empire intensified, including inflation, flowing from the need to finance wars on many fronts, among other factors.

[11] Davidson ("Safed's Sages," 7–12) quotes many descriptions of this crisis, the decline in the population of Safed, and the departure of Torah scholars. For example, he brings the description of R. Samuel de Uçeda, a younger contemporary of R. Moses, interpreting the opening verse of Lamentations: "In our times, we have seen that in every place under the rule of his majesty the sultan, there is no country with as many taxes and levies on the Jews as the Land of Israel. ... Despite coins being sent from all districts to pay off their taxes and levies, the Jews were not able to reside there because of the tax burden." Samuel de Uçeda, *Leḥem Dim'ah* (Venice, 1600), Lam 1:1. See also n. 16, below.

[12] Meir Benayahu, "Rabbi Israel Najara," [in Hebrew], *Asufot* 4 (1990), 205–6; Najara, *Miqveh Israel*, 23.

[13] This is implied by what his son R. Israel Najara said about him. See Israel Najara, *Meimei Israel* (Venice, 1600), 164b.

[14] We know the date of his death from his son, who writes that his father died "during the watch of the first day of the month of *Tamuz* 5341." See Najara, *Meimei Israel*, 164b; idem, *Miqveh Israel*, 388 n. 1; Ḥayyim David Azulai (Ḥida), *Shem ha-Gedolim ha-Shalem*, ed. Menahem Mendel Krengel (Jerusalem, 1994), *mem*:57.

[15] For the text of the eulogy, see Najara, *Miqveh Israel*, 411–22.

supporting him and helping him to succeed. The only personal (if not uncommon) touch, which is central in the eulogy, is her yearning for the Land of Israel. R. Israel described her longing for the Land of Israel and her aversion to being called a resident of Damascus:

> My mother never wanted to be referred to as a resident of Damascus, but rather as from the Land of Israel. And her efforts to travel to the Land of Israel every year were energetic. Moreover, every time she prayed, she included a prayer for this. Any oaths she took always included, "May I merit burial in the Land of Israel." Nevertheless, she did not merit it.[16]

The matter of her burial in Damascus, despite her yearning to be buried in the Land of Israel, is a considerable part of the eulogy. R. Israel bemoans the fact that her request was not fulfilled, even though she made efforts to arrange for her passing to occur at a time when she was in the Land of Israel, so that she would be buried there.[17] He found some consolation in the view that it was the will of God that his mother be buried next to his father, who also died in Damascus and was buried there.[18]

R. Moses's Early Studies in Safed

According to one scholarly view, R. Moses was one of the students of R. Joseph Karo, but this is unlikely.[19] Others, following R. Ḥayyim Vital

---

[16] Najara, *Miqveh Israel*, 414. Expressions of fierce yearning of the Jews of Safed who underwent difficult tribulations before leaving the Land of Israel are characteristic in writings of that period. See Mordechi Pachter, "The Land of Israel in the Homiletic Literature of Sixteenth-Century Safed" [in Hebrew], in *The Land of Israel in Medieval Jewish Thought*, ed. Moshe Hallamish and Aviezer Ravitzky (Jerusalem, 1991), 290–319.

[17] Her son wrote in his eulogy: "However, what I lament and bewail most, besides my deprivation from losing her, is that she died outside of the Land of Israel, especially because she troubled herself with this her entire life. Whenever she saw that she was feeling weak, she would travel to the Land of Israel, for the possibility of being buried there. But despite all that tenacious effort, she did not accomplish it" (Najara, *Miqveh Israel*, 412).

[18] Ibid., 418–19.

[19] See Abraham David, *To Come to the Land: Immigration and Settlement in 16th-Century Eretz-Israel*, trans. Dena Ordan (Tuscaloosa, AL, 1999), 128–29. Benayahu wrote that R. Moses and several other scholars "were no doubt part of the circle close to R. Joseph Karo, perhaps even his students"; Meir Benayahu, "The Controversy Between the Schools of Moses di Trani and R. Joseph Karo" [in Hebrew], *Asufot* 3 (1989): 45. However, Benayahu did not list R. Moses as one of R. Karo's known students (Benayahu, "Controversy", 187–327). This possibility seems implausible, for several reasons: (1) There is no direct documentation of this. (2) In his book *Leqaḥ Ṭov* (discussed in detail below), R. Moses identifies his teacher

---

in his diary known as *The Book of Visions*,[20] have seen him as a student of
R. Isaac Luria, who arrived in Safed in 1570 and died there in an epidemic on
the fifth of Av, 5332 (1572).[21] As is well known, even though Luria resided
in Safed only briefly, he influenced a great many individuals during his short
period of activity there. Be that as it may, R. Moses was around sixty years
old when Isaac Luria arrived in Safed, and he certainly must have considered some scholar from the previous generation—with whom he studied as a
young man and who helped him reach the status of a Torah sage and member
of the rabbinical court—as his mentor and rabbi.

In his book *Leqaḥ Ṭov*, published in Constantinople in 1575, R. Moses
cites several insights that he heard from his teacher. However, he does not
mention the teacher's name, and the teacher's identity is not easily clarified.[22] The teacher is usually mentioned together with the Aramaic abbreviation נר"ו (*naṭrei rahamana' u-farqei*, "may the Merciful One preserve and
redeem him") or the Hebrew abbreviation י"צ (*yishmerenu ẓuro*, "may his
Rock watch over him"), which are blessings used for living persons.[23] This
indicates that at the time the book was published, or at least when it was
written, his teacher was still alive. However, on two occasions, his teacher
is mentioned together with a blessing used for people who are deceased:
"My teacher and Rabbi ז"ל (*zichrono levrakha*, "may his memory be for a

as the author of a book of Rabbinic sayings. No such book by R. Joseph Karo is known. (3)
He does not mention the writings of R. Joseph Karo in his book *Leqaḥ Ṭov*, despite his anonymous Rabbi being cited numerous times in the work. (4) A halakhic question of R. Moses is
preserved in the responsa of R. Moses di Trani. It would seem unlikely that if he were a student of R. Joseph Karo, he would bring a question specifically to di Trani, who was R. Karo's
main rival. See also below, n. 62.

[20] Morris M. Faierstein, ed., *Book of Visions: The Diary of Rabbi Hayyim Vital* [in Hebrew],
(Jerusalem, 2005), 189–90. See below, the text annotated by n. 91. Similarly, Azulai, *Shem
ha-Gedolim, ma`arekhet gedolim, mem*:161, p. 160.

[21] There is one sentence in R. Moses's book *Leqaḥ Ṭov* that hints that he learned Torah from
R. Luria. The hint is in R. Israel Najara's poetic praise on the final page of the book: "How
much sweeter than honey, good taste and knowledge, a honeycomb, pleasant words worth
their weight in gold. ... And how much fiercer than a lion is the strength of the author, who
has scraped the honey from the carcass of the lion." Cf. Judges 14:8–9. Isaac Luria is widely
known by the nickname "the Lion."

[22] A facsimile reproduction of the book was published in Jerusalem in 1974, with the addition
of biblical chapter and verse numbers in the margins. At the end of the book, along with some
words of praise for the author, the anonymous publisher noted: "Many times in the book he
writes 'My teacher and Rabbi, may the Merciful One protect and preserve him, wrote ... ' and
the like, without mentioning his Rabbi's name. I have been unable to clarify who said Rabbi
is."

[23] Places where he mentions his teacher with a blessing used for a living person: 3b; 6b;
23a; 24b; 36a–b; 42a; 43a; 43b; 99a; 117a; 120a; 127a; 133b; 136b; 137b; 143a; 144b. Places
where he mentions his teacher without a blessing: 15b; 36b; 39b; 80b; 87a; 90a; 124a.

blessing")."[24] And yet, eleven lines later, commenting on the same biblical verse and still discussing the same topic, the teacher is mentioned as a living person: "This saying is explained in the book of sayings of my teacher and Rabbi, may the Merciful One preserve and redeem him."[25] This phenomenon is known from other books.[26] Many times it indicates that the individual in question died shortly before or during the publication process, resulting in inconsistent editing of the places where he is mentioned. However, we will see that this is not the case here.

Identification of the "book of sayings" of said teacher is not an easy task. "Book of sayings" is not a book title, but a very broad genre in the sixteenth century in which the author explains statements of *Hazal*, usually incorporating them into a Bible commentary, or into sermons or homilies. The "book of sayings" is mentioned in R. Moses's comments on the Torah portion of *Bereshit* (the first five chapters of Genesis), which stands as a distinctive unit separate from the rest of his work, and one other time in his commentary on the Torah portion of *Lekh Lekha* (Genesis 12–17).[27] In the other sections of the book, he cites his teacher with the phrase "My teacher and Rabbi interpreted ..." A review of R. Moses's citations from the "book of sayings" and comparison to the writings of scholars of the period suggests that it is possible, and indeed probable, to associate the "book of sayings" with his father-in-law, R. Israel di Curiel.[28] What we find here is the common phenomenon of a student who marries his teacher's daughter.[29]

R. Israel di Curiel died in 1577.[30] This data point is consistent with the fact that in the printed edition of *Leqah Tov*, R. Moses's teacher is mostly

---

[24] Moses Najara, *Leqah Tov* (Jerusalem: 1974), 4a.

[25] Ibid., 6b.

[26] For example, in Menahem de Lonzano's *Derekh Hayyim* (Constantinople, 1575) the name of R. Yosef Karo is mentioned three times: the first two times with a blessing for a living person and the third time with a blessing for a deceased person, after news of Karo's death had reached the author. See Joseph Hacker, "Agitation Against Philosophy in Istanbul in the Sixteenth Century: Studies in Menahem de Lonzano's *Derekh Hayyim*" [in Hebrew], in *Studies in Jewish Mysticism, Philosophy and Ethical Literature Presented to Isaiah Tishby on his Seventy-Fifth Birthday*, ed. Joseph Dan and Joseph Hacker (Jerusalem, 1986), 533–36.

[27] Najara, *Leqah Tov*, 15b.

[28] See the publisher's preface to the 1999 edition of *Leqah Tov*, claiming that R. Moses's teacher was R. Israel di Curiel, based on parallels between the teacher and his student (ibid., 33–6). R. Moses's book includes some citations from his teacher that have no parallel in R. Israel di Curiel's extant collection. However, there is evidence that R. Israel di Curiel authored additional collections that are no longer extant; see publisher's introduction to *Israel di Curiel: Derashot u-Ma'amarim*, ed. Shaul Regev (Jerusalem, 1992), 26.

[29] See Davidson, "Safed's Sages," 251–5.

[30] Haim Bentov, "Autobiographical and Historical Register of Rabbi Josef di Trani [in Hebrew], *Shalem* 1 (1974), 201–2, 206.

referred to as a living person. However, how can we account for the fact that on two occasions where R. Israel di Curiel was identified as the author of the "book of sayings" he is referred to as deceased?[31] Perhaps in these two instances it is a publisher's error, in which the expression "of blessed memory" was mistakenly inserted.

R. Moses traveled to Constantinople specifically to handle the publication of his book. We know this from the preface, which is signed אבי״י, the initials of Abraham ben Isaac Jabez, from the publishing house of the brothers Solomon and Joseph Jabez.[32] In the book's introduction, Jabez writes regarding the author and his work:

> There is a time to act for the Lord! He came with his staff and travel bag, abandoning his resting place ..., to preserve his learning in his hand. ... He wrote it on a tablet and inscribed it in a book, lest strangers feast on his strength and plunder his labor,[33] and his labor, which was done with wisdom, knowledge, and efficacy, be attributed to a man who did not labor for it.[34]

Even though the journey to Constantinople was arduous, R. Moses wanted to oversee the publication process to make sure that his creation would not be plagiarized and promulgated under the names of others. In addition to this supervisory visit to Constantinople, we know that R. Moses also visited Salonika at some uncertain date after the publication of the book. We know this from an Oxford manuscript that includes some passages of Don Tam Ibn Yahya, in which the poet R. Saadia Longo describes meeting R. Moses:

> The holy man of God, namely the sage Rabbi Moses Najara (may God preserve him!), resident of Safed, author of the book *Leqah Tov*, visited us. Spending time with him on the upstairs porch, we passed from topic to topic and from story to story. He said, "Who can bring me water to drink from the fountain on the *Qadi*'s grounds?[35] I can hear it, and have a passionate desire to drink from it."[36] At that point my thoughts broke into the realm of poetry, and

---

[31] Najara, *Leqah Tov*, 4a and 6b.

[32] Abraham Yaari, *Hebrew Printing at Constantinople: Its History and Bibliography* (Jerusalem, 1967), 26–32.

[33] Cf. Prov 5:10, Ps 109:11.

[34] Najara, *Leqah Tov*, publisher's preface. Cf. Eccl 2:21.

[35] That is to say, the fountain was adjacent to the residence of the *Qadi* [*Shari'a* judge]. The poetic expression alludes to King David's request, "Who will give me water to drink," and his three warriors who penetrated enemy lines to fetch it for him (2 Sam 23:15–6).

[36] Although water can be interpreted allegorically, here it seems that the reference is to actual water. Regarding water supply in Salonika during that period, the poet Abraham Reuben wrote:

I wrote these three poems and sent them to him, together with a flask of water from that fountain. ... The third poem consoles him for his wanderings, praises his book *Leqaḥ Ṭov*, and wishes him tranquility and a return to the Holy Land—or in any case, a swift end to eating salted bread and drinking rationed water.[37]

R. Saadia Longo refers to R. Moses as an "inhabitant of Safed." This characterization fits with a period between 1575 and the year 1579, by which time he had already settled in Damascus. The third poem is intended to raise the spirits of R. Moses with praise for his book and expresses the hope that this difficult period, associated with poverty, will pass quickly. It is possible that the economic hardship prompting these words of consolation influenced his departure from Safed and migration to Damascus.

Judge in Safed

R. Moses served as a judge on a rabbinical court in Safed for more than twenty years.[38] He also served for a long period as a judge in the *beit ha-vaʿad* (council representing all of the congregations) of the city, in which capacity he replied to many questions that were sent from various Jewish communities.[39] Of the impressive number of rulings issued by the court on which he sat, particularly striking is the response of a panel of judges, of which R. Moses was a member, to criticism by R. Moses di Trani (Mabit) that they did not provide sufficient proofs for their legal decisions: "Is it possible

---

"When I saw people selling water for a Dinar [or] Sela, ... and when I needed to buy some in Salonica, it bothered me enormously. I took up my parable: How great was the miracle of old, the visionary extracted water from a rock (*selaʿ*)! And today I will extract water from this selaʿ." See Shenhav Bartov, "Abraham ben Reuven: A Sixteenth-Century Poet" [in Hebrew], *Peʿamim* 159–60 (2019]): 107–8.

[37] Oxford Bodleian MS Pococke 74, fol. 95a–b. I thank Joseph Hacker for calling my attention to this source. On Don Tam Ibn Yaḥya and this manuscript, see Joseph Hacker, "Portuguese Jews in Salonica: The Correspondence between the Beit Halevi and the Ibn Yaḥia Families" [in Hebrew], *Sefunot* 26 (2019): 243, 247, 253, 257. "Salted bread and rationed water" is a reference to M Avot 6:4, *pat ba-melaḥ to'khal u-mayyim bi-meshurah tishteh* ("eat salted bread and drink rationed water"). Based on the content of the third poem (which is included later in the manuscript), it is possible that the allusion is to R. Moses having been in a hurry to continue his journey and, therefore, having been satisfied with a simple meal that was not much bother for his host. In addition, it is possible that he is expressing the wish that R. Moses's troubles, and the poverty he was enduring, would soon end.

[38] See n. 8 above.

[39] Yaakov S. Spiegel, "A Debate between Moses Alsheikh, R. Moshe Najara, R. Isaac Ibn Arḥa, and R. Joseph Karo Against Moses di Trani in the Matter of Isaac Amigo" [in Hebrew], *Min Hagenazim* 7 (2016): 6–9.

for community judges who issue fifty rulings in half a day to have the leisure to write out all of the proofs for each ruling at length?"[40] A number of extant rulings bear R. Moses's signature alongside those of various other scholars. We also have evidence of his involvement in the matter that was referred to R. di Trani for a halakhic ruling. The following are the rulings in which R. Moses is known to have been involved:

1. R. Moses is mentioned in the responsa of R. Isaac Lattes as being a member of a rabbinical court in Safed on 18 Nisan 5323 (April 11, 1563). This ruling was sent to the scholars and communal leadership of "Avignon and its surroundings" regarding the matter of a resident of Carpentras by the name of Bondeon Crescas, who performed the *halitzah* ceremony[41] after the death of his brother. His brother's widow later remarried, and Crescas eventually married her daughter—which is prohibited by Jewish law.[42] The ruling, which urges the communities of the region to use all available means to induce Crescas to divorce her, reflects the power and authority of the rabbinical court of Safed to which R. Moses had been appointed. A number of scholars besides R. Moses were signatories of the ruling, although some of the names are corrupted, probably by the publisher: R. Joseph Karo, R. Moses di Trani, שמואל קוויררקא (probably R. Samuel Ibn Verga), אברהם ארואינו (probably R. Abraham Arueti), יצחק ב'ר אברהם ארח (probably R. Isaac ben Abraham Arḥa), R. Moses Cordovero, R. Joel ben Jacob Ashkenazi, and R. Isaac ben Moses Dayan Halevi.[43]

2. Another ruling to which R. Moses is a signatory concerns a dispute known as the "Tamari-Venturozzo Divorce," which transformed from a local matter at a rabbinical court in Venice into a broad controversy involving many rabbis from a number of Jewish communities. The ruling was issued around the Shavuot holiday in 1568, signed by R. Moses, together with R. Solomon Absaban, R. Moses Galante, and R. Moses Alshich.[44]

---

[40] Ibid., 13–4.

[41] The *halitzah* ceremony is routinely performed by the brother of a married man who dies childless. The purpose of the ceremony is to free the surviving brother from the biblical obligation of levirate marriage to the widow of the deceased.

[42] In the case of *halitzah*, the marriage eligibility restrictions for the surviving brother and his former sister-in-law are the same as in the case of divorce: "He is prohibited to her immediate relatives, and she is prohibited to his immediate relatives" (M Yevamot 4:7).

[43] Max Hermann Friedländer, ed., *Resp. R. Isaac ben Immanuel de Lattes* (Vienna, 1860), 16–7.

[44] In Jewish law, a writ of divorce (*get*) requires the willing cooperation of the husband. There is an extensive halakhic literature discussing what measures may or may not be taken to pressure a reluctant husband to cooperate in order to free the woman to remarry in the event that the husband refuses to issue a *get*. The "Tamari-Venturozzo Divorce" affair revolves around such an incident of *get* refusal, in which R. Meir Katzenellenbogen induced the husband to issue a

3. R. Moses signed as concurring on a responsum written by R. Moses di Trani, together with R. Jacob de Qullier, R. Moses Alshich, and R. Elisha Gallico. The responsum concerns the obligations under the rabbinic laws of custodianship of a man who was asked to bring money from one place to another but was robbed on the way.[45]

4. Another ruling was issued by a judicial panel on which R. Moses sat with R. Moses Alshich and R. Isaac Ibn Arḥa, published by Yaakov Spiegel, concerning a monetary matter.[46] The members of the rabbinical court ruled against a defendant named Isaac Amigo, under the authority of the *beit ha-va`ad* of Safed, and imposed excommunication on him for failing to comply with their ruling. R. Moses di Trani disagreed with the ruling, and his rebuttals were published without mentioning the names of the rabbis from whom he dissented.[47]

5. In another responsum of R. Moses di Trani, R. Moses Najara is the person who sent the legal question to him. The responsum begins, "A student by the name of Moses Barukh came to me with a will in his hand and said that the *Ḥakham* Rabbi Moses Najara had sent him to show me the will."[48] Regarding R. Moses's conduct in this incident, R. Moses di Trani rebuked him, criticizing his handling of the consultation and adjudication.[49]

---

get through a combination of adversarial measures and mediation. After a time, the husband traveled to Mantua to challenge the validity of the *get* and met with R. Moses Provincalo, who cast doubt on its validity and called for a second *get*. That is to say, the dispute transformed quickly into a broad controversy. R. Moses and his colleagues ruled that another *get* was required, in agreement with R. Moses Provincalo. On the "Tamari-Venturozzo Divorce" affair, see, e.g., Shlomo Simonson, "The Scandal of the Tamari-Venturozzo Divorce" [in Hebrew], *Tarbiẓ* 28 (1959): 375–92; Ephraim Kupfer, "Further Clarifications Concerning the Scandal of the Tamari-Venturozzo Divorce" [in Hebrew], *Tarbiẓ* 38, 1 (1968): 54–60; Yitzhak Yudlov, "Bibliographical Notes on the Tamari Venturozzo Affair" [in Hebrew], `Alei Sefer* 2 (1976): 105–20. On the ruling of R. Moses and his colleagues, see Zvi Gertner, "The Case of the Tamari Venturozzo Divorce: New Details from the Beit Midrash of R. Joseph Karo" [in Hebrew], *Moriah* 16, 3–4 (1988): 9–18.

[45] Moses di Trani, *Resp. ha-Mabit*, 2 vols. (Venice, 1629–1630), 2:100; facsimile Jerusalem, 1990.

[46] Spiegel, "Debate." The responsum that Y. S. Spiegel published was taken from a manuscript owned by the Jewish community of Mantua, no. 88 (Institute of Microfilmed Hebrew Manuscripts at the National Library of Israel, f 874), 157a–164b.

[47] *Resp. ha-Mabit*, 2:213. See Spiegel, "Debate," 1–3.

[48] *Resp. ha-Mabit*, 1:281.

[49] See Meir Benayahu, *Yosef Beḥiri: Raban R. Yosef Qaro* [in Hebrew] (Jerusalem, 1991) 43–5. R. Moses di Trani also adopted sharp language against R. Moses and R. Moshe Alsheikh in the ruling on Isaac Amigo mentioned above. Based on these two sources, it would appear that he did not hold him in high regard (see Spiegel, "Debate," 4–6). It is not clear whether the consultation regarding the will was done as part of the legal decision-making process of the *beit ha-va`ad* or under a different framework.

The fact that R. Moses was among the signatories on rulings sent out on behalf of the sages of Safed to Jewish communities of the diaspora in the 1560s, during the lifetimes of R. Joseph Karo and R. Moses di Trani, demonstrates his centrality as a scholar and halakhic authority in the city. The responsa show that he was a member of the *beit ha-va`ad* of Safed, and one can assume that he was a member of the rabbinical court of one of the congregations as well. These sources illustrate the milieu in which R. Moses worked and his standing in the social stratum of the sages of his own generation, as well as his standing among the great leaders of the older generation, led by the students of R. Jacob Berab.

Leqaḥ Tov

The goal of R. Moses's Torah commentary *Leqaḥ Tov* is to collect all of the laws and *mitzvot* that the Rabbis derived from Torah verses into one place. The work of publication began in Constantinople on the fourth day of the month of *Shevat* 5335 (January 15, 1575),[50] in the publishing house of the brothers Solomon and Joseph Jabez.[51] The book includes a publisher's preface signed by Abraham ben Isaac Jabez, followed by a short introduction by R. Moses discussing the importance of the work. The book consists of 169 folios, concluding with a poetic epilogue praising the book and its author by the author's son, R. Israel Najara. A facsimile reproduction was published in Jerusalem in 1974 with the addition of verse references in the margins. A new edition with an introduction, corrections, and references was published in Jerusalem in 1999.[52]

Some scholars of subsequent generations have cited the work,[53] but over the course of time the book has not been widely used. It is mostly a broad collection of sources, showing exceptional scholarship and immense effort, with only a minority of the material created independently by the author. One can gather a small amount of information about the circulation of *Leqaḥ Tov* from a letter written by R. Israel Najara from Safed to R. Betzalel Ashkenazi

---

[50] As is common for traditional Hebrew books, the publication date must be calculated based on the numerical value of the Hebrew letters (*gemaṭria*) of an acronym given on the title page. The calculation for *Leqaḥ Tov* is a little more complex than usual, involving adding the number of letters of one of the words (four) to the sum of the values of the letters of the acronym.

[51] Yaari, *Hebrew Printing at Constantinople*, 26–32.

[52] References in this article are to the 1974 edition. The identity of the publisher is unknown. The 1999 edition was published by the Shuvi Nafshi Yeshiva. It includes an introduction about R. Moses that discusses many of the same issues evaluated here, but they have approached them quite differently. Cf. *Leqaḥ Tov*, 1999 edition, 27–44.

[53] See, e.g., nn. 82 and 83 below.

in Egypt. The friendly relationship between the two probably stems from
R. Ashkenazi's studies in Safed in the yeshiva of R. Israel Najara's grand-
father, R. Israel di Curiel. As we suggested above, R. Israel Najara's father
R. Moses Najara also studied at that yeshiva.[54] In the letter, R. Israel Najara requested that R. Ashkenazi transfer to him some funds obtained from
the sale of his father's book distributed in Egypt. After lengthy praise of the
addressee, R. Israel Najara writes:

> I come, perhaps improperly, ... to lay down this supplication ... to
> collect the price of my father's books there from him for me. Then
> I will know that I have found favor in his eyes.[55]

Leqaḥ Ṭov does not belong to one of the prevalent genres of Torah works of
the period. It was quite an impressive project, in which R. Moses reviewed every verse and noted every word and letter that was interpreted by the Rabbis.
In addition to the halakhic aspect that is central to his work, he also incorporated midrashic and exegetical material. This project required R. Moses to
write concisely and in a laconic and methodical style that did not leave room
to incorporate anecdotal remarks or extensive information on his thought,
conceptions, and values. This is how R. Moses introduces his work:

> I humbly prepared my heart and my eyes to seek and to search
> out, to know the interpretation of the Torah, as it has been received
> with its interpretation from the sages of the Mishnah and the Tal-
> mud. ... And I said, let me turn to the great commentators of the
> Torah. ... But I did not find enough to quench my thirst ... to know
> the interpretation of each verse with all of its precise hermeneu-
> tics. ... Therefore, God stirred my spirit and gave me the heart to
> seek and to search out in the Talmud, the Mekhilta,[56] the Sifra,[57]
> and the Sifre,[58] to find pleasing words and write them in a book,
> as clearly and concisely as I was able. And God delivered of the
> interpretations and hermeneutics of the Rabbis into my hand, for
> every verse, through an extra word or letter and the like—whatever

---

[54] See Meir Benayahu, "Introduction" [in Hebrew], in *R. Israel di Curiel: Derashot u-
Ma'amarim*, 13.

[55] Najara, *Meimei Israel*, 142b.

[56] The midrash halakhah known as *Mekhilta d'Rabbi Yishmael* to the book of Exodus was
published in Constantinople in 1515.

[57] The midrash halakhah to the book of Leviticus, known as Sifra or *Torat Kohanim*, was
published in Constantinople around 1510. R. Aaron Ibn Ḥayyim, a younger contemporary of
R. Moses, wrote a commentary on Sifra, publishing it under the name *Qorban Aharon* (Venice,
1609).

[58] The midrash halakhah to the books of Numbers and Deuteronomy known as Sifre was
published in Venice in 1546.

  Springer

touches upon understanding the verse precisely. When there is disagreement between *tannaim* or *amoraim*, I have taken the correct halakhic interpretation as written by Maimonides. If there is an opinion that disagrees with him, I sometimes also bring the other opinion.[59]

The book has a systematic design, following the order of the verses of the Torah. R. Moses drew from rabbinic literature: the Babylonian Talmud, Jerusalem Talmud,[60] midrash halakhah, and occasionally midrash aggadah. Similarly, he brings legal and exegetical material from early and late medieval commentaries. He brings practical halakhah that is derived from biblical verses, "as written by Maimonides," with reference to dissenting opinions, and specifically the glosses of R. Abraham ben David of Posquières. It is natural that R. Moses did not make the *Shulḥan ʿArukh* of R. Joseph Karo, published ten years earlier, into the halakhic basis of his book, because unlike Maimonides' *Mishneh Torah*, the *Shulḥan ʿArukh* does not cover areas of Jewish law that are no longer practiced, such as the laws of sacrifices, which make up a substantial part of R. Moses's work as a Torah commentator. However, the fact that none of the works of R. Joseph Karo is ever mentioned in *Leqaḥ Ṭov* is striking and requires investigation.[61]

Just as R. Moses bases the halakhic realm on Maimonides' *Mishneh Torah*, he follows Maimonides's *Sefer ha-Mitzvot* in enumerating the *mitzvot*. *Sefer ha-Mitzvot* is the most famous and widely available among works enumerating the *mitzvot* and constitutes the basis for the glosses of Naḥmanides.[62] R. Moses regards the study of *mitzvot* and *halakhot* that are

---

[59] Najara, *Leqaḥ Ṭov*, 2a.

[60] R. Moses's access to the Jerusalem Talmud is not to be taken for granted, because the work was almost lost, and there are few manuscripts. It was printed once prior to the publication of *Leqaḥ Ṭov* (Venice, 1523). On the circulation of the Jerusalem Talmud and its associated commentaries, see Saul Lieberman, "The Old Commentators of the Yershalmi" [in Hebrew], in *Alexander Marx Jubilee Volume on the Occasion of His Seventieth Birthday*, ed. Saul Lieberman (New York, 1950), 287–319. On the French commentators on the Jerusalem Talmud Solomon Sirilio and Elazar Azikri, see Lieberman, "Old Commentators," 301–13. On the manuscripts of the Jerusalem Talmud and the printed text, see Yaakov Z. Mayer, "From Material History to Historical Context: The Case Study of MS Vatican Ebr. 133 of the Palestinian Talmud" [in Hebrew], *Zion* 83 (2018): 277–321, esp. 309–10.

[61] He mentions the *Sefer Mitzvot Gadol* of R. Moses ben Jacob of Coucy and the *'Arbaʿah Turim* of R. Jacob ben Asher, but he does not mention the *Shulḥan ʿArukh* or the *Beit Yosef* of R. Joseph Karo. He mentions the commentaries on Maimonides's *Mishneh Torah* of R. Abraham ben David of Posquières and R. Vidal de Tolosa (*Maggid Mishneh*), but does not mention R. Joseph Karo's *Kesef Mishneh* at all. The fact that he mentions his anonymous teacher and mentor numerous times, but does not mention R. Joseph Karo at all, strengthens the assumption that he was not a student of R. Joseph Karo.

[62] See R. Moses's introduction (Najara, *Leqaḥ Ṭov*, 2a).

no longer practiced or are practiced infrequently—such as the laws of the Temple, sacrifices, the laws of purity and impurity, and laws applicable only in the Land of Israel—to be quite important. He speaks out against scholars who see laws that are no longer practiced as less important. He criticizes scholars that give short shrift to

> *mitzvot* that are not practiced, which are the very essence of the Torah.[63] As the Rabbis said in the first chapter of tractate *Ḥagigah*, "Civil law, Temple rituals, ritual purity, and forbidden relations are the very essence of the Torah." Even the most learned of the scholars of our time, when he is asked to explain a given verse as it is explained in the Talmud or in *torat kohanim*, etc., regarding sacrifices, or leprous lesions, or *ohalot* [ritual impurities inside a tent], or dedicated property, and many others, will not know it in depth. For there can be multiple detailed hermeneutical inferences from a verse, from which numerous regulations and laws are derived, as one who surveys this book will see, God willing.[64]

R. Moses emphasizes that there is something unsatisfactory about the fact that scholars focus on commonly practiced laws, but when asked to explain a verse about laws that are not commonly practiced, they cannot properly expound upon it. His criticism echoes a recurring criticism among other scholars of those that apply intricate, in-depth analysis to commonly practiced laws, while neglecting laws that are not commonly practiced, even though they are "the very essence of Torah."

> The statement of the Rabbis is known, that at the time when a man is ushered in to his Judgement, he is asked: "Did you conduct business faithfully? Did you designate times for Torah study? ... Did you engage in the dialectics of wisdom or understand one matter from another?"[65] But if they would ask him if he knows the weekly Torah portion as it is understood and explained, he would not know. Woe for that humiliation! How could he be considered wise in his own eyes, a teacher of intricate in-depth analysis when he is asked ... "Explain one verse correctly, with all of the precise inferences and hermeneutics received in the Talmud and midrashim, regarding sacrifices, ritual purity, and prohibited relations," which are the very essence of Torah?[66] If he responds to us that these are no longer practiced, we will say to him, "Does that

---

[63] See, e.g., BT Shabbat 32a.

[64] Najara, *Leqaḥ Ṭov*, 2a.

[65] BT Shabbat 31a.

[66] Cf. M Avot 3:18.

exempt us from occupying ourselves with them?" On the contrary, we should make them primary, so that study will be considered like the practice before God. As the Rabbis have said, "One who occupies himself explaining the burnt offering is as if he had sacrificed a burnt offering."[67] ... Since, for our sins, the Temple has been destroyed, and we are unable to fulfil them in practice, we can merit to study and occupy ourselves with them, and it will be as if the Temple were built and we have fulfilled all of the *mitzvot*, "and we will pay you our sacrificial bulls with our lips."[68]

Regarding its characteristics, R. Moses mixes two domains into the work: Bible commentary and Halakhah. In the realm of Bible commentary, in keeping with Sephardic tradition, he gives Rashi and Naḥmanides a central place, and frequently cites R. Elijah Mizraḥi, mainly in reference to Rashi. Similarly, he cites interpretations of R. Abraham Ibn Ezra,[69] R. Samuel ben Meir of Troyes (Rashbam),[70] and R. Hezekiah ben Manoah (Ḥizkuni).[71] Also, he quotes scholars from the generation of the expulsion from Spain, mainly *Zeror Hamor* of R. Abraham Saba,[72] *Aqedat Yiẓḥak* of R. Isaac Arama,[73] and *Toledot Yiẓḥak* of R. Isaac Karo.[74] Notable for their absence are the interpretations of R. Isaac Abarbanel, which may not have been available to him.[75] In the realm of Halakhah, he gives a central place to Maimonides' *Mishneh Torah*, the glosses of R. Abraham ben David of Posquières on the *Mishneh Torah*, and Naḥmanides' glosses to Maimonides' *Sefer ha-Mitzvot*. Also, he frequently discusses classical commentaries on the Talmud and the rulings by major halakhic authorities: R. Isaac Alfasi (Rif),[76] Rashi, Tosafot, R. Asher ben Jehiel (Rosh), R. Moses ben Jacob of Coucy (Smag), R. Solomon ben Abraham Ibn Adret (Rashba), R. Jacob ben Asher (*ba`al ha-turim*),[77] the

---

[67] Cf. BT Menaḥot 100a.

[68] Hos 14:3. Najara, *Leqaḥ Ṭov*, 2a.

[69] See, for example, Najara, *Leqaḥ Ṭov*, 9a.

[70] Ibid., 122b.

[71] Ibid., 22b.

[72] Ibid., 141b.

[73] Ibid., 2b, 7a, 13b, 24b.

[74] Ibid., 10b.

[75] Although Abarbanel's commentaries on most biblical books and some of his other books had already been printed by the early sixteenth century, his commentary on the Torah was first printed in Venice in 1579.

[76] Najara, *Leqaḥ Ṭov*, 91a.

[77] Ibid., 25b.

commentary of Nissim of Girona (Ran) on the *Ha-Halakhot* of R. Isaac Alfasi, the *Maggid Mishneh* by R. Vidal of Tolosa,[78] and others.[79]

On occasion, R. Moses will bring his opinion with phrases such as "It seems to me … " and the like. In some places he offers a novel interpretation of midrash halakhah. For example, on the issue of whether Transjordan is part of the Land of Israel (a question with halakhic implications), most authorities rule in the affirmative, but struggle with a midrash in Sifre (*Mas`ei* 61):

> "They shall be as cities of refuge for you." This only implies those that provide asylum in the Land of Israel. From whence do I derive those outside of the land? From "They shall be …

This implies that Transjordan is outside of the Land of Israel. R. Moses comments on this:

> That is to say, even those that are in Transjordan, which is outside of the Land of Israel, provide asylum. But those that are totally (*mamash*) outside of the Land of Israel, in other places, certainly do not provide asylum, because the law of sanctuary cities applies only in the Land of Israel.[80]

That is to say, R. Moses is creating a new concept, so that there are now three categories: "The Land of Israel," "outside of the Land" (Transjordan, which is still part of the Land of Israel), and "totally outside of the Land."[81]

R. Moses and Kabbalah

The place of Kabbalah in *Leqaḥ Ṭov* is quite limited. Interpretations from the Zohar and kabbalistic matters that touch on biblical interpretation appear only occasionally.[82] The book mentions a few kabbalistic matters that touch

---

[78] Ibid., 29a, 145b. This commentary on Maimonides' *Mishneh Torah* is mentioned numerous times in the book. R. Moses directs the reader to it under the assumption that it is easily accessible. See, for example, Najara, *Leqaḥ Ṭov*, 97b.

[79] There are isolated mentions of several commentators from earlier generations. Some examples are Isaac ben Asher Halevi (Najara, *Leqaḥ Ṭov*, 30b), R. Aaron Halevi of Girona [Ra'ah] (ibid., 128b), R. Obadiah Bartenura (ibid., 121b). From the Geonic period, it seems that he mentions only Saadia Gaon (ibid., 24b, 26a).

[80] Ibid., 106b.

[81] See Ḥayyim David Azulai (Ḥida), *Birkei Yosef*, 2 vols. (Livorno, 1774–1776; facsimile, Jerusalem, 2001), *Oraḥ Ḥayyim* 489, who discusses the dispute, and brings many opinions from the sixteenth and seventeenth centuries, including that of R. Moses.

[82] For example, in explanation of the fact that in a Torah scroll the letter א (*'alef*) in the word *vayyiqra'* ("And [God] called"), the first word of the book of Leviticus, is traditionally written

on Halakhah, which should be seen against the background of the widening influence of Kabbalah on Jewish law. The influence of Kabbalah on halakhic decisions can already be found in the fifteenth century, before the expulsion of the Jews from Spain, and strengthens in the sixteenth century. Although not included in guidelines for making rulings, Kabbalah gradually became part of rabbinic discourse in the halakhic realm.[83] In general, it appears as an element in halakhic deliberations when there is reason to fear contradicting the Zohar, particularly when there is no standard ruling or when the wording of the Zohar is particularly harsh.[84] Regarding the issue of whether to put on *tefillin* on intermediate festival days, on which authorities' opinions are divided, and which the Zohar prohibits with harsh language—seeing one who

---

smaller than the other letters of the word, R. Moses comments that the reason for this practice is known "by those who know hidden wisdom" (Najara, *Leqaḥ Ṭov*, 42b, on Lev 1:1). The commentary of R. Jedidiah Norzi (ca. 1560–1630) on the masoretic text of the Torah makes use of *Leqaḥ Ṭov* on this topic; see Jedidiah Norzi, *Minḥat Shai on the Torah* [in Hebrew], ed. Yosef Ofer (Jerusalem, 2005) to Leviticus 1:1. The Zohar is mentioned several dozen times in the book. See, e.g., Najara, *Leqaḥ Ṭov*, 6a, 6b, 7b, 8a, 8b, 9a, 11a, 14a, 17a, 22b, 23b, 34b, 41b, 43a, 86a. In general, he does reference midrashim on the weekly Torah portion that are mentioned in the Zohar, and on one occasion he references the *Ra`ya' Meheimna* section of the Zohar (ibid., 87b).

[83] The first efforts to create a link between the details of Jewish laws and the teachings of the kabbalists can already be found in the thirteenth century, and perhaps even earlier; see Meir Kadosh, "Kabbalistic Jewish Laws in Responsa from the 13th Century to the Early Years of the 17th Century" [in Hebrew], (PhD diss., Bar-Ilan University, 2004), 8–58; Gershom Scholem, "Responsa Attributed to R. Joseph Gikatilla" [in Hebrew], in *Festschrift Dr. Jakob Freimann zum 70. Geburtstag* (Berlin, 1937), 163. In the fifteenth century, one can find a substantial penetration of Kabbalah into the halakhic system and halakhic works. That is the case in the siddur *Zekher Ṣaddiq* of R. Joseph ben Tzaddik, which includes notes and practices, including some kabbalistic practices. Similarly, the commentary of Isaac Aboab II of Castile to the *'Arba`ah Turim* of R. Jacob ben Asher brings Kabbalah to bear on several halakhic matters, including the arrangement of the fingers during the Priestly Blessing, saying *taḥanun* at night, and saying "the Lord, your God, is true" after reading the *Shema*. See Yoel Marciano, "The Status and Dissemination of the Kabbalah in Jewish Society in the Iberian Peninsula in the Late Middle Ages" [in Hebrew], *Sefunot* 26 (2019): 160–4.

[84] In the responsa attributed to R. Joseph Gikatilla (written in the late fourteenth or early fifteenth century), there are nine responsa relating to Kabbalah, of which the first seven concern halakhic issues. On the question of removing the *tefillin* prior to the *musaf* prayer, the author rules according to Kabbalah, concluding, "And if this is the opinion of the Zohar, who would not fear?" (See also R. Joseph Karo, n. 86 below.) On the question of the prohibition of marital relations in the *sukkah*, he writes: "You should know that there is no authority who has ever mentioned the prohibition of this. ... But we have heard from those who speak truth (*magidei 'emet*) that the Zohar prohibits it, and if the Zohar prohibits it, who can permit it? Who can navigate between these towering mountains? So, we will accept the Kabbalah (Scholem, "Responsa Attributed to R. Joseph Gikatilla," 163–70). See David Tamar, "Bio-bibliographical Notes on a Few Rabbis, Sabbatians, and Kabbalists" [in Hebrew], *Qiryat Sefer* 47 (1972): 323–25.

does so as "mutilating the shoots" and deserving of death—R. Joseph Karo writes:

> Since our Talmud does not explicitly explain this law, who will indemnify us to dare to actively violate the words of Rabbi Shimon bar Yochai, who prohibits putting them on so vehemently?[85]

In a few places, R. Moses mentions statements from the Zohar that touch upon Halakhah, but not in connection with a halakhic ruling. For example, he writes that according to Maimonides, R. Asher ben Jehiel (Rosh), and most authorities, it is only the eating of the sciatic nerve (*gid ha-nasheh*) that is prohibited, but that one may otherwise benefit from it; "however, it says in the Zohar that all benefit from it is prohibited, even [throwing it] to the dogs."[86] He continues on to cite the Zohar's explanation of the reason that the Torah uses the term *"gid ha-nasheh"* to refer to the sciatic nerve,[87] expands a little on its significance in Kabbalah, and concludes with the words "and [the Zohar] discusses amazing things in connection with this matter."[88]

One might expect that a book written by a scholar of the second half of the sixteenth century who is known as a kabbalist and as one of the students of R. Isaac Luria would reflect a distinctly kabbalistic orientation. However, this is not the case. *Leqaḥ Tov* is written in a Talmudic-rabbinic style, and the Zohar is the only book of kabbalistic literature mentioned in it. R. Moses's mastery of the Zohar is evident, but he does not show preference for material taken from it over material from other sources, and he often cites it as an additional midrash from the Rabbinic period. In this respect, he follows the practice of the *Derashot u-Ma'amarim* of his father-in-law and teacher, R. Israel di Curiel.[89] This is especially prominent in his interpretation of the Torah portion of *Bereshit*, which (as explained below) features conceptual commentary on the creation story, in which he interprets verses without focusing on kabbalistic issues, and without mentioning interpretations of the early Sephardic kabbalists or the Kabbalah of R. Isaac Luria. He does not even make use of kabbalistic terminology in this fundamental discussion. These facts give rise to the questions: Was R. Moses a student of R. Isaac Luria? Was he a kabbalist? An affirmative answer would seem to be called for based on his being mentioned as one of R. Luria's students in R. Ḥayyim

---

[85] Joseph Karo, *Beit Yosef*, Oraḥ Ḥayyim 32, comment beginning with *"ve`akhshav."* Rabbi Shimon bar Yochai is traditionally attributed as the author of the Zohar.

[86] Najara, *Leqaḥ Tov*, 16b–17a, on Gen 32:33.

[87] *Sefer ha-Zohar* (Jerusalem, 1964), *Vayishlaḥ*, I, 170b. On this passage from the Zohar, see Isaac Arama, `*Aqeidat Yizḥaq*, 2 vols. (Jerusalem, 1984), Genesis § 26 (reprint of Pressburg, 1849; see 1:225b).

[88] Najara, *Leqaḥ Tov*, 17a.

[89] See the discussion of Regev in the introduction to di Curiel, *Derashot u-Ma'amarim*, 26.

Vital's *Book of Visions*, and based on his being on the list of authors of one of the several collections of Lurianic ideas and methods known as *Kanfei Yonah* (Dove's Wings). However, this evidence is not unambiguous and is no more convincing than the evidence to the contrary in *Leqaḥ Ṭov*. This is how R. Ḥayyim Vital described the different groups of R. Isaac Luria's students:

> Now I will list the initiates who came in with us to study. ...My group, which met right after midnight [which included] ...R. Joseph Arazin, ...was the group known as *penimiot ha-moḥin shel ha-da`at* ("the Inner Consciousness of Knowing"). There is another group called the *levushim* ("Divine Garments"), that includes my teacher R. Moses Alshich, R. Moses Najara ...R. Jacob Massoud ...and the late R. Moses Mintz.[90]

To what extent should we consider this excerpt from the *Book of Visions* to reflect historical reality? This is a serious question that requires some analysis, due to the author's mystical depictions and mixing of the world of spiritual visions with physical-historical reality. Thus, for example, if we compare this evidence with evidence from *Sefer Toledot ha-'Ar"i* (Book of the Lineage of Isaac Luria, which according to Meir Benayahu "is similar to the sources, into which much historical work has been sunk, that we have from the circle of Isaac Luria"), we see a clear contradiction between the two sources. "Some [of these sources] are accurate, and some are cloaked in legend and introspection."[91] It is noteworthy that R. Moses Alshich, who is mentioned in the *Book of Visions* as one of the students of R. Isaac Luria, alongside R. Moses, is not counted as one of R. Luria's students in the tradition handed down in *Sefer Toledot ha'Ar"i*. On the contrary, he is described as someone who had endeavored to study with R. Luria, but was turned away:

> R. Moshe Alshich's soul longed for this wisdom. He went along, crying, to the Rabbi [Isaac Luria], kissed his feet, and said, "What is my offense, and what is my sin, that my lord does not wish to bring me close, to be one of his students?" ...The Rabbi said to him that his soul had come into this world only to write those books that he had written according to the plain meaning ..."so do not trouble yourself any more with this matter." ...And from that day forward, he never thought of studying the Kabbalah.[92]

---

[90] Vital, *Sefer ha-Ḥezyonot*, 189–90. In the quotation, I extracted only those names that are discussed below.

[91] Meir Benayahu, *Sefer Toledot ha-'Ar"i* (Jerusalem, 1967), 123–4.

[92] Ibid., 123–4. For a more detailed account, see idem, 169–71.

Which tradition reflects reality? Both works (*Book of Visions* and *Sefer Tole-dot ha-Ar"i*) are quite complex from a historical perspective. However, even if we accept the testimony of R. Ḥayyim Vital that R. Moses studied Kab-balah under R. Isaac Luria, did he come as a colleague with an interest in R. Luria's teachings? Did he come to study as a student? If he came as a student, was he a close disciple? Does not the fact that R. Ḥayyim Vital re-ports himself to have been a member of the *penimiot ha-moḥin shel ha-da`at* group, in contrast to R. Moses Alsheich and R. Moses having been part of the *levushim* group, imply that the latter had a more limited connection to R. Luria's revelation of secrets and Torah teachings?

The complexity of the question is evidenced by the fact that only one member of the *levushim* group (R. Yaakov Massoud) is a signatory of the written pact of the students of R. Ḥayyim Vital. The signatures of R. Moses, R. Moses Alsheich, and the other members of the *levushim* are not included. Most of the signatories are from the *penimiot ha-moḥin shel ha-da`at*. The main point of the document, signed in 1572, is agreeing to an oath (*shavu`ah*) not to reveal the secrets of the Kabbalah that they have heard from R. Isaac Luria and from R. Ḥayyim Vital.[93] It is reasonable to assume that R. Ḥayyim Vital, as R. Luria's chosen disciple, included his closest circle of students as signatories on this document, in an attempt to establish control over the dissemination of the secrets of R. Luria's Kabbalah.

In any event, it seems that some of R. Luria's teachings reached R. Moses and that he also collaborated with R. Joseph Arazin and R. Moses Minz on *Kanfei Yonah*, a collection of R. Luria's ideas.[94] Why, then, did he not include anything from R. Luria's teachings—or from any other kabbalistic literature—in his book *Leqaḥ Ṭov?*

Based on the image portrayed in his book, there are not enough kabbalistic teachings and material to show that he was a kabbalist. Although he had an interest in Kabbalah as a supplementary source of religious knowledge,

---

[93] On the document, its dating, and terms, see Meir Benayahu, "Pact Documents of Kabbalists of Safed and Egypt" [in Hebrew], *Asufot* 9 (1995): 145–49.

[94] This book is parallel to, though distinct from, a better-known book named *Kanfei Yonah* by R. Moshe Yonah which also contains a summary of teachings learned from R. Isaac Luria. On these works, see Yosef Avivi, *Lurianic Kabbalah* [in Hebrew], 3 vols. (Jerusalem, 2008) 1:96–100, 111–13, 127; 2:740–41. In addition to this work, there are several other extant texts authored by R. Moses, such as *kavanot* ("intentions" for the worshipper to think about during prayer) for the blessings of the *amidah* prayer that were in the possession of R. Ḥayyim Vital and were incorporated into unpublished notebooks that were copied and circulated. From there R. Moses's material made its way into other works. See Avivi, *Lurianic Kabbalah*, 2:218. Ronit Meroz is of the opinion that *Kanfei Yonah* is the text of lectures given by R. Isaac Luria when he first arrived in Safed. See Ronit Meroz, "R. Yisrael Sarug – Luria's Disciple: A Research Controversy Reconsidered" [in Hebrew], *Da`at* 28 (1992): 42.

Kabbalah did not become a part of his identity and outlook. He apparently did not see it as the axis around which he would fulfill his religio-spiritual conception, as one might have expected from a Safed kabbalist.[95]

R. Moses the Preacher

One section of *Leqaḥ Ṭov* stands out from the rest of the book: the commentary on the *parasha* of *Bereshit*. It would seem that considering the purpose of the book, the commentary on this section should be brief—as was his practice with the other portions of the book of Genesis—because there is only one commandment in the entire book, with little halakhic midrash. However, R. Moses explains in the introduction to the book that when he began writing the work, he wrote in a lengthier style on this Torah portion, and even though it diverges from the goals of the book, he decided to include it:

> At the start, when my spirit willed me to come near to this work, I started with the portion of *Bereshit*, to note issues in the verses and reconcile them with the words of the Rabbis and make their words the core and basis. I intended to continue in this manner with all the other portions of this kind, because of my great desire to know that which was not explained in any book—these are the very essence of the Torah. But for now, I have set aside what I had started, until such time as we merit help from heaven. Nevertheless, that which I already took the trouble to write on that Torah portion, I will not leave out of this book, and will publish it, with God's help.[96]

The phrase "to make their words the core and basis" and his ambition to write a future commentary on other Torah portions "of this type," "which are the very essence of the Torah," refers to religio-conceptual commentary, for which the book of Genesis is fertile ground. The commentary on *Bereshit*, which extends to twenty-four pages, provides a glimpse into R. Moses's conceptual writing, based on interpretations of the Rabbinic period. As he writes

---

[95] R. Mordekhai Dato summarized his impression of the scholars of Safed, after visiting there in 1560, in these words: "All propositions of true and righteous wisdom that issue from the scholars of Safed (may it be speedily built and preserved and may God preserve them!) are based on the words of the Zohar. Their words are the same as its words and come from its splendor (*mi-zoharo*), and no one lifts a hand of investigation or foot of inquiry without it." See Boaz Huss, "The Zoharic Communities in Safed," in *Shefa Tal: Studies in Jewish Thought and Culture Presented to Bracha Sack*, ed. Zeev Gries, Haim (Howard) Kreisel, and Boaz Huss (Be'er Sheva, 2004), 149.

[96] Najara, *Leqaḥ Ṭov*, 2a.

at the beginning of the book: "I have come to interpret verses according to Rabbis, as I understand the simple meaning of their words, without deviating to the right or the left. This is the basis of my book, with God's help."[97]

R. Moses's exegetical approach is characterized by a fixed format in which questions and objections are posed on the text and its meaning (*he`arot*, "notes" in his terminology), followed by a systematic answer. One can compare his writing on *Bereshit* with the exegetical approach of his teacher R. Israel di Curiel,[98] which was influenced as a rule by the Sephardic style of scriptural exegesis of the generation of the expulsion from Spain. R. Israel Najara emphasized the fact that the training that R. Israel di Curiel provided to his students influenced their writings:

> His students who poured water over his hands, who were born on his knees, bowed down on their knees to drink water from his well and from the depths of his interpretations, *and they walked in his footsteps, making cakes for the work of homily, and* [*the water*] *flowed down onto the edge of his robes. Through him they gave birth, sprouted, and bore fruit.*[99]

This description echoes not only the stylistic and structural influence on their presentation of the material, but also the many references to the teachings of R. Moses Najara's mentor that are embedded in his book. He is also similar to his teacher in the limited role of Kabbalah in his work, not conveying the impression of being a kabbalist.[100] Although he demonstrates familiarity with the Zohar and with the kabbalistic dimension, it does not change or shape his approach. He is first and foremost a man of Halakhah, and that is what most interests him. He is interested not only in the Halakhah that is needed to manage the community and day-to-day life, but also in laws that are no longer practiced—to such an extent that he saw explaining them and studying them to be a central motivation for writing his book. He describes his yearning for and interest in the realm of Halakhah and *mitzvot* with these words: "My soul has been singed with desire for many years, from my youth,

---

[97] Ibid., 2b.

[98] Di Curiel, *Derashot u-Ma'amrim*.

[99] Najara, *Miqveh Israel*, 125.

[100] Benayahu, who sees R. Moses as a prominent kabbalist in the circle of R. Isaac Luria, is puzzled by the gap between R. Israel di Curiel and his son-in-law regarding the Kabbalah. According to him, it seems implausible that a scholar as distant from Kabbalah as R. di Curiel would marry off his daughter to a kabbalist from the school of R. Isaac Luria (see Benayahu, "Introduction," *Derashot u-Ma'amarim*, 15). As discussed above, it seems that the gap was smaller than Benayahu estimated. They both were familiar with kabbalistic literature and were acquainted with kabbalists and their ideas but were not kabbalists in the full sense of the word.

to approach this work, for it is great. My heart has been heated within me by the flame of my yearning, to find pleasing words."[101]

R. Moses's pretense of collecting every halakhah learned from the verses of the Torah makes it a unique work for its period. While many others wrote biblical commentary, commentary on midrash, homiletical literature, and halakha, this work of great erudition blends these domains all in one place. He presents as a scholar with broad knowledge and command of Torah literature, who integrates his own insights into the presentation of the material. However, one should not see these additions as possessing the originality and style that can be seen in the writings of the great figures of his generation in Safed such as R. Moses Alshich.

We know that in his later years R. Moses served as a preacher in Damascus, and it is reasonable to assume that he had held that position in one of the congregations in Safed. However, we do not know in which of the congregations he preached.[102] His spiritual activity as a rabbi in Damascus, including as a rabbi for the community, as a preacher, and as a *talmid ḥakham* among the scholars of the yeshiva can be seen in the eulogy given by his son, which, by nature, is full of praise:

> The entire city, from all quarters, are participating in this heavy grieving, whether the individuals of the congregations who hear his sermons every Sabbath, or people of the yeshiva who occupy themselves in Torah in his company, or members of his household who stand at the threshold, in the shadow of the Almighty. ...I say that not even one resident of this city remains outside of the mourning in order to comfort us from this sorrow. As I said regarding the verse, "not a man among us is missing"[103] who is not participating in this grieving.[104]

R. Moses had broad Torah erudition, held judicial positions in Safed, and was a member of the *beit ha-va`ad* of the city. In the era of the blossoming of Kabbalah in Safed he took a passive part, remaining within the traditional boundaries of Torah commentary and halakhic work. The goal that he set for himself in *Leqaḥ Ṭov* was unique, and impressive in scope. This work anticipated a hermeneutical school that developed later as part of traditional and Orthodox Judaism's grappling with Reform and with biblical criticism. In the nineteenth and twentieth centuries, a series of commentaries were written based on the connection between the written Torah and the

---

[101] Najara, *Leqaḥ Ṭov*, unnumbered first page following the title page.

[102] On the multiple congregations in Safed, see n. 1 above.

[103] Num 31:49.

[104] Najara, *Miqveh Israel*, 393.

oral Torah, including *Ha-Ketav veha-Qabbalah* of Yaakov Tzvi Mecklenburg (1785–1865),[105] *Torah Temimah* of Baruch Halevi Epstein (1860–1942),[106] and *Torah Sheleimah* of Menachem Mendel Kasher (1895–1983).[107] These commentaries and others like them are written in a different style, and with different motivations. Nevertheless, the common denominator with *Leqaḥ Ṭov* is broad. R. Moses is the harbinger of this genre.

The fact that sages like R. Moses were active in Safed in an extraordinary generation, in which several spiritual giants lived, overshadows them almost to the point of obscurity and shrouds their contribution. Study of figures like R. Moses shows not only the man and his work, but also sheds light on a wide stratum of learned sages, a stratum that constituted an important part of the spiritual-religious standing and power of the city of Safed in its golden age.

Publisher's Note Springer Nature remains neutral with regard to jurisdictional claims in published maps and institutional affiliations.

---

[105] Yaakov Tzvi Mecklenburg, *Ha-Ketav veha-Qabbalah* (Leipzig, 1839).

[106] Baruch Halevi Epstein, *Torah Temimah* (Vilnius, 1902).

[107] Menachem Mendel Kasher, *Ḥumash Torah Sheleimah*, 12 vols. (Jerusalem, 1992–1995).

Jewish History (2021) 35: 405–432
https://doi.org/10.1007/s10835-021-09427-x

Jews, Economic Metaphors, and the Healthy Body Politic: The Jewish Role in Christian Economic Narratives and the Birth of Modern Economics

GIACOMO TODESCHINI

University of Trieste, Trieste, Italy
E-mail: todeschinigiacomo@gmail.com

Accepted: 9 July 2020 / Published online: 17 December 2021

Abstract The linguistic structure of the Western Christian discourse about economics as resembling and symbolizing the entire logic of earthly government and order was closely connected to the shaping of the Christian discourse about Jews and Judaism as a religious and legal system as seen in the framework of the Christian "economy" of Salvation. Seeing the Christian representation of Jews and Judaism from this viewpoint, it becomes evident that a close historical relationship has existed between the history of Western anti-Judaism and the shaping of the Western Christian way of analyzing and representing public and private economic organization. Otherwise stated, there is a close relationship between European anti-Judaism and Western economics.

Keywords Jewish economic activity · Christian economics · Economic lexica · Anti-Judaism

An Historiographical Introduction

In the 1950s, the famous Austrian and American economist and economic historian Joseph Schumpeter introduced a new way of representing the history of economic theories. In what might be called the history of Western economic rationality, he combined the evolutionary perspective with a representation of economic discourses as historical realities. Schumpeter was convinced that ancient Greek philosophers and late medieval Christian jurists and theologians (the Scholastics) had produced a true economic science and discovered certain economic principles. He considered these ancient and late medieval economic doctrines as the prefiguration, or the primitive root, of modern and contemporary economic theories. He audaciously concluded that "a considerable part of the economics of the later nineteenth century might have been developed from those bases more quickly and with less trouble than it actually cost to develop it, and that some of that subsequent work was therefore in the nature of a time- and labor-consuming detour."[1]

Chapter 8 was originally published as Todeschini, G. Jewish History (2021) 35: 405–432. https://doi.org/10.1007/s10835-021-09427-x.

[1] Joseph Schumpeter, *History of Economic Analysis*, ed. Elizabeth Boody Schumpeter (New York, 1954; repr. 2006), 93.

In other words, according to Schumpeter, late medieval economic doctrines, even though they were produced in a vastly different conceptual universe, had a deep understanding of some basic economic truths. Schumpeter's paradigm circulated widely in the fifties and sixties. Raymond de Roover, the great Belgian American economic historian, emphasized it strongly in several books and articles. De Roover used it especially in his work on the economic doctrines of the Franciscan friar Bernardino of Siena and the Dominican bishop Antonino of Florence, two well-known Scholastic theologians who lived in the first half of fifteenth-century Italy.[2] Yet Schumpeter, like many other historians of economic thought, was not interested in the historical and linguistic contexts from which these texts emerged.

The interpretation of premodern economic concepts as the primitive form, or the first stage, of modern scientific economic thought was advanced by Schumpeter and, at the beginning of the century, by Sombart and Weber. It was then challenged from the 1960s on by important historians of economic thought and economists such as Mark Blaug[3] and Friedrich August von Hayek. In brief, they countered the thesis of continuity in Western economic thought with a thesis of discontinuity, claiming that medieval and early modern economic thought lacked "a technical [economic] vocabulary" and maintained a moral orientation that would have prevented the understanding of essential economic laws.[4] For example, according to Hayek, the Aristotelian idea of the sterility of money was the basis for the medieval and early modern moral prohibition of lending on interest. This conceptualization, consequently, made it difficult for premodern thinkers to understand the productivity of capital.[5]

The idea of a break between premodern and modern economic rationalities has been the most widely circulated representation of the genealogy of modern economic theory. Nowadays this widespread narrative is reassuring because it confirms the representation of economic modernity as something abstract and aseptically apolitical. This vision is commonly adopted by professors of economics and is the basis for the pervasive representation of modern explanations of economic laws as "revolutionary," owing to the genius of an outstanding economist, as in the case of the discovery of "marginal utility" by Jevons, Walras, and Menger.[6]

---

[2]Raymond de Roover, *S. Bernardino of Siena and Sant'Antonino of Florence: The Two Great Economic Thinkers of the Middle Ages* (Boston, 1967); idem, *La pensée économique des scolastiques: Doctrines et méthodes* (Montreal, 1971).

[3]Mark Blaug, *Economic Theory in Retrospect*, 4th ed. (Cambridge, UK, 1985).

[4]Ibid., 11.

[5]Friedrich A. von Hayek, "The Fatal Conceit: The Errors of Socialism," in vol. 1 of *Collected Works of F. A. von Hayek*, ed. W. W. Bartley III (London, 1988), 47.

[6]Blaug, *Economic Theory in Retrospect*, 294.

Nevertheless, mainly from the 1990s on, there has been a reappraisal of the evolution of Western economics proposed by Schumpeter and others, in such dissimilar works as those by Murray Rothbard and Odd Langholm, for example.[7] In these cases, deeper historical research and much better knowledge of medieval and early modern economic thinkers has allowed for a reappraisal of the construction of Western economic rationality as the gradual evolution of the understanding of economic laws. The reappearance of this evolutionary paradigm has been facilitated by the shattering of classic, historical certitudes about the medieval and early modern concept of the sterility of money, which misunderstood and refused to accept the principle of the fertility of money. The discovery of forms of medieval and early modern economic culture explicitly stating and appreciating the notion of the productivity of capital now enable historians to regard premodern economics as the primitive stage of Western economic rationality that culminated in the industrial revolution and capitalism.

It is possible to begin to challenge this representation of modern economics as the natural evolution and growth of economic theories (as increasing economic rationality). At the same time, it is possible to undermine the idea of a total break between premodern and modern economic ways of thinking. One can do so by paying closer attention, as historians of law and economic language actually do, to the formalizations of exchange and credit relations as the outcome of semantic strategies deeply interconnecting (what we today call) "economics" with other conceptual vocabularies, especially the theological and metaphysical ones.

In fact, economists and historians of economics—whether espousing an evolutionary model, like Schumpeter, de Roover, Langholm, or rejecting it, like Blaug, von Hayek, and their followers—typically speak about premodern economic concepts and their operative functioning. At the same time, they ignore the fact that these "concepts" are expressed by images, metaphors, and words,[8] entirely embedded in an epistemology and a well-defined historical language (medieval theological Latin, early modern juridical Spanish, or Latin, etc.). For example, in the cases of Antonino, Bernardino, Molina, De Lugo, and the other presumed "primitives" of Western economic thought, this semantic context was a theological context. That means, on the one hand, that

---

[7] Murray Newton Rothbard, *Economic Thought before Adam Smith*, (Brookfield, VT, 1995); Odd Inge Langholm, *The Aristotelian Analysis of Usury* (Bergen, NO, 1984); idem, *Economics in the Medieval Schools: Wealth, Exchange, Value, Money, and Usury according to the Paris Theological Tradition, 1200–1350* (Leiden, 1992); idem, *The Legacy of Scholasticism in Economic Thought: Antecedents of Choice and Power* (Cambridge, UK, 1998).

[8] George Lakoff and Mark Johnson, *Metaphors We Live By* (Chicago, 1980); Hans Weder, *Die Gleichnisse Jesu als Metaphern: Traditions- und redaktionsgeschichtliche Analysen und Interpretationen* (Göttingen, 1978).

economic reasoning made use of the conceptual syntax shaped by theology (e.g., indebtedness semantically fluctuated between metaphysical and daily meanings; obligation was at the same time a notion dependent on trustworthiness and faithfulness) and, on the other hand, that theological discourses could be meaningful in the economic field. The very notions of indebtedness as an economic condition and of money as an economic object full of potential could be clarified through the theological images of the eternal debt binding humankind to God and of the consecrated host repaying human sins. The "sacred host" as a metaphoric coin apt to measure invisible values and Christ's passion as the metaphorical beginning of a condition of spiritual indebtedness are two of the most powerful economic constructions produced by Western Christian theology.[9]

In light of the semantic context, the assertion of a continuity, or a break, between medieval and modern economic thought contains a structural and conceptual weakness rooted in the rigidity of an evolutionary model. The history of Western economic rationality could be more fruitfully explained by paying attention to the linguistic genealogy of economic notions (i.e., concepts, words, images) and lexicons, as well as abandoning the evolutionary ideology, which holds to the notion of the eternal progress of economics. This ideology is based on the representation of economics as a timeless rational structure, the understanding of whose laws evolves from naive to scientific. Rather, the history of Western economic rationality should be approached less abstractly by paying attention to the concrete-linguistic construction of Western economics. This would consequently mean admitting the "modernity" of many premodern economic concepts and, at the same time, admitting the "medievalism" of many aspects of the modern economic way of thinking and speaking and rationalizing.

It is then possible to underline the close connection existing between the ambiguous and contradictory theological construction of what we today call "economics" and the shaping of medieval anti-Judaism[10] and modern antisemitism in Western Christianity.[11] From this perspective, late medieval

---

[9]Giacomo Todeschini, "Money, Ritual, and Religion: Economic Value between Theology and Administration," in *A Cultural History of Money in Medieval Times*, ed. Rory Naismith (London, 2019): 57–78.

[10]David Nirenberg, *Anti-Judaism: The Western Tradition* (New York, 2013); Maurice Kriegel, "L'esprit tue aussi: Juifs 'textuels' et Juifs 'réels' dans l'histoire," *Annales. Histoire, Sciences Sociales* (2014): 875–99.

[11]Giacomo Todeschini, *La ricchezza degli ebrei: Merci e denaro nella riflessione ebraica e nella definizione cristiana dell'usura alla fine del Medioevo* (Spoleto, 1989); idem, *Il prezzo della salvezza: Lessici medievali del pensiero economico* (Rome, 1994); idem, *I mercanti e il tempio: La società cristiana e il circolo virtuoso della ricchezza fra medioevo ed età moderna* (Bologna, 2002); idem, *Les Marchands et le Temple: La société chrétienne et le cercle*

anti-Judaism and its economic implications do not appear as the transhistorical manifestation of an everlasting economic racism. Instead, more specifically, they appear as the punctual historical beginning of the European and Christian economic paradigm strictly connecting the very notion of economic rationality to the concept of cultural belonging.

The "Economy" of Salvation and the Jews

Indeed, the linguistic structure of the Western Christian discourse about economics as resembling and symbolizing the entire logic of earthly government and order was closely connected to the shaping of Christian discourse. This discourse centered on Jews and Judaism as a religious and legal system as seen in the framework of the Christian "economy" of salvation.[12] From this perspective, one can consider as two sides of the same coin the economic thought shaped by patristic and scholastic argumentation, respectively in the late antique and high medieval periods, and the multiple-polemics against Jews and Judaism advanced by the church fathers from the fourth to the seventh century and by the scholastic doctors from the twelfth to the fifteen century. Among many examples, certain extremely influential passages of Augustine of Hippo and Ambrose of Milan are especially relevant. In fact, both Augustine's representation of the authenticity of human beings and human faith in monetary terms (*homo moneta est dei*, "man is the coin of god") and Ambrose's description of Judaism as a coin that is devalued in consequence of the Jewish misinterpretation of Scriptures (*De Tobia*, 19, 64: "[Judaei] pecuniam habent et non habent, quia usum eius ignorant, pretium eius nesciunt, figuram eius et formam non cognoverunt"), robustly contributed to introducing into the Christian way of thinking a close association between human authenticity, right faith, and Christian identity, systematically organized through monetary metaphors.

The very notion of "authenticity," of being righteous, that is, of authentic worth, and consequently of truly belonging to the political community,

vertueux de la richesse du Moyen Âge à l'Époque moderne (Paris 2017); idem, *Ricchezza francescana: Dalla povertà volontaria alla società di mercato* (Bologna, 2004); idem, *Franciscan Wealth* (Saint Bonaventura, NY, 2009); idem, *Visibilmente crudeli: Malviventi persone sospette e gente qualunque dal medioevo all'età moderna* (Bologna, 2007); idem, *Au pays des sans-nom: Gens de mauvaise vie, personnes suspectes ou ordinaires du Moyen Age à l'époque moderne* (Paris, 2015); idem, *Come Giuda: La gente comune e i giochi dell'economia all'inizio dell'epoca moderna* (Bologna, 2011); idem, *La banca e il ghetto: Una storia italiana (secoli XIV–XVI)* (Rome, 2016).

[12] Valentina Toneatto, *Les banquiers du Seigneur: Evêques et moines face à la richesse (IVe–début IXe siècle)* (Rennes, 2012); Peter Brown, *The Ransom of the Soul: Afterlife and Wealth in Early Western Christianity* (Cambridge, MA, 2015).

was deeply affected by the recurrent use of these economic and monetary metaphors. Different shapes of religious otherness or "deviance"—from Judaism to Arianism and Manicheism—were perceived and represented as forms of human inauthenticity, that is, as lacking similitude to divinity. The divine, in turn, was frequently represented as the authority validating coins through its mark and as the metaphysical Minter. The Augustinian analogy between the Roman emperor sealing and authenticating coins through his own image and divinity minting, sealing, and authenticating men through its own image powerfully established Christian discourses on faith and unfaithfulness expressed through economic vocabularies and a financial syntax. That, as we shall see, will have notable consequences.

This "archaeology" can introduce us to a deeper understanding of the medieval and late medieval development of Christian polemics against Jews and Judaism. These polemics and discussions were not simply the expression of an explicit conflict concerning religious truths. Beyond the fight about the conversion of the Jews to Christianity, Christian theologians and jurists implicitly produced a polemical representation of economics that, in itself, represented Jews and Judaism as a perverted form of humanity. The core of this interplay between "economics" and the "economy of salvation" was shaped by the (theological) rhetorics and vocabularies concerning the value and the Value of Christ's body. The main consequence of that interconnection between discourses about Christ's metaphysical value and ordinary exchange values is represented and synthetized by Christian narratives related to the selling of Christ by Judas to the Jews and to the price paid for this selling by the Jews to Judas.[13]

The archetypal figure of the double and dialectical representation of the Jews (as infidels to convert and as economic obstacle to the social happiness of the elected ones) can be found in the variegated rhetorical representations of the economic incompetence (that is to say, economic perversity) of Judas Iscariot by the Greek and Latin church fathers. Judas's selling of Christ was represented as a form of economic stupidity and ineptitude, deriving from his unfaithfulness and untrustworthiness. In the patristic narratives about the selling of Christ by Judas, the emphasis on the contradiction shaped by the incommensurability of Christ's Value and the small sum of money paid to Judas directly points to Judas's unreliability in both the religious and economic spheres. His incapacity to appreciate the value/Value of Christ is the sign of his infidelity and degenerate human nature. In other words, since the patristic era, both Judas's untrustworthiness as administrator of the apostolic substance (as represented by the Gospel of John) and Judas's selling of Christ

---

[13] Todeschini, *Come Giuda*, chs. 3 and 7.

are described as two sides of the same coin. They are seen as two complementary manifestations of Judas's and Jewish incapacity to appreciate true
value and to distinguish sacred value from everyday value. The equation of
economic ignorance with infidelity meant that Jewish resistance to conversion could be represented as a form of economic ineptitude, easily associated
with greedy behavior and summed up by the keyword avarice (*avaritia*).[14]

The Jews as Economic Threat

A second stage in the evolution of this binary representation is found in the
anti-Jewish writings of the ninth through twelfth centuries, which described
Jews as stubborn infidels actively threatening the patrimony of the churches
and, at the same time, insidiously infiltrating the daily economic sphere of
Christians. From Agobard of Lyon[15] to Peter the Venerable of Cluny,[16] Jewish deviance is portrayed as a manifestation both of refusal to convert and of
perfidious economic activities. This manifests—according to Christian bishops and abbots—as the selling of ritually impure and then "vile" meats to
Christians, the buying of sacred objects (and the complicity with sacrilegious
thieves),[17] and the acquisition of sacred properties through lending on mortgage. In each case, the Latin keyword *tenacia* (whose synonym was *avaricia*)
was often used to denote obstinate Jewish attachment to a devalued truth as
well as to earthly things and riches.

The economic linguistics structuring medieval anti-Judaism becomes
even clearer when we pay attention to the syntax and words shaping the ongoing Christian construction of the Jews as both enemies of Christians and as
an economic threat to the holy goods of churches and the Church. Seeing the
Christian representation of Jews and Judaism from this viewpoint, it begins
to become evident that a close historical relationship has existed between
the history of Western anti-Judaism and the shaping of the Western Christian
way of analyzing and representing public and private economic organization.

---

[14] Ibid.

[15] Bernhard Blumenkranz, *Les auteurs chrétiens latins du Moyen Age sur les Juifs et le
Juidaïsme* (Paris, 1963), 152–68.

[16] Yvonne Friedman, "An Anatomy of Anti-Semitism: Peter the Venerable's Letter to Louis
VII, King of France (1146)," in *Bar-Ilan Studies in History* 1 (1978): 87–102; eadem, "Anti-
Talmudic Invective from Peter the Venerable to Nicholas Donin (1144–1244)," in *Le brûle-
ment du Talmud à Paris, 1242–1244*, ed. Gilbert Dahan (Paris, 1999), 171–89.

[17] Giacomo Todeschini, "The Origin of a Medieval Anti-Jewish Stereotype: The Jews as Re-
ceivers of Stolen Goods (Twelfth to Thirteenth Centuries)," in *The Jewish-Christian Encounter
in Medieval Preaching*, ed. Jonathan Adams and Jussi Hanska (New York, 2015), 240–52.

In other words, there is a close relationship between European anti-Judaism and Western economics.

The twelfth-century political and economic change in Jewish-Christian relations[18] is often described by historians as the true beginning of Western antisemitism. Eventually this change contained in its core a deep link between discourses on Christian economic organization as the development and growth of a sacred Body and discourses concerning Jews as a disturbing economic presence and an obstacle to the growth of the Christian social organism. On the one hand, twelfth-century Canon Law includes more and more subtle descriptions of economic strategies, used to make fruitful the sacred goods of churches and sacred institutions. On the other, in Christian theological, juridical, and political representations after 1120, Jews living in Christian lands emerged as uncanny economic actors threatening the well-being of Christians. Yet during the twelfth century the charge of usury did not concern Jews.[19] During this phase, the economic injuries attributed to Jews were not yet identified as usury. In conciliar constitutions about usurers and lending on interest in the second and third Lateran Councils (1139 and 1179), the accusation of usury and the ban on usurers clearly and uniquely concerned Christian usurers, the so-called *usurarii manifesti*, the "public usurers."[20] When, at the end of twelfth century, the Parisian master Peter the Chanter[21] labeled the Christian usurers as "our Jews," his intention was to make Christian lenders despicable, to underscore the unfaithful and untrustworthy behavior of Christian lenders on interest. The Christian usurer was represented as a fake Christian, that is to say like a "Jew."

---

[18] Anna Sapir Abulafia, "Theology and the Commercial Revolution: Guibert of Nogent, St Anselm and the Jews of Northern France," in *Church and City, 1000–1500: Essays in Honour of Christopher Brooke*, ed. David S. H. Abulafia, Michael J. Franklin, and Miri Rubin (Cambridge, UK, 1992), 23–40; idem, *Christian Jewish Relations 1000–1300: Jews in the Service of Medieval Christendom* (London, 2014).

[19] T. P. McLaughlin, "The Teaching of the Canonists on Usury," *Mediaeval Studies* 1 (1939): 81–147; 2 (1940): 1–22; Bernard Schnapper, "La répression de l'usure et l'évolution économique (XIIIe–XVIe siècles)," *Tijdschrift voor rechtsgeschiedenis* 37 (1969): 47–75; Diego Quaglioni, Giacomo Todeschini, and Gian Maria Varanini, *Credito e usura fra teologia, diritto e amministrazione: Linguaggi a confronto (sec. XII–XVI)* (Rome, 2005); Giacomo Todeschini, "Usury in Christian Middle Ages: A Reconsideration of the Historiographical Tradition (1949–2010)," in *Religion and Religious Institutions in the European Economy, 1000–1800*, ed. Francesco Ammannati (Florence, 2012), 119–30.

[20] F. Schaub, *Der Kampf gegen den Zinswucher, ungerechten Preis und unlauteren Handel im Mittelalter: Von Karl dem Großen bis Papst Alexander III; Eine moralhistorische Untersuchung* (Freiburg, 1905); Karl Weinzierl, "Das Zinsproblem im Dekret Gratians und in den Summen zum Dekret," *Studia Gratiana* 1 (1953): 549–76.

[21] John W. Baldwin, *Masters, Princes and Merchants: The Social Views of Peter the Chanter and His Circle* (Princeton, NJ, 1970), 296–301.

During these years, the problem was not specifically lending on interest but, more generally, and confusingly, what Peter the Venerable, abbot of Cluny, called the Jewish *male parta pinguedo*, a wickedly gained wealth. In this depiction of the Jews as economically dangerous, the key-lexicon actually was characterized by the use of the vocabulary of theft, that is by words like *fur, furtum, furtive, furatus, fraudulenter* (thief, theft, furtively, stolen, fraudulently).[22] In other words, the emphasis was placed on the presumed treacherous, deceptive, and murky nature of the economic transactions performed by the Jews (and, consequently, on the presumable illegality of Jewish wealth), rather than on specific economic practices and contractual forms. This point is particularly important to grasp the conceptual and lexical link connecting this representation of Jewish wealth as the outcome of obscure and treacherous economic activities. On the one hand, there was the ancient Christian vocabulary of the "unlawful seizure" (*invasio*) of sacred properties (*res ecclesiarum*) by infidels, heretics, and especially by the controversial kind of heretics shaped by the group or sect of the so-called simoniacs (*symoniaci, symoniani*). On the other, was there the vocabulary of the *tenacia Judaeorum* that is the resistance of the Jews to conversion depicted as a form of greediness and materialism comparable to the literal interpretation of the Holy Scriptures.[23]

In fact, the keyword and concept of *invasio* of sacred properties perpetrated by the enemies of churches, a keyword/concept that we first find in conciliar canons of the fourth century, has a long history. It first appears in relation to conflicts between different forms of Christianity during the Christianization of the Roman Empire. There the rival episcopal ruling powers would be represented in terms of an abusive, irregular, or unlawful occupation of ecclesiastical (that is, consecrated) land. This concept was modified many times, especially after the beginning of the Carolingian age, and finally

---

[22]Mario Sbriccoli, "Nox quia nocet: I giuristi, l'ordine e la normalizzazione dell'immaginario," in *La note: Ordine, sicurezza e disciplinamento in età moderna*, ed. Mario Sbriccoli (Florence, 1991), 9–19; Valerie Toureille, *Vol et brigandage au Moyen Âge* (Paris, 2006); Todeschini, *Come Giuda*, 2.2.

[23]Humbert of Moyenmoutier (of Silvacandida), "Adversus simoniacos libri tres," in vol. 1 of *Libelli de lite imperatorum et pontificum*, ed. Friedrich Thaner (Hannover, 1897), 100–253; Joseph H. Lynch, *Simoniacal Entry into Religious Life from 1000 to 1260: A Social, Economic, and Legal Study* (Columbus, OH, 1976); Giacomo Todeschini, "'Judas mercator pessimus': Ebrei e simoniaci dall'XI al XIII secolo," *Zakhor: Rivista di storia degli ebrei in Italia* 1 (1997): 11–23; idem, "Christian Perceptions of Jewish Economic Activity in the Middle Ages," in *Wirtschaftsgeschichte der mittelalterlichen Juden: Fragen und Einschätzungen*, ed. Michael Toch and Elisabeth Müller-Luckner (Munich, 2008), 1–16; Anna Sapir Abulafia, *Christians and Jews in the Twelfth-Century Renaissance* (New York, 2013).

semantically enlarged and complicated between the eleventh and twelfth century during the Investiture controversy.[24] In this period the notion of "invasio" and plunder of sacred properties by enemies and thieves became more functional in political terms. Originally, it referred to a perverse injury that characterized infidels and imperfect Christians. It was then used to indicate the political adversaries of the Gregorian Reform. Finally, it evolved into the idea that infidels and especially Jews among them could be viewed as an economic threat to the sacred economy of Christians. The representation of infidels (i.e., non-Christians) included fake Christians and Jews as sneaky, treacherous agents whose main goal was the depredation of Christian wealth, namely, the *invasio* of sacred Christian lands and the robbery (or laying waste) of sacred goods.[25] This suggests that, from the universalistic Christian perspective, the very existence of infidels and Jews (and, more broadly, non-Christians) could be viewed in terms of loss and privation. The immaterial and material treasure consisting of souls and terrestrial goods could appear in this light as a Christian economic sum, a complex "patrimony," which infidels and Jews would have devalued both by resisting to become Christians and by occupying and using Christian sacred goods and lands.

The very economic notions of "profit" (*lucrum*) and "sum" (*summa, mons*) began to be affected by this semantic ambiguity. The fact that both the sum of ecclesiastical properties and the "accumulation" of the true believers could be perceived and described as different shapes of the same "capital" made it possible to represent and to conceive of some basic economic concepts, such as abstract notions concerning both visible and invisible things.[26] For this reason, the idea that "infidels" obviously impoverished Christians began to be viewed both as a religious and economic truth. The semantic equation establishing a correspondence between infidelity and loss; decrease and impoverishment was summed up through the word *invasio*, formally denoting the intentional nature of infidels' behaviors, namely their own will to damage and reduce the amount of Christian sacred goods. In this linguistic context, from the twelfth century onwards, both Crusade ideology and the development of credit transactions and discourses jointly determined a new and more specific meaning of *invasio* as an economic category that included many different techniques employed by infidels and Jews to depredate and weaken the Christian social body.[27] It is important to remember that this

---

[24] Uta-Renate Blumenthal, *The Investiture Controversy: Church and Monarchy from the Ninth to the Twelfth Century* (Philadelphia, 1988).

[25] Giacomo Todeschini, *Gli ebrei nell'Italia medievale* (Rome, 2018).

[26] Todeschini, *Il prezzo della salvezza*; idem, *Ricchezza Francescana*, 126ff.

[27] Rebecca Rist, "The Power of the Purse: Usury, Jews, and Crusaders, 1198–1245," in *Aspects of Power and Authority in the Middle Ages*, ed. Brenda Bolton and Christine Meek (Turnhout, 2007), 197–216; idem, *Popes and Jews, 1095–1291* (Oxford, 2016), 136ff.

"body" was traditionally viewed as a mystical body and, more precisely, as the earthly manifestation of Christ's body.[28] Christian theologians and jurists described a series of factors as various manifestations of the infidel attitude to "invade" (*invasio*) and depredate Christian territories. These included the "occupation" of the Holy Land by Muslims; the participation in market and credit transactions by French, English, German, Spanish, and Italian Jews; and the political and professional presence of Jews in Christian cities as public administrators and doctors or surgeons.

The Jewish "invasion" of Christian lands and holy spaces was thus a profanation and desecration of the Christian mystical body and of the individual and familiar "bodies" constituting the Christian *respublica*.[29] The specific economic nature of that "invasion," moreover, was emphasized by the multiplication of market transactions during the twelfth century. The fact that Jews and Christians were together involved in this commercial and credit "revolution" offered the occasion to theologians like Peter the Venerable and Peter the Chanter, as well as to canonists like Bernard of Pavia and pope-jurists like Alexander III and Innocent III to represent Jewish business activities as the main form of Jewish presence in Christian countries.[30] The presumption that Jews in Christian lands were by nature invading and desecrating worked as a rhetorical *a priori* to represent Jews as economic villains; and this at a time when, from the twelfth century onwards, market interplays became the crucial path for organizing social relations and codifying relationships between individuals and governmental institutions.

Inner and Outer Economy: Credit and Usury

In this perspective, between the twelfth and thirteenth century, credit transactions began to be defined according to one of two typologies: either as legitimate and useful forms of lending and borrowing, acknowledged by sacred institutions, or as illegitimate and useless forms of credit commonly called "usury.[31]" In the first case, money and coins had a value that was controlled

---

[28]Caroline Walker Bynum, *Wonderful Blood: Theology and Practice in Late Medieval Northern Germany and Beyond* (Philadelphia, 2007); Linda Kalof, ed., *A Cultural History of the Human Body in the Medieval Age* (Oxford, 2012).

[29]Miri Rubin, *Gentile Tales: The Narrative Assault on Late Medieval Jews* (Philadelphia, 2004); Jonathan Adams and Cordelia Hess, eds., *The Medieval Roots of Antisemitism: Continuities and Discontinuities from the Middle Ages to the Present Day* (London, 2018).

[30]Toch and Müller-Luckner, *Wirtschaftsgeschichte der mittelalterlichen Juden*; Todeschini, *Christian Perceptions*, 1–16; Michael Toch, *The Economic History of European Jews: Late Antiquity and Early Middle Ages* (Leiden, 2013).

[31]Giacomo Todeschini, "Trésor admis et trésor interdit dans le discours économique des théologiens (XIe–XIIIe siècle)," in *Le Trésor au Moyen Âge: Pratiques, discours et objets*, ed. Lucas Burkart et al. (Florence, 2010), 33–50; idem, *Come Giuda*.

and legalized by the sacred and ruling institutions. In the second case, the Christian theologians and jurists described the value of money and coins as a value imposed by individuals whose public reputation was unknown and who consequently could not be viewed as truly belonging to the market communities, defined by religious and charismatic kinship. A good example of this distinction is offered by the pontifical letters of the last quarter of the twelfth century, in which the popes Alexander III and Innocent III ordinarily discuss and emphasize the importance of the credit relations binding Christian seigneurial powers with ecclesiastical institutions or bishops and abbots. In these cases, the real problem was not the legitimacy of paying interest but, on the contrary, both the delay or resistance to repaying loans.

Around the same time—namely, between 1139 and 1179—the second and third Lateran Councils firmly condemned Christian usurers, who were unmistakably depicted as fake Christians, heretics, and rebels against the will and commandments of God and the Church. Both the well-known bull *Vergentis in senium* (1199) of Innocent III and the confessional summa (ca. 1215) by the Parisian master Thomas of Chobham, explicitly claim that heretics have no right to possess economic goods and that usurers are rebellious and heretical outsiders fiercely and insolently fighting against the Church. This context clearly shows that immediately before and after the Fourth Lateran Council (1215), in which lending on interest by Jews was condemned, the concept of "usury" was well distinguished from the concept of "credit." Furthermore, the noun "usurer" (*usurarius*) normally referred to a specific kind of heretic as an aberrant and wicked Christian exposing his/her deviancy through his/her economic daily activities. In other words, until 1215 "usury" was not, from a canonical and, more generally, legal perspective, a synonym for credit and lending on interest. Rather, "usury" was a definition of a specific type of heretical deviancy whose core was defined by specific crooked economic behaviors, which directly linked usury transactions with crimes like theft, robbery and, more generally, cruelty and lack of charity.[32] The description of usury as a crime against nature, analogous to sodomy, was intimately connected with behaviors characterizing deviant or fake Christians and, consequently, also "infidels," or non-Christians. These individuals were represented as subjects acting against nature.[33] One of the deepest

---

[32] Harald Siems, *Handel und Wucher im Spiegel frühmittelalterlicher Rechtsquellen* (Stuttgart, 1992); Todeschini, *Il prezzo della salvezza*; idem, *I mercanti e il tempio*; idem, *Ricchezza francescana*; idem, *Come Giuda*.

[33] Giacomo Todeschini, "*Soddoma e Caorsa:* Sterilità del peccato e produttività della natura alla fine del medioevo cristiano," in *Le trasgressioni della carne: Il desiderio omosessuale nel mondo islamico e cristiano, secc. XII–XX*, ed. Umberto Grassi and Giuseppe Marcocci (Rome, 2015), 53–79.

consequences of this conceptualization was that the value of money (and exchangeable goods) had to be fixed, controlled, and balanced by those who officially represented and embodied Christian faith in the cities and markets. This included ecclesiastical ruling powers, seigneurial powers, and their representatives, from the local administrators to the so-called *probi viri*, those who were publicly recognized as expert merchants and brokers.

In this theological and economic climate, since the last years of the twelfth century, Jews were represented as infidels whose aberration and obstinacy assumed the shape of usury, the main economic Christian heresy. Indeed the Fourth Lateran Council (1215) accused Jews of dispossessing Christians, and especially their churches and monasteries, of their own immobile property through lending on interest. The concluding section of constitution 67 of the Fourth Lateran Council is entirely dedicated to forbidding the "immoderate usuries" of the Jews and offers a clear rationale for this shift.[34] The last lines of the canon forbidding usury are explicitly associated with the desire of the Church to regain the tithes that ordinarily had been paid to churches when a Christian possessed the land. Moreover, both the representation of the Jews as wealthy entrepreneurs and the stereotype of the Jews as usurers impoverishing Christians started between the twelfth and thirteenth century in the French-Italian area where the Gregorian Reform and its rhetorics had prevailed.

Indeed, it was not a consequence of the professionalization of Jews as usurers, which cannot be proven despite the claims of many historians, Le Goff among others. Rather, this representation of Jews was the endpoint of a theological and ecclesiological polemic against them that was gradually reformulated in economic and financial terms during the eleventh- and twelfth-century commercialization of Western Christian economy.[35] The presence of Jews among Christians was now seen as a very specific economic threat and, in consequence of the growing involvement of churches and monasteries in the new credit economy, as an explicit menace to the economic safety of these sacred institutions.

---

[34] Rowan Dorin, "Canon Law and the Problem of Expulsion: The Origins and Interpretation of Usurarum voraginem (VI 5.5.1)," *Zeitschrift der Savigny-Stiftung für Rechtsgeschichte: Kanonistische Abteilung* 99 (2013): 129–61; Rowan Dorin, *Banishing Usury: The Expulsion of Foreign Moneylenders in Medieval Europe, 1200–1450* (PhD diss., Harvard University, 2015); idem, "'Once the Jews Have Been Expelled': Intent and Interpretation in Late Medieval Canon Law," *Law and History Review* 34 (2016): 335–62.

[35] Julie L. Mell, *The Myth of the Medieval Jewish Moneylender*, 2 vols. (New York, 2017–2018). 1:155–316.

Jews and the Christian Social Body

During the thirteenth century, Christian discourses on usury, credit, the value of things and commercial exchange became ever more complicated. In particular, the analysis of money (and consequently its value and price, i.e., interests legitimately payable by borrowers to lenders) formed the core of a complex representation of markets as public spaces where the balance of justice and equity could be calculated in probabilistic terms.[36] In this context, experts of Canon Law such as Henry of Susa started to make a distinction between "usury" performed by public usurers and legitimate cases of payment of interest. The latter was defined as the compensation of damages suffered by various kinds of businessmen. The formation of the so-called "exceptions" to the prohibition of usury has been described by many historians as a sort of mitigation or softening of that prohibition.[37] These exceptions were codified around the middle of the thirteenth century in the *Summa aurea* by Henry of Susa, cardinal of Ostia, and then continually repeated for centuries by Christian lawyers, theologians, and legislators. I argue that those exceptions reshaped the classic description of usury by emphasizing the social and religious relevance of those who performed the contract of lending more than the substance of the contract itself.

This reorganization of the Christian discourse on lending and money was based on procedures of exception that firmly redefined the social and economic role of the Jews in the Christian world. The late medieval lawyers, on the one hand, described usury as an economic activity ordinarily performed by specific wicked subjects, the *usurarii manifesti*. But, on the other hand, they characterized many different forms of lending on interest as licit and legal transactions ordinarily performed by businessmen whose civic role was beyond all suspicion.[38] Some of the principal protagonists for whom interest was sanctioned are ecclesiastical institutions such as churches and monasteries managing their own lands, well-respected Christian merchants administrating their commercial credit investments, and fathers- and sons-in-law linked by delayed payments of invested dowries. In short, through the juridical mechanism of "exceptions to the prohibition of lending on interest," interest and lending on interest began to be described as legitimate forms of

---

[36]McLaughlin, "The Teaching of the Canonists on Usury"; Langholm, Economics in the Medieval Schools; Joel Kaye, *Economy and Nature in the Fourteenth Century: Money, Market Exchange, and the Emergence of Scientific Thought* (Cambridge, UK, 1998), 103ff.; John H. Munro, "The Medieval Origins of the Financial Revolution: Usury, Rents, and Negotiability," *International History Review* 25 (2003): 505–62.

[37]Jacques Le Goff, *La bourse et la vie: Économie et religion au moyen âge* (Paris, 1987).

[38]Giacomo Todeschini, "Eccezioni e usura nel Duecento: Osservazioni sulla cultura economica medievale come realtà non dottrinaria," *Quaderni storici* 44 (2009): 443–61.

compensation for the loss of a profit rightly due to different kinds of investors who, at the same time, were perceived and represented as public institutions and full citizens of the Christian "republic" (*respublica Christianorum*).

This reformulation of the ancient prohibition of usury clearly distinguished between lending on interest performed by vulgar people and infidels on the one hand, and credit transactions undertaken by honest and well-respected Christians, on the other. This distinction resulted in a new Christian perspective on monetary transactions that recognized and emphasized the potential value of money and riches (namely, their potential utility and potential to grow) around being owned by "true believers," that is to say, by distinguished Christians.[39] Christian wealth owned by merchants and bankers, churches and public authorities, as well as rulers could receive interest as a compensation for "accruing damage" (*damnum emergens*) or "losing a probable profit" (*lucrum cessans*).

This idea that the wealth of rich Christians could be estimated at a higher market value on account of its social utility became widespread from the second half of the thirteenth century onwards. In this way, credit and banking, when managed by "true Christians," could become one specialized part of the administration of the "common good." The welfare of cities, states, and kingdoms began to be represented, especially by canonists and theologians belonging to the Franciscan Order, as the outcome of many different social and economic strategies.[40] Among these strategies, the financial ones found their own space; the development of "credit exceptions" in jurisprudence opened up a discursive space for a new definition of credit transactions as a positive, public good performed by Christian businessmen and sacred institutions. A blatant example of this process can be seen in the fourteenth century legitimation of public debt in Italian cities such as Florence, Venice, and Genoa,[41] where the sums lent by citizens were refunded through the payment of periodical interest. Indeed, the entire bureaucratic and financial machine surrounding the "public debt" was declared legal and ethical on the

---

[39]Nirit Ben-Aryeh Debby, "Mendicant and Jews in Florence," in *The Jewish-Christian Encounter in Medieval Preaching*, ed. Jonathan Adams and Jussi Hanska (London, 2015), 282–95.

[40]Todeschini, *Ricchezza Francescana*, 136ff.

[41]Anthony Molho, *Florentine Public Finances in the Early Renaissance, 1400–1433*, (Cambridge, MA, 1971); idem, *Tre città-stato e i loro debiti pubblici: Quesiti e ipotesi sulla storia di Firenze, Genova e Venezia*, in *Italia 1350–1450; Tra crisi, trasformazione, sviluppo* (Pistoia, 1993), 185–215; Julius Kirshner, "Privileged Risk: The Investments of Luchino Visconti in the Public Debt (monte comune) of Florence," in *Politiche del credito: Investimento, consumo, solidarietà* (Asti, 2004), 32–67; David Chilosi, *Risky Institutions: Political Regimes and the Cost of Public Borrowing in Early Modern Italy*, London School of Economics, Working Papers No. 177/13 (London, 2013).

basis of its importance as a tool for the attainment of the "common good" (*bonum commune*) of Christian society. In other words, "public debt" was understood as an economic strategy to improve the health of the Christian mystical Body.[42] The logic of this complex Christian reformulation of the connection between finance, public good, and the health of the social Body, that is to say, of the State Body (normally represented through the image and metaphor of Christ's Body), increasingly implied a neat separation between inner and outer economy.[43] The very notion of economic relations changed deeply. The association of healthy economic growth with inner economy, on the one hand, and, on the other, of outer economy with economic failure and cessation of development in the economic/social body was one major consequence for the distinction between Christian and alien economies.

Against this background, Jews began to be commonly represented, first in Italy during the fourteenth and fifteenth centuries, as professionals in moneylending; and, consequently, city-states in central and northern Italy began to invite Jewish bankers to settle in towns in order to open private banks.[44] Many historians treat this phenomenon mainly as proof of Jewish specialization in money matters and usury at the end of Middle Ages. However, it is possible that European economic narratives and politics,[45] as well as Christian legal definitions of economic and financial transactions up to the turn of the thirteenth century, played a major role in creating both the stereotype of the Jewish usurer and Christian economic policies that sought a solution to liquidity problems in the supposed monetary wealth of Jews.[46] The vague Christian understanding of Jewish legal and economic culture,[47] as well as of the institutional nature of Jewish communities, facilitated the public perception of Jewish society as epitomized by its wealthiest elite and the assignment

---

[42]Giuseppe De Luca and Angelo Moioli, *Il potere del credito: Reti e istituzioni nell'Italia centro-settentrionale fra età moderna e decenni preunitari*, in *Storia d'Italia. Annali* 23 (Turin, 2007): 212–55.

[43]Jonathan G. Harris, *Foreign Bodies and the Body Politic: Discourses of Social Pathology in Early Modern England* (Cambridge, UK, 1998); Gianluca Briguglia, *Il corpo vivente dello Stato: Una metafora politica* (Milan, 2006).

[44]Leon Poliakov, *Les banchieri juifs et le Saint-Siège du XIIIe au XVIIe siècle* (Paris, 1965); Michele Luzzati, "Banchi e insediamenti ebraici nell'Italia centro-settentrionale fra tardo Medioevo e inizi dell'Età moderna," in vol. 1 of *Gli ebrei in Italia*, ed. Corrado Vivanti (Turin, 1996), 173–235; Ariel Toaff, "Banchieri" cristiani e 'prestatori' ebrei?" in vol. 1 of *Gli ebrei in Italia*, 265–87; Marina Romani, "*Pegni, prestito e condotte (Italia centro settentrionale secc. XIV–XVI)*," *Mélanges de l'Ecole française de Rome: Moyen Âge* 125 (2013): 365–81.

[45]Francesca Trivellato, *The Promise and Peril of Credit: What a Forgotten Legend about Jews and Finance Tells Us about the Making of European Commercial Society* (Princeton, NJ, 2019), 37–48.

[46]Mell, *Myth of the Medieval Jewish Moneylender*, 2:3–112.

[47]Todeschini, *Christian Perceptions*, 1–16.

of economic tasks to this limited minority that Christian banking companies and international Christian bankers neither would nor could take on.

The strange encounter between, on the one hand, oligarchic economic policies, which distinguished the splendor of Christian credit businesses from the daily wretchedness of local lending on interest (gage and mortgage loan) performed by "infidels" and vile, little people and, on the other hand, the actual political and economic presence of Jews inside Christian territories, produced a new Christian perspective on economy and the beginning of a Christian economics. The idea that a well-ordered economic body (State, church, city, monastery, i.e., a governed space) could be disturbed by an external, pathogenic agent stopping the circulation of wealth and harmonious growth became an ordinary economic concept. Jews, in this context, began to be viewed no more uniquely as prototypical infidels menacing Christian faith, but also as an abstract economic element disturbing the civic organism.[48]

Devaluated People

At this point, we can grasp a little more clearly how the panoply of Christian images and metaphors involving Jews[49] structured late medieval and early modern economic discourses on the common good and public utility, and thereby implicitly created some concepts that later will be typical of modern economic rationality. What we are dealing with is a transfer of images and categories occurring without being (in most cases) explicitly defined in doctrinal terms.

A good example of this process is offered by the close association between the images and discourses associating Jews and the poor as "minors" (namely as semi-citizens or noncitizens) between the twelfth and the fifteenth century.[50] Through an accurate analysis of texts and images, it is possible to find many examples that show how the religious imaginary concerning the minority of the Jews actually worked.

An interesting and meaningful case can be found in the technique in illuminated manuscripts of the thirteenth and fourteenth century of representing

---

[48] Trivellato, *The Promise and Peril*, 49–65.

[49] Sara Lipton, *Dark Mirror: The Medieval Origins of Anti-Jewish Iconography* (New York, 2014).

[50] Brian Pullan, *Poverty and Charity: Europe, Italy, Venice, 1400–1700* (Aldershot, UK, 1994); Barbara A. Hanawalt, *"Of Good and Ill Repute": Gender and Social Control in Medieval England* (New York, 1998); Pierre Boglioni, Robert Delort, and Claude Gauvard, eds., *Le petit peuple dans l'Occident medieval: Terminologies, perceptions, réalités* (Paris, 2002); Sharon A. Farmer, *Surviving Poverty in Medieval Paris: Gender, Ideology and the Daily Lives of the Poor* (Ithaca, NY, 2002).

Judas and Lazarus as both prototypes as well as stereotypes of a danger-ous, Jewish marginality and as types representing the menacing inferiority of the poor. The small physical size of Judas and Lazarus, as well as their place-ment in front of the table behind which Jesus and the Apostles, or the wealthy and powerful are sitting, is the figural beginning of a long-lasting discourse on the suspect nature and problematic social utility of those defined as mi-nors and as powerless. How were these kinds of representations connected to the structuring of the modern notion of "common good" (= "public utility" and "common interest")? What was the meaning of "minor" and "powerless" from the perspective of the common good and public interest?

The late medieval civil and canon law described the "infamy" of Jews and the poor as the basis for their untrustworthiness and, as in other cases of "infamy," of their political unacceptability, clearly evident from their in-admissibility as witnesses in the courts of law.[51] If one pays attention to this new juridical doctrine, it becomes clear that the representation of the minority of Jews and the poor (namely through the physical "littleness," representing social "littleness") conveyed the implicit conceptualization of their unrelia-bility in regard to contracts, that is, their association with low and despicable forms of economic activity.

We can also consider the late medieval Western Christian texts that used the rhetoric of public ethics and moral theology to describe the problematic civic identity of tradesmen. The latter referred to salaried workers, ordinar-ily represented as shameless, corrupt, and dishonest people. This widespread discourse attempted to justify the low price of work performed by common-ers,[52] while it also formulated more general arguments explaining the eco-nomic reasons for the low or high price of professional skills, as well as of

---

[51] Peter Landau, *Die Entstehung des kanonischen Infamiebegriffs von Gratian bis zur Glossa ordinaria* (Cologne, 1966); Walter Pakter, *Medieval Canon Law and the Jews* (Ebelsbach, DE, 1988); Julian Théry, *Fama: L'opinion publique comme preuve judiciaire; Aperçu sur la révo-lution médiévale de l'inquisitoire (XIIe–XVe siècle)*, in *La preuve en justice de l'Antiquité à nos jours*, ed. Bruno Lemesle (Rennes, 2003), 119–47; F. R. P. Akehurst, "Good Name, Repu-tation, and Notoriety in French Customary Law," in *Fama: The Politics of Talk and Reputation in Medieval Europe*, ed. Thelma S. Fenster and Daniel Lord Smail (Ithaca, NY, 2003), 75–94; Daniel Lord Smail, "Témoins et témoignages dans les causes civiles à Marseille du XIIIe au XIVe siècle," in *Pratiques sociales et politiques judiciaires dans les villes de l'Occident à la fin du Moyen Age*, ed. Jacques Chiffoleau, Claude Gauvard, and Andrea Zorzi (Rome, 2007), 424–37.

[52] Giacomo Todeschini, "Servitude et travail à la fin du Moyen Âge: La dévalorisation des salariés et les pauvres 'peu méritants'," *Annales. Histoire, Sciences Sociales* 1 (2015): 81–89; idem, "Wealth, Value of Work and Civic Identity in the Medieval Theological Discourse (XII–XIV c.)," in *Reichtum im späteren Mittelalter: Politische Theorie, ethische Handlungsnormen und soziale Akzeptanz*, ed. Petra Schulte and Peter Hesse (Stuttgart, 2015), 55–68.

more visible goods. These archetypal representations of various social statuses, and of their value in shaping the public good for the utility of the state, were also metaphors for value itself, since they linked worthlessness and devaluation with abundance and high value with shortage. In this kind of discourse, salaried workers, the so-called *mercenarii*, are represented both as a crowd of dishonest and wicked people and as subjects well-disposed to be hired by infidels and knavish strangers. Their "avarice," namely their greed for gain, was frequently described as analogous to the greed of Jews and alien enemies. Thus, between the central Middle Ages and early modernity, the dubious and devalued identity of Jews, the poor, tradesmen, and other social minors and powerless people shaped a major economic concept, that of devaluation, by linking depreciation with uselessness and worthlessness with exclusion. This economic concept, however, was based on the living metaphor of devaluation and worthlessness embodied by Jews and powerless people.

To fully grasp these associations, it is useful to recall that the Western Christian theological mind, from Augustine on (as we saw before) contained a powerful monetary metaphor for humankind.[53] According to this metaphor, humans are God's coins, and just as a coin loses its value if the

---

[53]Raymond Bogaert, "Changeurs et banquiers chez les Pères de l'Eglise," *Ancient Society* 4 (1973): 239–70; Paola Radici Colace, "Moneta, linguaggio e pensiero nei padri della chiesa tra tradizione pagana ed esegesi biblica," *Augustinianum* 30 (1990): 405–22; Todeschini, *I mercanti e il tempio*; idem, *Trésor admis et trésor interdit*. See Augustinus, *Sermones de vetere testamento (1–50)*, ed. Cyrille Lambot, *Sermo*, CCSL 41 (Turnhout, 1961), 125–26:

> Nam etiam imagines in hominibus diversae sunt. Filius hominis habet imaginem patris sui, et hoc est quod pater eius, quia homo est sicut pater eius. In speculo autem imago tua non hoc est quod tu. Aliter est enim imago tua in filio, aliter in speculo. In filio est imago tua secundum aequalitatem substantiae, in speculo autem quantum longe est a substantia! Et tamen est quaedam imago tua, quamvis non talis qualis in filio tuo secundum substantiam. Sic in creatura, non hoc est imago dei, quod est in filio qui hoc est quod pater, id est, deus verbum dei per quod facta sunt omnia. Recipe ergo similitudinem dei, quam per mala facta amisisiti. Sicut enim in nummo imago imperatoris aliter est et aliter in filio - nam imago et imago est, sed aliter impressa est in nummo; aliter habetur in filio, aliter in solido auro imago imperatoris - sic et tu nummus dei es, ex hoc melior quia cum intellectu et cum quadam vita nummus dei es ut scias etiam cuius imagine geras et ad cuius imaginem factus sis, nam nummus nescit se habere imaginem regis.

See Cyrille Lambot, "Une série pascale de sermons de saint Augustin sur les jours de la création," *Revue Benedictine* 79 (1969): 213: "Quomodo enim nummus, si confricetur a terra, perdet imaginem imperatoris, sic mens hominis, si confricetur libidinibus terrenis, amittit imaginem Dei. Venit autem monetarius Christus, qui repercutiet nummos…"

mint mark is obliterated, humans lose their value and identity if the image of God with which they have been imprinted is obliterated by sin. This image shaped by Augustine was contained in his ninth sermon, which largely circulated by handwritten tradition. Augustine's emphasis on the connection between the authenticity of faith, namely individual trustworthiness, and the degree of self-consciousness possessed by the Christian, the living coin of the metaphor, created a clear link between the possibility of validating a Christian identity as authentic or counterfeit and the idea of proving this identity through a close examination of the inner mind.

The transformation of this monetary metaphor defining individual credibility into a strategy of validating identity was made possible from the twelfth century through the semantic translation of Augustine's discourse in the textual domain shaped by canon law. Canon law actually amplified and spread the Augustinian image by relating it to the problem of usury, that is to the puzzling identification of the Christian usurer as a fake Christian (and a pseudo-Jew). First, Gratian's *Decretum*, citing a passage of Pseudo-Chrysostom's commentary on Matthew, utilized Augustine's image of the monetary authenticity of *fideles* stamped with God's imprint (*caragma*), to distinguish them from usurers (the worst "merchants"; "super omnes mercatores plus maledictus est usurarius", *Decretum Gratiani*, LXXXVIII 11) whose "coinage" (that is, their human identity) was counterfeit. In this way, the wicked economic and monetary practice called *usura*, though not yet well codified and elucidated by Gratian, was connected to the usurer's dishonorable and contemptible identity: the alien nature of *usura* was explained and illuminated through the depiction of the alien and isolated identity of the "fake" Christian performing the crime.[54]

Similarly, in a text of Ambrose that we have seen before, Jews' resistance to conversion and their determination to maintain their own faith was represented as the obtuse will to preserve and hoard a treasure of devalued coins (and, therefore, it was a form of greed). Consequently, in the texts shaping canon law after the Gregorian Reform (around 1073–1096), that is after the struggle against simony and for the Roman Primacy, economic abuse began to be represented as a transgression very close to simony and heresy and, similar to these perverse errors, as a form of deviancy mainly practiced by

---

[54] Manlio Simonetti, "Origene e i mercanti nel tempio," in *Recherches et tradition: Mélanges patristiques offerts à Henri Crouzel*, ed. André Dupleix (Paris, 1992), 271–84; Giacomo Todeschini, "Linguaggi economici ed ecclesiologia fra XI e XII secolo: Dai 'Libelli de lite' al Decretum Gratiani," in *Studi in onore di Mario del Treppo*, ed. Gabriella Rossetti and Giovanni Vitolo, 2 vols. (Naples, 2000), 1:59–87; Emmanuel Bain, *Église, richesse et pauvreté dans l'Occident médiéval: L'exégèse des Évangiles aux XIIe–XIIIe siècles* (Turnhout, 2014).

alienigenae, "strangers,"—that is, by bogus Christians or other agents "coming from the outside," like Jews, whose dishonesty and questionable humanity could be summed up well by the image of a counterfeit coin.

The obsession over the devaluation of coins was clearly visible in fourteenth-century polemics about the forced devaluations imposed by kings and landlords, as well as in the huge importance attributed to the art of money-changing in medieval markets.[55] This obsession corresponds to the late medieval fear of defamation and loss of belonging that could transform the member of a well-renowned kinship into a despised outsider.[56] Against this backdrop, Jews become a prototype of fakeness and the stereotypical example of many different kinds of devalued humanity. At the same time, the polemical reduction of the complexity of actual daily Jewish life, culture, and economic activities to a simplified abstraction summed up by the slanderous word "usury" fit well with the metaphorical representation of Jews as devalued and counterfeit coins: "bad money driving out good."

The Jews as an Economic Obstacle: The Beginning of Christian Economics

Consequently, if we look at the political and linguistic structure of the economic discourse in Christian cities during the fourteenth and fifteenth centuries, we learn something new and rather surprising. Indeed, organic economic metaphors, such as the blood/money metaphor used to signify the constant and healthy circulation of wealth, become current between the fourteenth and fifteenth century in France, England, and Italy—in other words, in countries characterized by increasing economic growth and growing social disparity, and thus countries obsessed by the problem of the value/Value of things and humans.[57] This phenomenon can be described as the birth of

---

[55]Raymond de Roover, *Money, Banking and Credit in Medieval Bruges: Italian Merchant Bankers, Lombards and Money Changers* (Cambridge, MA, 1948); idem, *L'évolution de la lettre de change (XIVe–XVIIIe siècle)* (Paris, 1953); Jacques Le Goff, *Marchands et banquiers du Moyen Age* (Paris, 1956); Peter Spufford, *Money and its Use in Medieval Europe* (Cambridge, UK, 1988); Edwin S. Hunt, *The Medieval Super-Companies: A Study of the Peruzzi Company of Florence* (Cambridge, UK, 1994).

[56]Francesco Migliorino, *Fama e infamia: Problemi della società medievale nel pensiero giuridico dei secoli XII e XIII* (Catania, IT, 1985); Fenster and Smail, *Fama: The Politics of Talk*.

[57]Jerah Johnson, "The Money=Blood Metaphor, 1300–1800," *Journal of Finance* 21 (1966): 119–22; Philip Mirowski, ed., *Natural Images in Economic Thought: "Markets Read in Tooth and Claw"* (Cambridge, UK, 1994); Nicolaas T. O. Mouton, "Metaphor and Economic Thought: A Historical Perspective," in *Metaphor and Mills: Figurative Language in Business and Economics*, ed. Honesto Herrera-Soler and Michael White (Berlin, 2012), 49–76.

a public rhetoric (rooted in a previous theological lexica), which aimed at denoting Christian economy and markets as functions of that complex organism: the Christian "republic." This public rhetoric automatically hinted, as never before, at the existence of economic accidents slowing and blocking the ordinary growth and expansion of the economic Body of Christianity. A good example can be found in the polemics, current in France and Italy during the fourteenth century, against royal or seigneurial monetary policies, and more generally in the economic nature of the late medieval discourses against tyranny.

The fourteenth- and fifteenth-century Italian representations of political enemies as greedy usurers can be clearly seen in Dante's *Divine Comedy*. They can also be seen in the circulated libels and defamatory frescoes on the walls of communal palaces representing defeated political adversaries as a "man with a moneybag hung around his neck," an obvious evocation of "avarice."[58] This imagery strongly confirms the fact that the so-called "economic revolution" of Western Christendom has been characterized by the idea that the Christian mystical Body, the "Body Politick,"[59] had to thoroughly fight against economic antagonists, who in turn could be visualized as the origin of mortal disease and dangerous infection. The problem already was how to maintain and perpetuate the "beneficent fluid [of wealth and money] circulating among the various members of society"—many centuries before the birth of political economy or anatomy and before their conceptual and lexical interplay. In the late medieval stage of this process, the Christian imaginary concerning the economic role of Jews in Christian society worked in a perfectly visible way and was clearly expressed.[60]

A good vantage point from which one can consider this phase of the construction of (what some centuries after will be called) "economics" is the specific historical context of fourteenth–fifteenth century Italy, which links the economic activities performed by Jews with the economic/ethical analysis and description of the Italian civic economies. This linkage was conveyed by the Franciscan, Dominican and, more generally, contemporary ecclesiastical treatises and sermons, as well as by local legislation, aimed at discussing and reforming the economic policies of city-states.[61] The historiographical misunderstanding of the economic role played by the Jews in Christian Europe

---

[58]Giuliano Milani, "Avidité et trahison du bien commun: Une peinture infamante du XIIIe siècle" *Annales. Histoire, Sciences Sociales* (2011): 705–39; idem, *L'uomo con la borsa al collo: Genealogia e usi di un'immagine medievale* (Rome, 2017).

[59]Ludovic Desmedt, "Money in the 'Body Politick': The Analysis of Trade and Circulation in the Writings of Seventeenth-Century Political Arithmeticians," *History of Political Economy.* 37 (2005): 79–101.

[60]Desmedt, *"Money in the 'Body Politick',"* 80; Johnson, "The Money=Blood Metaphor."

[61]Todeschini, *I mercanti e il tempio;* idem, *Ricchezza Francescana,* 159ff.

and specifically in Italy at the time, that is, the widespread historiographical certitude about Jewish concentration in banking activities during this period, has much to do with the historiographical habit of anachronistically reading these discussions, analyses, and legislation as objective and impartial, namely, nonideological sources.[62] On the contrary, the multifaceted economic and political condition of Jews in late medieval Italy, are evident when one closely considers the documentary sources.[63] These sources clearly show that the authors and public rulers producing these texts made use of Christian rhetoric, which (since the end of the twelfth century) traditionally portrayed the Jews as experts of money (that is, as suspect "strangers" expert in what seemed to be both attractive and alien in the new Christian market economy), and thus were perceived as both useful and dangerous for Christians' welfare.

In fact, there is a huge difference between the real economic presence of Jews in the Italian cities and states between the fourteenth and fifteenth century and the institutional representation of the Jewish economic presence created by the agreements (*condotte*) formally binding Christian cities and Jewish moneylenders.[64] Even if, as most historians have believed, these documents seem to summarize the entire economic story of Jews in Italy at the end of the Middle Ages, many other Christian and Jewish sources allow us to see that lending on interest during this period was only a small part of the multidimensional Jewish participation in the social, cultural, and economic life of Italian city-states at the beginning of the Renaissance. Indeed, the *condotte* itself contains a hint of this more complex reality. The word *condotte* came from the Latin *conducere*, to hire, which points to the fact that the Jews were "hired" by the Christian city-states in order to lend on interest, in exchange for temporary citizenship.[65] Between the fourteenth and fifteenth

---

[62]Maristella Botticini and Zvi Eckstein, *The Chosen Few: How Education Shaped Jewish History, 70–1492* (Princeton, NJ, 2012).

[63]Daniele Carpi, ed., *Bibliotheca italo-ebraica. Bibliografia per la storia degli ebrei in Italia, 1964–1973* (Rome, 1982); Aldo Luzzatto, ed., *Biblioteca italo-ebraica: Bibliografia per la storia degli Ebrei in Italia, 1974–1985* (Milan, 1989); Shlomo Simonsohn and Manuela M. Consonni eds., *Biblioteca italo-ebraica: Bibliografia per la storia degli ebrei in Italia, 1986–1995* (Florence, 1997); Shlomo Simonsohn, *A Documentary History of the Jews in Italy* (Jerusalem, 1982); idem, *The Apostolic See and the Jews: Document, 492–1404* (Toronto, 1991).

[64]Joseph Shatzmiller, *Shylock Reconsidered: Jews, Moneylending, and Medieval Society* (Berkeley, 1990); Flora Cassen, *Marking the Jews in Renaissance Italy: Politics, Religion, and the Power of Symbols* (Cambridge, UK, 2017); Giacomo Todeschini, "Jewish Usurers, Blood Libel, and the Second-Hand Economy: The Medieval Origins of a Stereotype (from the Thirteenth to the Fifteenth Century)," in *The Medieval Roots of Antisemitism: Continuities and Discontinuities from the Middle Ages to the Present Day*, ed. Jonathan Adams and Cordelia Hess (London, 2018), 341–51.

[65]Toch and Müller-Luckner., *Wirtschaftsgeschichte der mittelalterlichen Juden.*

century, in the heart of the financial revolution led by the most renowned Italian merchant bankers, the inner infidels par excellence, the Jews began to be formally invited by Christian oligarchies to open banks and lend money in exchange for a temporary residence permit, namely, for an incomplete citizenship.

In other words, in Italy (and Europe) the stereotype of Jewish usury as a symbol encapsulating the whole system of Jewish economic activities was grounded in the difficulty Christian institutions had managing local and daily credit forms and, at the same time, in the perception of the most "familiar strangers" as wealthy experts in what looked like the most extreme form of economic otherness: both money's metallic and hypothetical value. To fully grasp this point, it is crucial to remember that during this phase (fourteenth–fifteenth century) powerful Christian families of merchant bankers (such as the Medici, Strozzi, Davanzati, and many others) dominated the European markets by building a financial network based on familial and political connections, in short, an economic system bound together by various kinds of trust relationships (from parental kinship to religious faithfulness). Christian financial economy, however, was noticeably troubled by money and coins, since on the one hand (according to Aristotle), money was a sterile, metallic object, but on the other hand could appear as a fruitful (and abstract or potential) value according to many distinguished thirteenth-century canonists and theologians.[66]

The main outcome of this contradiction was an ever-clearer separation (both conceptual and practical) between the economic sphere of international or institutional finance and the economic sphere of local credit epitomized by lending on interest, which in turn was characterized as a necessary, but vile and vulgar transaction—a kind of business characteristic of low status or infamous persons. The widespread Christian idea that "Jews" were a temporary solution to this conundrum was, on the whole, the endpoint of a long chain of theological and political associations denoting "Jews" as greedy and, consequently, as wealthy aliens whose sinful condition and minority status or "serfdom" (*servitus*) could be viewed as usable and functional: a form of good (economic) use of a people who were intrinsically wicked (*bene uti malo non est malum sed bonum*, as the Augustinian tradition incessantly repeated). From this perspective, the deal proposed by Christian oligarchies to some more or less wealthy Italian Jews during the financial revolution of the late Middle Ages (receiving temporary citizenship in exchange for their role as public usurers) turns out to be both an ideological and a practical experiment. In the "Italian laboratory" created by north-central city-states between

---

[66]Langholm, *Economics in the Medieval Schools*.

the fourteenth and the fifteenth centuries, credit policies became a governmental technique. Hiring Jews as moneylenders, according to this logic, formally made local credit relationships a degraded and easily controlled arena, actually a delimited financial sphere controlled and ruled by important families, oligarchies, and lords. At the same time, the delegation of the task of lending on interest to some wealthy Jewish families strongly affirmed both the stereotype of Jewish arrogant carnality and the subordinate and questionable nature of economies that were not directly managed by Christian rulers and public powers.[67]

The ambiguous role played by the Jewish bankers in exchange for the concession of civic rights to their families and communities undeniably became the factual starting point of the global stereotyped Christian representation of the Jews as greedy infidels and paradigmatic public usurers.[68] Concurrently, both the ideological and practical designation of Jews as official moneylenders (as it was established by Christian public powers) deeply transformed the very notion of economic organization and rationality. Henceforth, the very idea of economic growth was qualified by the crucial idea that exogenous and potentially dangerous elements could be useful, for a while, for running the economic machinery, at least until the rulers of the machinery would become able to make it work without them.

Blood and Wealth Circulation: Jews, Economic Diseases, and the Growth of the Common Good

Moreover, since the middle of the fourteenth century, this economic physics was clearly reinforced by the spread of the aforementioned narratives portraying the administrative life of Christian cities, states, and kingdoms as a condition of health or illness maintained in a state of unstable equilibrium. These narratives made increasing use of images and metaphors of the circulation of fluids and humors to denote the health or disease affecting the public Body. The well-known work of Nicolas Oresme on money (*De moneta*) offers a good example of this new intellectual (and political) tendency to use medical metaphors to illustrate the balanced or unbalanced functioning of markets and cities, the presence or absence of liquidity, and generally the economic development or crisis of Christian economies. The previous Christian doctrinal tendency to represent the economic growth of the Christian mystical Body in terms of well-being or degeneration was now advanced through the

---

[67]Todeschini, *La banca e il ghetto*, 103ff., 196ff.
[68]Mell, *Myth of the Medieval Jewish Moneylender*.

recourse to the medical vocabulary of the Aristotelian and Galenic doctrine comparing the public Body to a human body:[69]

> The state or kingdom, then, is like a human body, and so Aristotle will have it in Book V of the Politics. As, therefore, the body is disordered when the Humors flow too freely into one member of it, such that that member is often thus inflamed and overgrown while the others are withered and shrunken, and the body's due proportions are destroyed and its life shortened; so also is a commonwealth or kingdom when riches are unduly attracted by one part of it. For a commonwealth or kingdom whose princes, as compared with their subjects, increase beyond measure in wealth, power, and position, is as it were a monster, like a man whose head is so large and heavy that the rest of his body is too weak to support it. And just as such a man has no pleasure in life and cannot live long; neither can a kingdom survive whose prince draws to himself riches in excess.[70]

Coins and their movements began to be described in terms of health or illness. Consequently, some economic policies could be represented as "chronic sicknesses," being especially dangerous because they were imperceptible.

> And as some chronic sicknesses are more dangerous than others because they are less perceptible, so such an exaction [the monetary mutation, namely the devaluation of money] is the more dangerous the less obvious it is, because its oppression is less quickly felt by the people than it would be in any other form of contribution.[71]

---

[69] Joel Kaye, *A History of Balance, 1250–1375: The Emergence of a New Model of Equilibrium and its Impact on Thought* (Cambridge, UK, 2014), 362.

[70] Nicolaus Oresme, *Tractatus de origine, natura, iure et mutationibus monetarum*, ch. 25: "Est igitur respublica sive regnum, sicut quoddam corpus humanum, et ita vult Aristoteles V Politicae. Sicut igitur corpus male disponitur, quando humores excessive fluunt saepe ex hoc inflatur et nimium ingrossatur, reliquis exsiccatis et nimis attenuatis, tolliturque debita proportio, neque tale corpus potest diu vivere; ita conformiter est de communitate vel regno, divitiae ab una eius parte attrahuntur ultra modum. Communitas namque vel regnum, cuius principantes, in comparatione ad subditos, quantum ad divitias, potentiam et statum, enormiter crescunt, est sicut monstrum unum, sicut unus homo, cuius caput est ita magnum tam grossum, quod non potest a reliquo debili corpore sustentari. Quemadmodum igitur talis homo non potest sese iuvare, neque sic diu vivere, ita neque regnum permenere poterit cuius princeps trahit ad se divitias in excessu, sicut fit per mutationes monetae." See newly revised edition, Tommaso Brollo and Paolo Evangelisti, eds. (Trieste, 2020).

[71] Ibid., ch. 20: "Et quemadmodum quaedam aegritudines chronicae sunt aliis periculosiores, eo quod sunt minus sensibiles, ita talis exactio, quanto minus percipitur, tanto periculosius exercetur."

It was in this historical context that Jews began to be represented not merely as enemies of Christian prosperity, welfare, and economic growth, or as an exogenous obstacle to Christian happiness, but rather (through even more specific metaphors) as pathogenic agents and, more generally, as an economic disease affecting the Christian Body Politic. Especially during the fifteenth century, the Franciscan economic school contributed to this semantic shift through the social and economic analyses of some major Franciscan jurists and theologians by strongly emphasizing the importance of the circulation of money and wealth in order to insure both the economic and religious order of the Christian *respublica*.

One of the first and principal uses of what would be an extensively disseminated metaphor of money circulating in the public body like blood in a human body is found in the work of one of the most famous Franciscan preachers of the fifteenth century, Bernardino of Siena.[72] Some historians have represented this author as a skillful premodern economist. However, if we pay attention to the words and phrases in his writings, we can see that the economic discourses he shaped and the economic metaphors he utilized were not "economic theory" in the modern sense. Rather, his language and vocabulary joined theological assumptions and economic prescriptions, so that ultimately the economic metaphors he used were not politically neutral nor economically aseptic. On the contrary, his economic conceptualizations illustrated by physical images highlighted (in ethical and political terms) the opposition between productiveness and unproductiveness, health and illness, circulation and stagnation, common good and common evil. Indeed, in the text of one of his most renowned sermons, Bernardino compared the circulation of wealth within the Christian city to the circulation of "natural heat" (*naturalis calor*) in the human body. One hundred and fifty years after Bernardino, Bernardo Davanzati in his widespread treatise on money will interpret Bernardino's circulation of "natural heat" as blood circulation.[73] Bernardino thereby came to describe Jewish moneylending as a mortal disease assailing the civic body by causing a detrimental interruption of the circulation of its heat/blood. The conclusion deriving directly from the logic of the metaphor was that Jews and Jewish moneylending were like the kind of tumor or abscess (*apostema*) that medieval manuals of medicine suggested should be "surgically" removed.

This was the beginning of a long-lasting economic/political and religious discourse. The economic metaphor based on the anatomical image of

---

[72] See Giacomo Todeschini, "'Au ciel de la richesse': Le coeur théologique caché du rationnel économique occidental," *Annales. Histoire, Sciences Sociales* 74 (2019): 1–4; idem, *Come l'acqua e il sangue: Le origini medievali del pensiero economico* (Rome, 2021), 47ff.

[73] Bernardo Davanzati, *Lezione delle monete* (1588), in vol. 2 of *Scrittori Classici Italiani di Economia Politica*, ed. Piero Custodi (Milan, 1804): 19–55, 36–38.

heat/blood's circulation was the inauguration of an economic model that used natural/medical language to imply that the natural flow of the circulation of money could be stopped by some human or nonhuman obstacle, an obstacle that would have to be removed to allow the realization of a "healthy economy." The circulation of the fundaments of such Western and Christian economic discourse started thanks to the first economic/theological summaries and manuals, such as Summenhart's impressive work on contracts in the early decades of the fifteenth through the sixteenth century.[74]

It was against this background that Jews and other actors perceived as non-Christian or not-full Christian (that is, "alien") were shaping economics that in the eyes of Christians could appear nonhuman, irrational, and savage[75] and, ultimately, a major hindrance to the development of a superior economic rationality.

Acknowledgments I presented part of this text in 2018 at the North Carolina Jewish Studies Seminar and in a lecture at the Institute for Israel and Jewish Studies at Columbia University. I am grateful to Julie Mell for the English editing of the first version of this manuscript and to Federica Francesconi for her editorial assistance.

Publisher's Note Springer Nature remains neutral with regard to jurisdictional claims in published maps and institutional affiliations.

---

[74]Conrad Summenhart, *Opus septipartitum de contractibus* (Hagenau, 1513).
[75]Eric Wilson, *The Savage Republic: De Indis of Hugo Grotius, Republicanism and Dutch Hegemony within the Early Modern World-System (c. 1600–1619)* (Leiden, 2008).

Milton Keynes UK
Ingram Content Group UK Ltd.
UKHW020800181023
430769UK00006B/223